PARENTAL DISCRETION IS ADVISED

PARENTAL DISCRETION IS ADVISED

THE RISE OF N.W.A
AND THE DAWN OF GANGSTA RAP

GERRICK D. KENNEDY

ATRIA BOOKS

NEW YORK LONDON TORONTO SYDNEY NEW DELHI

ATRIA BOOKS

An Imprint of Simon & Schuster, Inc.
1230 Avenue of the Americas
New York, NY 10020

First Atria Books hardcover edition December 2017

ATRIA BOOKS and colophon are trademarks of Simon & Schuster, Inc.

For information about special discounts for bulk purchases, please contact Simon & Schuster Special Sales at 1-866-506-1949 or business@simonandschuster.com.

The Simon & Schuster Speakers Bureau can bring authors to your live event. For more information or to book an event, contact the Simon & Schuster Speakers Bureau at 1-866-248-3049 or visit our website at www.simonspeakers.com.

Interior design by Laura Levatino

Manufactured in the United States of America

10 9 8 7 6 5 4 3 2 1

Library of Congress Cataloging-in-Publication Data
Names: Kennedy, Gerrick, author.
Title: Parental discretion is advised : the rise of N.W.A and the dawn of gangsta rap / Gerrick Kennedy.
Description: First Atria Books hardcover edition. | New York: Atria Books, 2017.
Identifiers: LCCN 2017032780 (print) | LCCN 2017033278 (ebook) | ISBN 9781501134937 (eBook) | ISBN 9781501134913 (hardcover) | ISBN 9781501134920 (pbk.)
Subjects: LCSH: N.W.A. (Musical group) | Rap musicians—United States—Biography. | Rap (Music)—History and criticism.
Classification: LCC ML421.N25 (ebook) | LCC ML421.N25 K46 2017 (print) | DDC 782.421649092/2 [B]—dc23
LC record available at https://lccn.loc.gov/2017032780

ISBN 978-1-5011-3491-3
ISBN 978-1-5011-3493-7 (ebook)

For Jermaine, Charles, and Robert. I am, because of you.

CONTENTS

PARENTAL
DISCRETION
IS ADVISED

PROLOGUE

A maze of metal barricades was stuffed with hundreds of rap fans waiting to file into San Manuel Amphitheater. Inside, heavy, pounding bass from the DJ's turntable drowned out the piercing beeps of metal detectors that greeted early arrivers. It was opening day of Rock the Bells, an annual hip-hop festival that was launched in Southern California and toured throughout the world during its decade run. Twenty thousand fans made the pilgrimage to the hills of the Inland Empire desert, roughly an hour and a half outside of Los Angeles, for two days of music performances. The mix of underground genre outliers; revered elder statesmen; and young, chart-topping wunderkinds allowed Rock the Bells to enjoy a status as the preeminent destination for hip-hop fans well before massive music gatherings like Coachella, Bonnaroo, and Lollapalooza diversified their lineups to reflect rap's surging mainstream dominance. A gust of wind swept dust through the security line as workers confiscated prohibited paraphernalia from disappointed fans who unsuccessfully hid marijuana blunts or glass one-hitters they hoped to bring into the festival. It was well over 100 degrees on this Saturday afternoon, but more palpable than the triple-digit temperature was the anticipation from fans waiting to get inside.

The bill was a heady, extensive representation of several generations of hip-hop acts that traversed mainstream and alternative lanes of the genre. Common; Jurassic 5; Kid Cudi; Pusha T; KRS-One; Talib Kweli; Kendrick Lamar; Tech N9ne; Earl Sweatshirt; Slick Rick; Juicy J; Too Short; Immortal Technique; E-40; Tyler, the Creator; Doug E. Fresh; Lecrae; J. Cole; Rakim; A$AP Rocky; Danny Brown; the Internet; and Wu-Tang Clan were all booked for a weekend that marked the landmark tenth anniversary of the festival.

Also on the marquee was Eazy-E, the "Godfather of Gangsta rap" and founder of the most notorious hip-hop group of all time, N.W.A.

Nearly two decades had passed since Eazy took his last breath, losing his battle with AIDS years after N.W.A crumbled amid accusations of shady contracts and bitter rivalries. Eazy was long expunged from the narrative of hip-hop, succumbing to the mores of irrelevance after his hard-core image morphed into a sort of zany caricature of itself. But today he would rap again.

In the months leading up to the festival, Rezin8, a San Diego–based company that specializes in immersive design, was hard at work resurrecting Eazy. A combination of green-screen motion capture, animation, multimedia, and Eazy's children's memories produced what was hyped as an "accurate, authentic reflection" of the rapper. Eric "Lil Eazy-E" Wright Jr. was used for the avatar's body. Derrek "E3" Wright provided the voice. And Eazy's "face" was constructed using an imprint of his daughter, Ebie Wright.

"You're not going to be looking at 1987 Eazy-E, you're going to be looking at 1994 heyday," Eazy-E's widow, Tomica Woods-Wright, said ahead of the festival. "You're going to get probably what most people remember of that last impression of that era he was in."

"We aren't trying to mimic something, you're creating something," Wright continued. "We're building, in the capacity, a reflection to carry on that's a piece of him. It's not going to be him, but it's going to be as damn close as you can get."

On what would have been Eazy's fiftieth birthday, the technology that brought Tupac Shakur, Ol' Dirty Bastard, and Michael Jackson back from the dead for another musical thrill introduced Eazy's digitized likeness for a "virtual performance" (as it was billed by the festival organizers).

A dozen incandescent bulbs cast a blue glow over the stage as plumes of dank marijuana smoke hung over the audience. Despite years of beef among the group, Bone Thugs-N-Harmony, the Cleveland rap posse Eazy signed to his Ruthless Records, reunited for the occasion and had just performed a set of its biggest hits when the lights came to a slow dim. From the amphitheater's rafters, a complex rig descended slowly as multiple smoke machines sent thick clouds of fog, pale red from a strip of lights, rolling across the stage. With the push of a button, there he was again, clad in his signature slate-gray Dickies that sagged slightly and a black hat with "Compton" stitched in white, Old English–font letters.

Eazy—or, more accurately, the digital composition of him—stood still, soaking up the rapturous applause from the crowd.

"*We Want Eazy! We Want Eazy! We Want Eazy!*" the crowd cheered.

When his former bandmate DJ Yella, behind a pair of turntables, cued up a beat as startling as an air-raid siren, Eazy started bobbing his head to the music and finding his swagger before addressing the crowd, many of whom hoisted smartphones in the air to record the moment. There were even gasps of disbelief as one of rap's earliest fallen heroes was resurrected.

"What's up, LA! Make some motherfucking noise," digital Eazy shouted.

Satisfied with the love he was receiving, Eazy launched into the verse that caps one of the most famous rap songs of all time, a record that transformed the genre forever.

". . . Straight outta Compton is a brotha that'll smother yo' mother," Eazy rapped amid the shrills of twenty thousand rap heads. An overwhelming number of Compton hats and T-shirts emblazoned with "N.W.A" in eerie red letters—or ones with the faces of its members in mug shot–like poses—could be seen in the audience. Throughout the weekend, Eazy's face was omnipresent, as scores of savvy street vendors camping out in the parking lot sold an array of homemade N.W.A paraphernalia for well below what merchants inside charged. Eazy would have appreciated the hustle.

"Dangerous motherfucker raises hell, and if I ever get caught I make bail," Eazy continued as his holographic likeness bounced alongside DJ Yella without missing a beat.

Without as much as a pause, Eazy then dove into another of his indelible, hard-core tales of street life, "Boyz-n-the-Hood"—a song that transformed the former drug dealer into an unlikely rap sensation. The crowd, some of whom were not even alive during the peak of Eazy's fame, joined in unison to chant the anthem's most famous bars:

> *Cruisin' down the street in my six-fo'*
> *Jockin' the bitches, slappin' the hoes*

For a moment Eazy was alive again, basking in the love that has largely evaded him since his death, as his legacy is often overlooked in the pantheon of fallen rap gods. Unlike Tupac and the Notorious B.I.G., he didn't go out a hip-hop martyr consumed by the violent street life dominant in his lyrics. But like his life and his career, Eazy's moment onstage was all too brief. Just as quickly as he had arrived, he vanished into a cloud of smoke. And the show went on.

COMPTON'S
N THE HOUSE

Of the many big bangs that have transformed rap over the decades, N.W.A's *Straight Outta Compton* is one of the loudest. It was a sonic Molotov cocktail that ignited a firestorm when it debuted in the summer of 1988. Steered by Dr. Dre and DJ Yella's dark production and Ice Cube and MC Ren's striking rhymes, and brought to life by Eazy-E's wicked charm, the record fused the bombastic sonics of Public Enemy's production with vicious lyrics that were revolutionary or perverse, depending on whom you asked. The world hadn't heard anything like it before. Radio stations and MTV refused to add the title song to their playlists. Critics didn't get it, couldn't see past the language, or, worse, refused to acknowledge it as music. Politicians even launched attacks, working to great lengths to condemn the music and its creators. N.W.A were to hip-hop what the Sex Pistols were to rock—and really, what's more punk than having a name that dared to be spoken or written in full, and music that incensed a nation? Red-faced and outraged Americans protested the group, police officers refused to provide security for its shows, and the FBI got involved, but that didn't stop *Straight Outta Compton*, N.W.A's debut album, from selling three million records without a radio single.

With *Straight Outta Compton*, N.W.A didn't just manage to put its hood on the map, the group forced the world to pay attention to the rap sounds coming out of the West Coast. It's an album that provided the soundtrack for agitated and restless black youth across America with its rough and raunchy tales of violent life in the inner city, expressed through razor-sharp lyrics. "It was good music," LA rap-radio pioneer Greg Mack said. "And the lyrics, they meant something."

The emergence of N.W.A—who billed itself as the World's Most Dangerous Group—in the late eighties provided a jolt to the rap industry. Public Enemy had already helped redefine the genre by ushering in aggressively pro-Black raps that were intelligent, socially aware, and politically charged. But N.W.A opted for an angrier approach. The group celebrated the hedonism and violence of gangs and drugs that turned neighborhoods into war zones, capturing it in brazen language soaked in explicitness. "Street reporters" is what they called themselves, and their dispatches were raw and unhinged—no matter how ugly the stories were.

Like the Beatles, N.W.A's lineup was stacked with all-stars: Eazy-E, Ice Cube, Dr. Dre, and MC Ren would become platinum-selling solo rappers, while DJ Yella helped Dre break ground on a new sound in hip-hop. They were the living embodiment of the streets where they were raised, and there was zero pretense about it. And when it came to subject matter, with N.W.A, politics took a backseat. Instead, frustrations about growing up young and black on the streets of South Central Los Angeles became the driving force behind their music. Gangs, violence, poverty, and the ravishing eighties crack epidemic swept through black neighborhoods like F5 tornadoes. People were angry and restless, and without a flinch N.W.A documented its dark and grim realities like urban newsmen.

Straight Outta Compton was a flash point that spoke for a disenfranchised community and disrupted the order of those who were confronted with the voices and images of a community they'd much rather ignore. Black teens and young adults immersed in street life, yet looking for something to hold on to, flocked to the album. And so did white, suburban, middle-class teens who knew nothing about the "hood" or a life inside it, but looked to rap as an outlet for rebellion in the same way their parents gravitated toward the angsty countercultural attitudes percolating in rock music during the 1960s.

As unapologetically violent, misogynist, and problematic as their lyrics often were, the group's harrowing depictions of urban nightmares provided a vital response to the growing disenfranchisement from the Regan-era politics that had transformed the nation and created an economic catastrophe for metropolitan Los Angeles. N.W.A introduced an antihero. The way Melvin Van Peebles's groundbreaking 1971 film *Sweet Sweetback's Baadasssss Song* used America's longstanding perception of black men as seething, violent hunks to politicize the image, N.W.A brought it to life by mixing reality with fantasy through its music—and the result was as terrifying as it was successful.

At its peak, Eazy's Ruthless Records—a label he started strictly as a means to get off the streets—was the number-one independent label in the industry and the largest black-owned indie since Berry Gordy's legendary Motown empire. Without Eazy laying down the foundation for hustlers-turned-record-executives, who knows if Death Row, Bad Boy, No Limit, or Cash Money could have existed. How would Jay-Z ever have known he could go from slinging crack cocaine to creating Roc-A-Fella had Eazy not done it less than a decade before?

Ice Cube once said the music took off because it was a moment in time bottled up and shaken until it burst. It's no surprise then that the group's most insidious track, "Fuck tha Police," became a rallying cry in LA after a group of white police officers were acquitted in the savage beating of unarmed black motorist Rodney King. Those three words became a mantra, shouted and painted on walls by those who pilfered and torched the city in the days after the acquittal, in what remains one of the deadliest, most destructive uprisings in American history. More than a quarter of a century before the Black Lives Matter movement and a new generation of youth turned to social-media activism as a means of protest against police brutality, N.W.A were screaming "Fuck tha police." Their lyrics were purposely confrontational. They shouted furiously to push back against racial profiling and offered insight into the daily tur- moil of inner-city youth through visceral storytelling, but they just as well promoted misogyny, homophobia, and sexual violence without abandon. "We had lyrics. That's what we used to combat all the forces that were pushing us from all angles: Whether it was money, gang-banging, crack, LAPD," Cube said. "Everything in the world came after this group.

"N.W.A was the World's Most Dangerous Group. We changed pop culture on all levels. Not just music. We changed it on TV. In movies. On radio. Everything. Everybody could be themselves. Before N.W.A . . . you had to pretend to be a good guy."

N.W.A shocked middle America, scared the government, and sparked conflict with law enforcement. Although their run together was short, N.W.A's music encouraged a generation of young, black emcees to explore their rawest thoughts, no matter how obscene or radical. Today, hip-hop is seen far differently than it was during N.W.A's rise. Hip-hop is credited as the single most influential genre in American pop music over the last half century, as its artists have long gone from persona non grata to pop stars, corporate pitchmen, actors, fashion designers, tech moguls, and executives—and it wouldn't have happened if a group of men from Compton and South Central didn't light the fire.

#

Compton wasn't even on a map in 1985. It wasn't that the mostly Afri- can American suburb in South Central Los Angeles was some deserted town or a Podunk dump in the shadows of the glamorous big city, but it may as well have been, considering that an official county publication outlining the cities, towns, and neighborhoods of LA inadvertently left it off. For those that didn't reside somewhere within its ten square miles or one of the surrounding cities touching its borders—Willowbrook, West

Compton, Carson, Rancho Dominguez, Long Beach, Paramount, or Lynwood—Compton was virtually nonexistent.

And it was easy to forget about Compton amid the landscape of Los Angeles, a city that's a literal representation of the California Dream, with its lush beaches, sunny weather, and glitzy industries. Compton is located just south of the concrete ribbons of freeway connecting downtown Los Angeles to the beaches of Santa Monica and Venice, to the entertainment capital of Hollywood, and to the opulence of Beverly Hills. Its geographic centrality to Los Angeles County gave it the name "Hub City." In the mid-1980s, Compton, then a city of nearly 90,000 residents, looked much like any other suburb. Wooden bungalows painted a multitude of colors with porches and sprawling yards lined streets dotted with towering palms and banana trees. During that time, middle-class black and brown families in Compton were hard at work toward their own version of the California Dream.

That's what Richard and Kathie Wright were in search of when they made the move to Compton from Greenville, Mississippi, during the Great Migration. The Wrights settled into a simple, traditional middle-class way of life. Kathie taught grade school and Richard became a postal worker. Unlike LA, however, life in Compton—and throughout South Central— was far from the glamorous way TV shows and films depicted. South Central communities struggled to rebound from the 1965 riots in Watts, which left a vital strip of the neighborhood's business district blackened to the point that it was rechristened "Charcoal Alley." President Richard Nixon's Comprehensive Employment and Training Act, a public program created to provide desperately needed jobs, helped South Central residents bounce back from the recession of the early 1970s. But when President Ronald Reagan moved into the White House in 1981 he nixed the initiative. By 1982, one year into Reagan's first term, South Central was in crisis. Unemployment and poverty tested families. Startling high school dropout rates drove up crime. Yet, more ominous elements were at play, as an epidemic of gangs and drugs started to ravish communities.

"If you sat on this porch at night and just listened real hard, you'd hear nothing but gunfire," Ice Cube said of his parents' South Central abode. "I've heard it so much in my neighborhood that I can't hear it no more. At night, you'll see the helicopter flying around here with the spotlight on, looking for somebody. If you hear a car with a beatbox booming at night, you know they're out looking for somebody. As long as you can't see where they're coming from, gunshots aren't scary. Now, if you see the fire from the gun, then you run . . ."

A dangerous mentality set in among Compton youth: "I grew up in the hood, I'm going to die in the hood." It was understandable. Jobs were hard to come by and people were just trying to survive.

The hope and promise felt by a generation of black migrants was replaced with despair and disillusion in their offspring. An area that was once a beacon of black middle-class achievement had become one of blight by the 1980s. Young black men in Los Angeles were six times as likely to be killed as their white peers, and Compton had a murder rate that was more than three times the per-capita rate of LA—a city of little more than three million people. "It was a dangerous time. Everybody was trying to get their hustle on. If you encroached on somebody else's territory, there's problems," remembered Vince Edwards, who grew up in Compton and goes by CPO Boss Hogg. "The gang culture was prevalent. You had all these dealers trying to get their money made so you had to worry about them—and you had to worry about crossing gang territory."

Decades of fraught racial tensions throughout Los Angeles also added to the ticking bomb that was inner-city life in South Central. Before an influx of black suburbanites flocked to Compton between the 1920s and the 1950s, the city was predominantly white. Integration of the city was met with resistance as home owners, real-estate brokers, civic leaders, and law enforcement worked in tandem to keep Compton white. Although a 1948 decision by the Supreme Court ruled against restrictive housing practices, the Federal Housing Administration routinely denied loans to blacks in areas not covered by restrictive covenants (alternative agreements that served to perpetuate residential segregation on private properties). As a matter of policy, these restrictions also extended to Asians, Mexicans, and Native Americans. Black families were forced into nearby neighborhoods like Watts. There were some residents around Compton who didn't resist the growing integration, and even profited off blacks by selling their homes for more than they would to a prospective white buyer. However, the enterprising practice came with great danger as white property owners received threats or, in more severe cases, were beaten by other whites for listing their properties with realtors who sold to both white and black buyers.

Of all the areas around Los Angeles where this practice was happening, Compton was disproportionately affected, and the city became a battleground of sorts. Whites pushed back against the thousands of black families trickling into the suburb during the 1950s and '60s, mostly coming from the South. White residents felt the uptick in black families negatively impacted their property values, and they turned to violence as a means of intimidating and pushing away their new non-white neighbors. Black Korean War veteran Alfred Jackson and his wife, Luquella, were met with a mob of white residents assembled in front of their moving van to demand they leave when the couple arrived in Compton in 1953. It took the brandishing of firearms by Alfred and a family friend who was there to help them move to turn the crowd away. Standoffs like these continued, and mobs of angry whites grew in their aggression. Soon they resorted to bombing and firing weapons into the homes of black families. Crosses were burned on lawns: the fiery declaration of war that was the hallmark of the Ku Klux Klan's intimidation tactics against blacks. White gangs like the "Spook Hunters" violently harassed black families. Mobs formed under the slogan "Keep the Negroes North of 130th Street." This defiant fight against inclusivity echoed back to the early years of World War II, when the Compton City Council forcefully resisted construction of a public-housing complex in the neighborhood because it was considered "Negro housing." The message was clear: protecting Compton's whiteness was essential.

Violent reactions among white communities took place across the nation as millions of blacks fled the South, where Jim Crow laws and lack of economic opportunity stifled their livelihoods. Cities like Oakland, Boston, Detroit, New York, and Los Angeles became choice destinations. Skilled black migrants in LA found employment that provided a middle-class income, making the idea of the California Dream a reality. A victory in the battle for housing parity came in 1963 with the California Fair Housing Act. Drafted by William Byron Rumford, the first black person from Northern California elected to serve in the legislature, and better known as the Rumford Act, it sought to end racial discrimination by landlords and property owners who refused to rent or sell to minorities. Under the act, ethnicity, religion, sex, marital or familial status, or physical handicap couldn't serve as the basis of denial. However, the relationships between blacks and whites in South Central, and across the country, never rebounded—not that the trauma from slavery, segregation, and centuries of institutionalized racism in this country will likely ever heal. Blacks continued to feel treated as second class—feelings that were compounded in south LA by inadequate access to public transportation, decent schools, affordable housing, or high-wage jobs, as well as being overlooked for opportunities of political influence in the community, and being discriminated against by the police strictly because of the color of their skin. It was enough to create a powder keg that would combust in Watts during the summer of 1965 on a sticky August afternoon.

It was a routine traffic stop with a familiar setting: A white cop pulling over a black motorist. California highway patrol officer Lee Minikus pulled over Marquette Frye after getting a report of a reckless driver. The twenty-one-year-old was behind the wheel of his mother's 1955 Buick Special with his older stepbrother, Ronald, weaving down a stretch of South Avalon Boulevard in Watts. Frye told the cop he was trying to avoid potholes but admitted to indulging in a few drinks earlier. He goofed his way through a sobriety test he couldn't possibly pass, shucking and jiving for the spectators lurking close by. The sobriety test failed, Minikus radios for the car to be impounded and he places the young man under arrest—typical DUI protocol. Ronald went to fetch their mother, Rena, to claim the car and immediately upon arrival she berated her son for driving under the influence. "I told you about drinking and driving," she seethed. "Let me smell your breath." Most accounts say Frye was cheery and joking with the responding officers—until his mother arrived. Frye's demeanor changed and he began cursing and shouting at the cops. His mother jumped on one officer's back and Marquette took a swing at another. An officer attempted to subdue Frye and swung his baton at his shoulder but missed and struck him in the head. Rena and her sons were hauled off to jail. The crowd of spectators swelled to nearly one thousand, and they became furious as talk of what happened turned to rumors and speculation—one widely spread, and incorrect, story was that the cops beat Rena. A mob formed. For many, this was the last straw, as they were already frustrated with law enforcement and being disenfranchised by city officials. The prior autumn saw the appeal of the Rumford Act, after the California Real Estate Association launched an initiative that pushed against it. Proposition 14, later to be found unconstitutional by state and US Supreme Courts, legalized discrimination under the guise of protecting property owners' absolute discretion of selecting renters and buyers. The *Los Angeles Times* endorsed the initiative, and it passed with 65 percent of the vote. Frye's encounter with the officers was a tipping point for the residents of Watts, who were fed up and angry with the police and their position in LA. They decided to fight back.

Rocks were hurled at police cruisers. Officers not pummeled with objects got pulled from cars and beaten. Store windows were smashed, and many businesses were set ablaze. Warfare enveloped the streets, intensifying over the course of six days. Nearly one thousand buildings were left damaged or destroyed. More than thirty people lost their lives with over one thousand more injured. Property damage was estimated at $40 million, and more than 3,400 people were arrested. "We all got pissed and went out and burned up our neighborhood," one demonstrator said. "We brought 'the man' onto their own land. That's the only way we could communicate." Following the riots, whites took flight out of South and West Los Angeles neighborhoods.

The civil unrest in Watts and across the country during the civil rights movement unmasked the racial angst felt by blacks in large cities like Detroit, Chicago, and New York—places once seen as a refuge. A generation of blacks were sick and tired of being treated as inferior to whites. No longer were they going to silence themselves or keep the peace the way their parents told them they needed to in order to get by. They had had enough.

Eric "Eazy-E" Wright and the men of N.W.A were a part of the next generation. And soon the anger and frustrations that boiled over from their parents and the people in their neighborhood would provide the inspiration for a musical revolution.

PANIC
ZONE

The world came to know him as Eazy-E—the man who blazed a trail with incendiary and profane music that shook America to its core, altered popular music seemingly overnight, and established the West Coast as a hip-hop capital. He was the embodiment of the black male America feared most: violent, menacing, criminal. The "godfather of Gangsta rap," Eazy built a rap start-up from the streets of Compton that, when adjusted for inflation, was generating over $20 million a month by today's standards. Before all that, though, he was Eric Lynn Wright, your local "street pharmacist."

The influx of crack cocaine in South Central kept Eric in demand and flush with cash and, really, what more could a hustler ask for coming up in Compton during an era when hangin', bangin', and slangin' was a way of life? In 1985, Eric was twenty-one years old and deep in the drug game. But his choice of profession didn't reflect his upbringing as much as it did the budding street-savvy business acumen that made him a multimillionaire.

A nurturing two-parent household wasn't enough to keep Eric away from the lure of the streets. He dropped out of Dominguez High School during his sophomore year. For a moment, he considered following in his father's footsteps by pursuing a career with the post office, but he hated "workin' for somebody else." Around the same time, a slick drug trafficker named "Freeway" Rick Ross was busy transforming South Central into a crack capital with wholesale cocaine—first as a powder, then as the smokeable "ready rock."

"Ready rock" was as addictive as it was cheap; however, its toll—physically and emotionally—was astoundingly destructive. While the typical one-gram package of powdered cocaine sold for $100 and was only 55 percent pure, one-tenth of a gram of crack only cost between five and twenty-five dollars and often was between 75 and 100 percent pure, making it far more potent than regular cocaine. Crack first showed up in the United States in 1981 in Los Angeles, San Diego, and Houston, according to the federal Drug Enforcement Administration. In just a few short years it reached pandemic levels. By 1996, crack was available in twenty-eight states—a number that spiked to forty-six the following year. It was widely accessible throughout the streets of South Central, from big-time dealers like Freeway; groups of Jamaicans, Haitians, and Dominicans; sophisticated networks organized by splinter groups from the Bloods and the Crips; and street entrepreneurs who realized the swelling profits available in the drug game. Eric was one of those street entrepreneurs.

At five foot four, he certainly didn't exactly look like your typical dealer, but nothing about his short exterior should lead you to believe he was one to test. "That boy could fight. He's all muscle. If he locked on to you, you're in trouble," said Greg Mack, LA rap-radio pioneer and friend of Eric's. Short, broad-shouldered with a clenched jaw that usually meant business, Eric was a formidable presence, despite his diminutive stature. And he made for a surprisingly disciplined drug peddler. He didn't get high. He didn't even really care for liquor. Each morning he woke up early and read the *Los Angeles Times* cover to cover. He then got dressed in his signature look: white T-shirt, tube socks, Dickies or jeans, and dark sunglasses known as locs—his Jheri curls spilling out of his baseball cap. He'd venture down South Muriel Avenue, a street filled with houses of red-and-brown brick or pale-colored stucco with manicured lawns and handsome brick-and-wrought-iron gates. "Everyone thought he was some radical street thug. That was his structure. Even early on, he was very business," recalled former girlfriend Tracy Jernagin.

Eric never went anywhere without a wad of cash stuffed inside his sock, his ankle warmed by $2,000 worth of bills at any given time. After checking his pager he'd walk from his house to the corner of Caress Avenue and Alondra Boulevard where he then used a pay phone to make his deals, returning calls to those he knew who hit his pager with the right code: for an eighth of an ounce, better known as an eight ball, the page needed an "8"; half an ounce was "12." The phone is still there today, dusty and unused. He often operated out of the Atlantic Drive apartment complex, a pink two-story building less than a mile from home on South Muriel. Close to a highway underpass, the building's horseshoe layout and tight driveway made it nearly impossible to see most of the units from the street. It made for an ideal, round-the-clock drug bazaar. The sign on the building's façade that warned "This is a crime watch area" wasn't nearly enough to deter dealers, particularly the number of Crips who descended upon the stucco complex to make deals. By the time Eric was in elementary school, the Crips and Bloods had carved out territory throughout much of South Central. Eric was down with the Kelly Park Crips, whose turf was on the east side of Compton near his home. Kelly Park was a lush grass field behind Colin P. Kelly Elementary School with brightly colored playground equipment, concrete benches, and a basketball court. Eric was known around the neighborhood as "Casual." He wasn't a hard-core gangbanger by any means, even if he later created a wildly exaggerated image of one in order to sell records. Eric got along with differing Crip factions in the neighborhood, not a surprise considering he sold them great rock at fair prices. He wasn't out snuffing adversaries via drive-bys or rolling the streets ready to drop you over gang beef, but he didn't back down from a fight, either. "If you looked at [his] knuckles, they were gone. They were dimpled. He had scars and shit," recalled Mazik Saevitz, who briefly worked with Eric's label as a member of hip-hop duo Blood of Abraham. Eric was guarded and said very little, keeping a grim expression on his face and sunglasses covering his eyes.

Despite how Eric carried himself, his propensity to snap when provoked, or the gangster tales he spit as a rapper, he was nothing at all like the Crips in his hood. And most certainly he was unlike Raymond Lee Washington and Stanley Tookie Williams, the Crips' infamous cofounders.

The intent of the Crips—which morphed out of a cluster of previous collectives—was to continue the revolutionary ideology of the 1960s and to serve as community leaders while aggressively protecting their neighborhoods from other, larger local gangs like the LA Brims and the Inglewood Chain Gang. Introduced by a mutual friend, Raymond Lee Washington and Stanley Tookie Williams formed an alliance to eliminate all street gangs and create a "bull force" neighborhood watch. "I thought, 'I can cleanse the neighborhood of all these, you know, marauding gangs.' But I was totally wrong. And eventually, we morphed into the monster we were addressing," Williams said. The Crips adopted the color blue and began to map turf in Compton. Near Centennial High School, on Piru Street, a street crew was formed by Sylvester Scott and Benson Owens as a way to challenge the insurgent gang and defend itself against the Crips. The Pirus (Owens established the West Pirus) were the first Bloods gang. Red was the gang's chosen color, as many of the non-Crip street gangs called one another "blood." In 1974, a twenty-one-year-old Washington was sentenced to five years at the Deuel Vocational Institution in Tracy, California, for second-degree robbery, the first Crip incarcerated there. Washington recruited his fellow inmates into the gang, much to the chagrin of black prison collectives such as the Black Muslims and the Black Guerrilla Family, groups whose ethics, morals, and values didn't align with what they had heard about the more volatile Crips outside of prison walls. When Washington was released from prison and returned to Los Angeles, he discovered that tensions between the Crips and the Bloods had erupted into all-out war.

Gunplay, instead of squaring up fist-to-fist, was now the norm to settle disputes. Recruits looking to build their credibility resorted to crimes that escalated in their senselessness and heinousness. Disillusioned, Washington, who strongly opposed guns, began distancing himself as he wanted the gang to cease internal feuding and work toward a truce with the Bloods.

But Washington didn't get to see that happen. On a late August night in 1979, he was hanging out on the corner of Sixty-Fourth and San Pedro Streets when a car pulled up and the unidentified occupants called him over. Washington usually didn't step up to cars if he didn't know who was inside, but he recognized the occupants and exchanged a few words with them before a passenger drew a sawed-off shotgun and blasted into Washington's stomach. He was rushed to Morningside Hospital and died in surgery. An arrest was never made. A few months later, Tookie vanished from the streets after being convicted of quadruple murder. He was sentenced to death and was later executed by lethal injection, after pleas for clemency and a four-week stay of execution were both rejected by Governor Arnold Schwarzenegger in 2005.

A decade after they were founded, the Crips and Bloods had become an unstoppable force, with both sects having grown exponentially. Blue and red territories were divided across LA and beyond, with splintered sects establishing borders alongside Latino gangs. Shared hand signals were used for identification. Pictographs etched in spray paint on walls and buildings sent messages, marked territory, and warned rivals not to fuck with them—if your name was painted on a wall and crossed out, chances are your days were numbered. Turf is a gang's prized possession, and no piece of land was off limits. Gas stations, schools, liquor stores, even Burger Kings became claimed territory. And warring over turf got bloody, fast.

"You couldn't wear blue over here, you couldn't wear red over there. I had to learn the color scheme," said Greg Mack. "I literally took a change of clothes for wherever I went so that I could change and be in the right color in the right area. Didn't want no mistakes."

Kids who had made it just beyond the throes of puberty were aggressively recruited. Just consider the milieu of South Central at the time to understand the appeal of falling in line with a gang. Work was scarce. Crime was spreading like a plague. Single-parent households struggled to stay afloat. Gangs provided a distraction. For these youths, there was a feeling of power, family, a sense of belonging, protection, strength, and pride. The growing spate of high school and junior high school students being drafted into various Crip and Blood sets went far beyond South Central. In Denver, for instance, about two dozen Crips from California arrived and drafted about four hundred members to establish new gangs named after Los Angeles sets. Police officials went as far as dubbing the surge "Criptomania." "When I first came to California it was a bit of a culture shock," said Tracy Curry, better known as the D.O.C. "The whole idea of the gangbanging shit was a bit much."

Where Hollywood romanticized gang culture with films like *Grease* and *West Side Story*, the realities of gangland were vicious, and usually ended in bloodshed. Forty or so gang sets had split up nearly every inch of Compton's ten square miles. In the war zone that was mid-1980s South Central, casualties were plentiful, as gang membership between various Crip and Blood sets across the city soared to an estimated fifteen thousand before the decade was over. By 1984 there were about two hundred gangland killings in Los Angeles County—a number that climbed to five hundred by 1988.

Bloody rivalries between gang members didn't go unnoticed. However, in the eyes of the law, the media, and those who lived in Los Angeles, the gang wars were a crisis relegated to lower-class, primarily black and brown communities—that is, until the slaying of Karen Toshima. The night of January 30, 1988, was one of celebration for Toshima. The twenty-seven-year-old graphic artist from Long Beach nabbed a massive promotion at her Studio City ad agency and planned to have a quiet dinner with a friend to toast the accomplishment. The pair dined in Westwood Village, a handsome, palm tree–lined cavalcade of movie theaters, chic restaurants, and hip boutique shops adjoining the UCLA campus on the affluent Westside of Los Angeles. After dinner Toshima and her companion were walking amid the throngs of Saturday-night strollers when gunfire erupted among rival South LA gang members who'd traveled to the area. A bullet pierced her temple, and she collapsed on the sidewalk near a popular eatery. She died in the hospital the following morning.

The murder of an innocent bystander caught in the crosshairs of gang fire wasn't an anomaly. Drive-by shootings were typical where Bloods and Crips operated. In some neighborhoods, a Cadillac creeping down the block brought fear to its residents, though not as terrifying as the sight of the barrel of a .30-caliber semiautomatic rifle poking through a passenger-side window and spraying a stream of hot bullets that may or may not have intended targets. "*What's up, cuz?!*" or "*What hood you from, cuz?!*" were questions one hoped never to be asked. Weapons—rifles, tire irons, knives, small-caliber handguns (or "Saturday night specials")—were wielded with abandon, turning plenty of innocent black and brown lives in South Central into collateral damage. But the idea of a gang-related killing happening outside of the inner city, let alone an affluent neighborhood such as Westwood, jolted naïve Angelenos, for whom gang violence was only a problem in certain neighborhoods. The media covered the story with fervor. Police patrols were tripled, including a spate of anti-gang programs by police and prosecutors. Thirty officers were assigned to the investigation of the young woman's murder, and Los Angeles mayor Tom Bradley—who made history as the first African American mayor of a major US city with an overwhelmingly white majority population—along with city council, agreed to spend millions for the extra patrols. But the attention given to the Westwood slaying outraged black and brown communities who felt authorities cared more about the one gang-related murder that happened in a posh neighborhood than they did about the thousands of murders across South and East Los Angeles. The optics certainly proved them right.

As gang crime continued to escalate in South Central, the LAPD was also faced with how to confront the invasion of crack cocaine. Before crack found its popularity, spliffs dipped in liquid PCP, known as Sherm sticks or angel dust, provided cheap highs that were popular on the streets. The discovery of crack cocaine, however, would unleash a crippling drug epidemic unlike anything seen before. Crack is cocaine processed into smokeable slivers or crystals through use of baking soda or ammonia. Smoking crack delivered a high far more intense than that of snorting cocaine—and did so without making the user's nose bleed. But its addictive nature brought a dark cloud to the streets of South Central. The rise of crack brewing alongside the proliferation of gangs made for a perfect storm.

"It just swept through the neighborhood," said rapper and actor Ice-T, an early pioneer of West Coast Gangsta rap. "[And] came with a tremendous amount of violence—then LA got really, really dangerous."

DOPEMAN

Eric may have never gotten into the drug game, or out of it, if it weren't for Horace Butler. Eric was always a hustler, but he started with petty burglaries—not slingin' dope. Butler, his first cousin once removed, lived close by and would often have Eric tag along with him. Butler showed Eric the ropes, making his then-teenage cousin a "runner"—the person who delivers the product to customers after drug deals were made. Eric greatly admired his cousin, but Butler would soon be met with the very fate so many in the drug game encountered. Late one night, he was driving his truck in Mid-City headed to the I-10 freeway. Butler and an unknown passenger in the car with him crept to a stop at the light. Before the signal changed, shots rang out.

Pop. Pop. Pop. Pop. Pop. Pop. Pop.

Seven bullets ripped through Butler, courtesy of the car's passenger, who escaped. The car rolled backward before it crashed. Butler's slaying rattled Eric to his core. It was a wake-up call, and he started to ask himself if it was all worth it. "I'd probably be dead right along with him," Eric admitted.

Slinging dope certainly came with its bounty of material riches. It was evident throughout South Central, and Eric was no exception. He had the thick gold chains, custom-made leather coats, and a Suzuki Samurai SUV dipped in red candy paint to show how well he had done. But fast money came with its perils. The battle for territory between gang subsets morphed South Central into an urban war zone. Even if you were lucky enough to evade being smoked by an adversary, you were still at risk of being fast-tracked to prison where all too often the occupants were—and continue to be—disproportionally black and brown. And it was a gamble that intensified with the War on Drugs.

During the 1960s, recreational use of marijuana, cocaine, LSD, and heroin were symbols of rebellion and antiestablishment views that were spreading rapidly in the United States and throughout the Western world. Nothing captured the spirit more than rock music, with musicians glamorizing the recreational drug use they exploited for artistic inspiration. It was a sign of the times, as rock lent a voice to the social upheaval and political dissent that resonated with America's youth. The rock-and-roll lifestyle grew synonymous with drugs, and its stars were celebrated for hard living and partying. The Rolling Stones, Grateful Dead, Pink Floyd, Jimi Hendrix, Janis Joplin, and Jim Morrison were just as famous for embracing hard drugs as they were for their music—although Hendrix, Joplin, and Morrison would all succumb to drugs at the age of twenty-seven. Even the Beatles, a band marketed as clean-cut and straight-laced, experimented. Bob Dylan is credited with introducing the Fab Four to cannabis during his 1964 tour of England, an experimentation that trickled into their work, making it more mellow and contemplative. The band would prove instrumental in shifting attitudes toward marijuana, since "whatever the Beatles did was acceptable, especially for young people." The Beatles even experimented with LSD, with Paul McCartney boasting it opened his eyes and made him "a better, more honest, more tolerant member of society."

Laws against drugs have been in existence in the US since San Francisco's antiopium law of 1875, with drug prohibition policies continuing in some fashion for the next century. The criminalization of psychoactive substances escalated once President Nixon decided to treat drug use and dependency as a crime issue rather than a heath one. "America's public enemy number one, in the United States, is drug abuse. In order to fight and defeat this enemy it is necessary to wage a new, all-out offensive," he famously declared in the summer of 1971. And Nixon, the country learned, meant business. The Drug Enforcement Administration was established to replace the Bureau of Narcotics and Dangerous Drugs and Nixon doubled down on his efforts to eviscerate drug abuse, which he called one of the most vicious and corrosive forces attacking the foundations of American society, a major cause of crime and "a merciless destroyer" of human lives. Yet Nixon's aggressive crackdown had more disturbing, ulterior motives: It was a way to target blacks and the antiwar left.

"We knew we couldn't make it illegal to be either against the war or black, but by getting the public to associate the hippies with marijuana and blacks with heroin, and then criminalizing both heavily, we could disrupt those communities," one of Richard Nixon's top advisers confessed years after Nixon left office. "We could arrest their leaders, raid their homes, break up their meetings, and vilify them night after night on the evening news. Did we know we were lying about the drugs? Of course we did."

Nixon's War on Drugs ushered in the era of mass incarceration. Before then, the US prison population had largely been flat. In 1970 there were 357,292 inmates in custody, a number that spiked by more than 200,000 people by the close of the decade, as law and order swept the nation in a failed bid to cease drug use or the global drug trade.

When President Reagan entered the White House he turned Nixon's rhetorical War on Drugs into a literal one in 1982. At the same time, high-grade Columbian cocaine was responsible for making Miami a massive drug capital and was being brought into South Central through a Bay Area drug ring that peddled cocaine to the Crips and Bloods. And it was that pipeline to Columbia's cartels that afforded gang members in South Central the wherewithal to purchase military-grade automatic weapons.

What dealers in South Central weren't aware of, however, was how the spread of crack through their sales helped finance a Central American war. "Freeway" Rick Ross would purchase product from Nicaraguan supplier Oscar Danilo Blandón Reyes, who in turn channeled the profits to a guerrilla army named the Fuerza Democrática Nicaragüense (Nicaraguan Democratic Force) or FDN, the largest of several anticommunist groves called the Contras. Blandón received protection from the CIA, as the rebel Contras worked to overthrow the leftist Sandinista government while receiving support from the Reagan administration through secret weapons sales to Iran, in what became known as the Iran-Contra Scandal. Blandón would be arrested, and he worked with the US government, resulting in the prosecution of Ross, who served thirteen years in jail.

The Iran-Contra Scandal has long been viewed as proof that the government was complicit in the crippling crack epidemic that tore through South Central. The government did acknowledge in 1986 that the money helped fund the Contra rebels, but maintained the smuggling of drugs was not authorized by the US government or resistance leaders.

Amid the Iran-Contra Scandal, Reagan passed the Anti-Drug Abuse Act of 1986 through Congress. Reagan's omnibus drug bill appropriated $1.7 billion to fight the drug crisis, earmarking $97 million to build new prisons and allocating $200 million for drug education and $241 million for treatment. The bill also included strict mandatory minimum sentencing guidelines for drug offenses. Possession of at least one kilogram of heroin or five kilograms of cocaine was now punishable by at least ten years in prison, while selling five grams of crack carried a mandatory five-year prison term. Imposing the same penalties for the possession of an amount of crack cocaine as for one hundred times the same amount of powder cocaine placed a wide disparity between how minorities and whites were punished for the same exact drug. Under Reagan's war, drug dealers and their clients were villainized. They were viewed as America's most-wanted criminals, with drugs blamed as the sole reason as to why areas such as South Central were struggling.

For young men like Eric, dealing often felt like the only viable way to make a living in South Central. Risks came with the job, but what were the employment options in the area at that time? He may have stumbled upon dealing by circumstance, but it's understandable the appeal to someone like Eric. He was a high school dropout that didn't want to answer to anybody but himself. It made him the perfect street hustler, but Eric was faced with a sobering choice after losing his beloved cousin: How much longer do you spend your days watching your back?

IF IT AIN'T RUFF

The media made sure Americans were tuned into the War on Drugs. Footage of drug raids became increasingly prevalent on the nightly news, and focused almost exclusively on urban streets. In fact, a survey of network news during the first five years of the 1980s showed the number of cocaine-related stories jumped from ten a year to an astounding 140. Research from the University of Michigan discovered that from 1985 onward, the number of whites shown using cocaine dropped by 60 percent—and the number of blacks rose by the same amount. Blacks and Hispanics most certainly didn't represent the majority of drug users, but cops weren't breaking down doors in Manhattan or Beverly Hills. The image of guys peddling vials of white crystal to crackheads or tattoo-covered thugs playing dominoes or sipping forties would have played much better to the fear of the drug than a white businessman loosening his tie at the end of a long day in the office and snorting a few lines from inside a luxury condo.

Los Angeles police responded with brute force. LAPD chief Daryl F. Gates, who went as far as condemning drug use as treason and believed even casual drug users ought to be "taken out and shot," ramped up efforts to rid the streets of drug users and their suppliers. Gates's sight was focused intently on black neighborhoods in South Central. Stop-

and-frisk became routine, especially for young black men who gave the slightest whiff of involvement in gangs. Red or blue attire automatically made you a suspect. Hand signs were monitored, as was the way men stood while they were in public.

The LAPD's Community Resources Against Street Hoodlums (or CRASH) unit began conducting sweeps, which led to thousands of presumed gang members being arrested, mug-shotted, fingerprinted, and held until someone came to bail them out. "We'd take them to jail for anything and everything we can," one officer said. Most often the men targeted were unaffiliated, and consequently damaged by the reality of a police record. Just being stopped by a cop could make all the difference to one's livelihood. Members of the task force compiled a "field identification card" on suspected gang members, even when they had no cause to arrest or cite them, and CRASH officers sometimes carried a throwaway gun or drugs to plant on suspects.

Gates's bid to control "the rotten little cowards" who belonged to gangs and terrorized South Los Angeles with drugs and guns led to nightly sweeps where hundreds of officers would canvas nearly sixty square miles of South Central looking for any- and everyone with gang ties. Gates approved overtime for one thousand officers to descend on neighborhoods as part of this mission. LAPD's literal war introduced the use of the battering ram, an armored vehicle weighing six tons and equipped with a fourteen-foot steel arm able to pierce through fortified and barred doors of suspected "rock houses" in a matter of seconds. The ram would burst through the door or smash through a window and a charge was thrown to stun those inside, as officers descended on surprised criminals. The battering ram brought a physical representation of the destruction authorities were fighting against. "It had such a psychological impact on all of us. Your house may have not got run over by the battering ram, but you know it's out there," Ice Cube said of growing up around the frequent sounds of smashed doors and windows. "That had an effect on everybody. It was like killing a fly with a sledgehammer. It showed how heavy-handed the LAPD were on us." On more than one occasion, an innocent resident saw their walls crumble. The battering ram added to the resentment against police brewing in black neighborhoods. It was enough to inspire Compton rapper Toddy Tee to record "Batterram," one of the earlier hit rap songs to come out of the West Coast:

Yeah rockman, you'll see it soon
And you won't hear a snatch, you'll hear a boom
You can't stop it, baby
The Batterram

The most famous of these so-called "Operation Hammer" stings happened on April 6, 1989, when Gates—at the time eyeing an entry into politics and set on a run for governor—showed former first lady Nancy Reagan how the battering ram worked. Reagan, who famously coined the phrase "Just Say No," gladly accepted the offer as she was looking for a way to maintain her visibility as an antinarcotics crusader now that she was out of the White House. A nasty heatwave pushed temperatures in South Central above 100 degrees the day she was set to observe the battering ram in action. As SWAT officers stormed a suspected "rock house" at Fifty-First Street and Main Street, Reagan and Gates sat in an air-conditioned luxury motor home with "The Establishment" emblazoned on the front, snacking on fruit salad. Reagan wore a blue LAPD windbreaker with "Police" lettered on the back and "Nancy" across the front. A throng of reporters and photographers, all tipped off hours in advance, had assembled. According to the *Los Angeles Times*, while SWAT officers roughly frisked and cuffed the fourteen men and women captured inside the small, heavily fortified stucco bungalow, Reagan was seen freshening her makeup for the waiting cameras. "These people in here are beyond the point of teaching and rehabilitating," Reagan sighed heavily while detailing the "very depressing" house she had walked through. In all, about a gram of crack was retrieved.

Years before the former first lady's overhyped media stunt, her husband's aggressive War on Drugs might have discouraged Eric from continuing to deal. Jail or getting shot and killed were all-but-guaranteed
outcomes of dealing, and so he began to question whether or not it
was the life for him. Eric also had kids to think about. A ladies' man, he
already had a handful of children with just as many women by the time
he was twenty-two. "He was family oriented, always been," his daughter
Erica Wright recalled. "Always had time for us, period." Eric knew the
drug game had its limits. The money was great and lots could be made,
as crack addiction pilfered its victims for every nickel and dime they had.
Eric had a nice safety net, saving about $250,000 from dealing—and he
soon decided he wanted out. "I seen that it wasn't really worth it, it wasn't
worth my life," he said. "I figured I could do something right for a change
instead of something wrong."

SOMETHING 2
DANCE 2

The dawn of the 1980s brought with it the explosion a new music genre that would become far more influential than the 1960s British Invasion, or the surge of synth-pop two decades later, and dictate the next half century of popular music as its artists continue to set trends and dominate radio airplay and record sales. Within the first five years of the decade, Madonna emerged and propelled bright dance-pop to the masses, Diana Ross reinvented herself, Whitney Houston took her place as America's sweetheart, Prince found superstardom with his magnum opus *Purple Rain*, and Michael Jackson—having ushered out disco with his brilliant *Off the Wall* album at the tail end of the seventies—released his behemoth *Thriller*, which became the best-selling album of all time. MTV crash-landed on televisions across America to serve as the official documentarians of the counterculture percolating among the youth. And on the East Coast, hip-hop took its first steps.

New York City was hip-hop's nucleus. DJs rocked block parties using turntables to chop and manipulate popular records for pop-lockers to bend and snap their bodies to, and rappers joined in to spit rhymes over instrumentals of groove-heavy beats and popping basslines to hype the party. DJs became the pulse of the party. House bands felt stale and irrelevant when compared to the excitement and originality of DJs. The popularity of DJs at clubs inspired emcees who would rap over beats. The verbal art form would soon transition from parties to recording studios. Early songs like 1979's "King Tim III (Personality Jock)" from the Fatback Band, the Sugarhill Gang's earth-shattering "Rapper's Delight" and Kurtis Blow's "The Breaks" were deeply funky joints that lit up dance floors. The music was free-spirited and perfect for dancing to, but it could also pack a punch that lasted far after the party ended. Inspired by funk innovator George Clinton and electropop pioneers Kraftwerk and Yellow Magic Orchestra, Afrika Bambaataa crafted the dazzling "Planet Rock," a sweaty dance-floor anthem blending synthesizer and vocoder sounds with breakbeats that served as a precursor to techno, house, and trance. Along with Grandmaster Flash and the Furious Five's 1982 hit "The Message"—a record that introduced sociopolitical commentary to hip-hop—"Planet Rock" laid the blueprint for hip-hop. DJ Kool Herc, Fab Five Freddy, Spoonie Gee, Marley Marl, Kool Moe Dee, the Fat Boys, Whodini, Doug E. Fresh, and Warp 9 were some of the genre's earliest architects and emcees like Run-D.M.C., LL Cool J, Public Enemy, Eric B. & Rakim, KRS-One, Slick Rick, Beastie Boys, EPMD, the Juice Crew, and Boogie Down Productions carried the second wave of the genre through the rest of the decade.

Nearly three thousand miles away from hip-hop's nexus, LA was in the midst of disco fever. Mobile DJ crews armed with crates of fast-paced dance and silky R & B grooves commanded the party scene, with varying crews dominating their own turf across the city—the Dream Team working South Central, Uncle Jamm's Army playing Culver City and eastward with an ambitious and enterprising kid named Alonzo Williams anchoring clubs and parties from Gardena to Long Beach. Although dance and R & B was the official soundtrack at parties, the streets told a different story, as East Coast hip-hop was blasting all over the West. "In South Central, all you had to do was open your window. You heard Run-D.M.C. or Sugarhill Gang or the Sequence or Kurtis Blow. Everybody was bumping it," said KDAY programmer Greg Mack. But despite its bicoastal prevalence, major labels still weren't checking for hip-hop.

✻

Alonzo didn't plan to DJ for a living. Raised in Compton, the Gardena High School graduate had dreams of becoming a broadcaster. He enrolled at the Los Angeles School of Broadcasting through LA's Regional Occupational Program to study the craft, but a lisp that had long ago earned him the moniker of "Daffy Duck" made that dream seem out of reach. While DJing might not have been his plan A, it was a fallback that took him further than he could imagine—and set the scene for the birth of an era of hip-hop that disrupted the zeitgeist.

Alonzo purchased two turntables and set up an account to rent equipment from Hogan's House of Music in Lawndale. He built his own turntable stand that converted into a rolling dolly, gluing wisps of fluffy pink material to make it look like he was DJing on a bright cloud. A friend at a Plexiglas shop made him a sign that read, "Disco Lonzo, Superstar DJ." At gigs, he'd don a gold chain etched with his name, a whistle, and a construction hat with a rotating siren light.

Lonzo made $150 a week performing at schools, house parties, nightclubs, and big dances. During a gig at the Long Beach Convention Center one night, Lonzo was approached by Roger Clayton and Andre Manuel, who both extended offers to help him out. Lonzo made Manuel part of his Disco Construction and Wrecking Crew, and taught him how to DJ. Clayton, who DJed under the name the Ace of Dreams, was cofounder of DJ group Uncle Jamm's Army and he got Lonzo a part-time gig in the warehouse of a record distributor. Clayton also hired Lonzo to DJ parties he threw under his Unique Dreams production company. Lonzo's father, after seeing his son perform to a packed crowd at a dance hall in Torrance called Alpine Village, asked what it cost to rent the place and was furious to learn it cost $1,000. "Too high," he told his son. Lonzo's dad hooked him up with a friend back in Compton who owned Eve's After Dark, a small social club in nearby Willowbrook. Though smaller, Eve's only cost half the fee Alpine charged. Lonzo now had a home base to launch his own DJ troupe.

Eve's After Dark was the only teen club in the city, with the exception of the Workshop on Ninety-First and Western. It was located near Compton—about a quarter mile away. Because it was located in the county of Los Angeles, it didn't fall under the purview of Compton or LA city proper, which meant the club could stay open until 6:00 a.m. Kids as young as sixteen—the place was alcohol-free—flocked to Eve's, although the club advertised its parties for an eighteen-and-over crowd (after midnight Eve's turned into an after-hours joint for attendees twenty and up). Eve's became so popular that Lonzo began hosting as many as four parties a night. The club was collecting nearly $10,000 a month. Although city law banished jukeboxes, singing, and live entertainment past a certain hour, Eve's kept the party going until morning, since the law didn't state anything about DJs. The crew expanded beyond Manuel, who had dubbed himself the Unknown DJ, to include Dr. Rock, a friend of Alonzo's, Billy T from Sacramento, Sweet Ron Ron from New York, and later West Compton native Antoine Carraby. Lonzo dropped the words "Disco Construction" from the group name and soon the Wrecking Crew became the Wreckin' Cru after an attorney for some group in the Midwest sent them a cease-and-desist letter because it had the same name. Inspired by athletes being described as "world class" while he watched the 1984 Olympics, Lonzo thought to flip the name a bit and add World Class to circumvent possible infringement.

While Lonzo's Wreckin' Cru built a loyal following at Eve's, Clayton moved around from one end of the Los Angeles basin to the other. Clayton's Uncle Jamm's Army was packing spots like the Veteran's Auditorium and the Sports Arena. Thousands of people flocked to see its stable of popular DJs, including Mr. Prince, Egyptian Lover, DJ Pooh, and Bobcat. The DJs based their personas on characters they created, such as an Egyptian snake charmer, and dressed in costumes of military fatigues, leather, or spikes. When Uncle Jamm gigs ended, those unafraid to commingle with Compton's gangs would continue the party at Eve's. "We walked in and my eyes just lit up. Ten thousand kids, and nothing but DJs," Greg Mack said of those Uncle Jamm parties at the Sports Arena. "I'd never seen that in my life. The place was just off the chain." At Eve's, the vibe was sophisticated. If you weren't clean-dressed, you weren't allowed in. Period. Ladies donned dresses, fellas were fitted in silk shirts with skinny ties and slacks. Colored handkerchiefs repping gang affiliations were strictly forbidden. The Unknown DJ served as the musical director for the club. Lonzo dressed the DJs in satin jackets and put together routines filled with Temptations-style choreography for the Cru to do during sets that were heavy on sweaty R & B, funk, and electro joints from Parliament, Donna Summer, Prince, and George Clinton's solo work. "People came out in droves," Lonzo recalled. "It was a constant party."

＊

In 1981, Andre Romelle Young was sixteen and barely focused on his studies at Compton's Centennial High School. Tall, broad-shouldered, and skinny with an afro, Andre was mostly interested in chasing girls, ditching classes, and kicking it with his homies. His peers were being lured into the fast cash of dealing and the camaraderie of gang affiliations, even if both most often ensured a life of constant peril.

Andre's mother, Verna, was committed to keeping her son off the streets. Though he was deep within the confines of Crip and Blood territory, Andre never joined because "there wasn't no money in it." Verna worked full-time, which meant he was often shuttled between home and his grandmother's place in New Wilmington Arms, a housing project in Compton that was a notorious drug bazaar. Verna moved the kids more than a dozen times across South LA, and at one time or another lived in places like Watts, Carson, and Long Beach. Eventually the family settled in

Compton, in a home that was just two streets over from Eric's family on South Muriel. Verna pushed strong values on Andre, and no matter where they lived, he was mostly able to keep his nose clean. She allowed Andre to transfer from Centennial to Fremont High School in South Central, where he excelled at swimming and diving. He loved drafting, and a teacher wanted him to enroll in an aircraft drafting apprenticeship program at Northrop Grumman, an aviation company. It was a prospect that excited him—especially considering the lucrative career it could lead to—but his grades made him ineligible and he dropped out of Freemont, enrolling in an adult school in Compton and later radio-broadcasting school.

Handsome, with a voracious appetite for women, Andre met a young lady named Lisa Johnson, whom he got pregnant. It was a secret relationship, out of respect for Lisa's mother, who thought her daughter was too young to be dating. She was livid to learn her daughter was expecting a child and threatened Andre during a call with Verna that ended with the women spewing venom toward each other. Lisa's mother was so upset she refused to inform Andre the baby had arrived. His daughter La Tanya Danielle Young was born on January 19, 1983, when he was seventeen, and Lisa fifteen. But La Tanya wasn't actually Andre's firstborn, that would be Curtis Young, born just over a year earlier in nearby Paramount to a woman named Cassandra Joy Greene. It would be two decades later when Curtis was a twenty-one-year-old rapper named Hood Surgeon before father and son actually met.

What Andre did have was a passion for music, something he shared with his mother. He would buy singles and listen to them as much as he could in his bedroom, spending hours analyzing the music. He loved the rap records coming out of the East Coast. But he's also a true soul and funk savant, raised on the records his mother kept in her prized collection. Music was so omnipresent in their house, Verna would often toss on a record before she turned on the lights when she came home from work at night. Marvin Gaye; Earth, Wind & Fire, Sly Stone; Parliament-Funkadelic; Isaac Hayes; and James Brown were in constant rotation. When he was fourteen Andre saw Parliament-Funkadelic perform at the LA Coliseum and was awestruck by George Clinton's euphoric showmanship. The show changed Andre, and funk would forever shape his musical viewpoint.

Inspired by Grandmaster Flash's seven-minute opus "The Adventures of Grandmaster Flash on the Wheels of Steel"—where Flash scratched and mixed pieces of Michael Viner's Incredible Bongo Band's "Apache," Chic's "Good Times," Queen's "Another One Bites the Dust," and Blondie's "Rapture" with dialogue from Flash Gordon—Dre decided he wanted to become a dancer. He shared his dream with his brother Tyree, who is three years younger, and is Verna's son from her second marriage after a tumultuous union with Andre's father, Theodore. Tyree excelled at football, basketball, and track, and was the first in the family to graduate from high school. While Tyree appeared to be on the track to future success, there was increased concern by friends and family over his frequent run-ins with local gang members.

*

Andre encouraged friends and fellow rap fans Darrin and June Bug to join him in forming a new dance crew. He was athletic when he felt like it, and he picked up pop-lock moves he'd seen on *Soul Train* for years. Verna, a part-time seamstress who had made a name for herself in the community for her elegant costumes, invested in her son's newfound hobby. She designed outfits for the crew and drove them to dance competitions. Verna was incredibly supportive; she had her own dreams of being an entertainer, and perfomed in an act called the Four Aces. Verna gave up the passion when she got pregnant by her boyfriend, Theodore. Two weeks after her sixteenth birthday, Verna gave birth to Andre. Musical ambitions extended to Theodore as well, and his son's middle name, Romelle, was chosen in honor of the group he sang with, the Romells, who never made it farther than their neighborhood.

Andre would get in front of the crowd and wave his arms, bend his knees and lunge himself to the ground as if he'd fallen before jerking himself back up and moving in robotic poses. His crew competed in a number of contests but never finished higher than second place. He then decided to try his hand at DJing, in the vein of Grandmaster Flash. He'd sit with old stereo components, tearing them apart and reshaping them into homemade mixers. Andre took his crudely made turntables and speakers out to a park around the corner from his house and spun records for the neighbors. For Christmas, he asked his mother for a music mixer, which he planned to attach to the music system and two turntables he had cobbled together. Verna and her then-husband Warren, whose son became rapper Warren G, scraped together the money to buy it.

"Andre was so excited when he unwrapped his mixer. He immediately got dressed and went out to show some of his friends before setting it up," Verna recalled. "He remained in his room all day, practicing with his mixer. I had to beg him to take a break just to eat." For Verna, it wasn't uncommon to find Andre asleep with music blasting into his headset.

At times neighbors complained about the loudness, but Verna didn't mind. It meant her child wasn't running the street or finding trouble. Her house became the party spot. Just about every kid on the block would come by. Verna didn't care so long as it kept the kids safe and out of foolishness. It was a fair trade, she thought. Andre launched a new music crew—a DJ group—called the Freak Patrol. They DJed at dances in the park near the house, and even booked club dances and house parties. Verna would pile Andre, Tyree, and as many of their friends as fit in her car and drive to Eve's After Dark, dropping them off at nine o'clock and setting an alarm for one in the morning, when she'd return to get them.

*

Andre began frequenting Eve's on the weekends. One night, a seventeen-year-old Andre caught a break when one of Lonzo's DJ's didn't show up, and his godmother's brother, Tim, persuaded Lonzo to let him show his skills. Andre pushed his way up to the turntables and, in a ballsy move, challenged Yella to a DJ battle.

Antoine "Yella" Carraby, born and raised in West Compton, was a standout DJ in the World Class Wreckin' Cru. Antoine joined under the name Bric Hard and earned his stage name from the Unknown DJ, who heard the Tom Tom Club's "Mr. Yellow" and told him, "That's what your name should be." Yella had mad skills. He helped bring full-scale scratching to the area after New York's Davy DMX, Kurtis Blow's DJ, spent two days teaching him how to spin—showing him how to hold the record, do the mixing, everything. It was the first time the West Coast had been exposed to the act of scratching.

Yella accepted the challenge from the young Andre. After Yella did his thing behind the ones-and-twos like usual, Andre mounted the stage like he had always dreamed. He reached for a headset and put them on. On one turntable he laid down Afrika Bambaataa's sizzling, futuristic dance-floor banger "Planet Rock" and placed the Marvelettes' Motown doo-wop classic "Please Mr. Postman" on the second turntable. The two records couldn't be more distant sonically, with widely differing tempos and moods. He tinkered with the tempos, adjusting them to meet in the middle. The crowd went wild.

Lonzo was taken aback. "Please Mr. Postman" mixed in perfect time with "Planet Rock," a record that ran twice as fast—it's a trick that's a cinch to pull off for today's DJs, with the advent of computer software, but back then was virtually unheard of. "He would lay a beat down, go over it with the a capella from another beat, and then he might take another beat from another record. It was just layers of different songs," remembered Greg Mack. "It wasn't just mixing, it was a production. As a matter of fact, he got criticized for it by some of the other regular DJs because they thought it wasn't mixing."

Andre began calling himself "Dr. Dre, the Master of Mixology," the "Dr." part lifted from his basketball idol, Julius "Dr. J" Erving. Lonzo knew ladies would go wild over the tall, handsome, and talented teenager and thought bringing Dre into the fold would help him compete with Uncle Jamm's Army, whose flashy ensembles made them electric draws. Dre was offered a spot in the Wreckin' Cru with Lonzo paying him $50 a night.

WORLD CLASS

Competition among DJ crews was fierce. Just like gang beef, rival crews were sensitive about their turf. When crews came across one another at the same venue, things often got heated and at times turned violent. But it was the fury that filtered in from the warfare between the Crips and Bloods that started to impede attendance at local dances, and eventually decimated the entire scene.

One of the worst incidents came during an August 17, 1986, stop on Run-D.M.C.'s Raising Hell Tour at the Long Beach Arena. As Brooklyn trio Whodini opened, a melee erupted between 300 to 500 black and Latino gang members. Fists, knives, and snapped-off chair legs ripped through the crowd. One fan was tossed over the balcony and onto the stage by a gang member. Assailants snatched gold chains and pummeled anyone in their path. "Please," one Whodini member said into the mic, "this is a place to party. This is a place to hear music." His plea was ignored and more than forty people were injured. Run-D.M.C. never made it to the stage.

Incidents like what happened in Long Beach and at other Run-D.M.C. shows that summer—such as the shooting death of a fourteen-year-old boy at a Bedford-Stuyvesant rap concert called Monster Jam '86 and fighting during screenings of *Krush Groove*, a seminal hip-hop film based on the early days of Def Jam Records released the year prior—pushed mainstream publications to vilify and associate rap music almost exclusively with violence. The music had drawn the ire of Parents Music Resource Center cochair Tipper Gore, who suggested that hip-hop influenced the youth that "it's all right to beat people up."

Inspiration struck the Wreckin' Cru when Lonzo booked Run-D.M.C. at Eve's in 1983. It was the group's first LA appearance, and their biting debut singles, "It's Like That" and "Sucker M.C.'s," were firebombs. The Hollis, Queens, trio, decked out in leather pants, leather hats, jackets, and tennis shoes, had a much harder street edge than the baggy pants and skinny ties the Wreckin Cru' rocked. Run-D.M.C. were fresh, no doubt, and Jam Master Jay even gave them advice on how to have a stronger, more commanding presence on stage. Yella and Dre were amazed—and the way the two saw it, they could do it too.

"This is it? It's not even a ten-minute show. We can do this," Yella said of that early Run-D.M.C. show at Eve's. "That's exactly how it started. 'We can do this.'"

During downtime, Yella and Dre hung out at the club and wrote their own material. Yella taught Dre how to master scratching, just as Davy DMX once taught him. The pair listened to records and experimented with an old four-track recording deck in Lonzo's back room. It was, Dre says, how he learned record production, as he would listen to records and think, "I would have done this different." Dre suggested they record for real, an idea that Lonzo initially thought was crazy, but he agreed, thinking the music could possibly blow up like Run-D.M.C.

In 1984, the group went to Audio Achievements, a Torrance recording studio run by engineer Donovan Smith. For a hundred bucks, they were able to record "Slice," which Yella spearheaded, and "Kru Groove." The records were deeply indebted to "Planet Rock" and the fast, synthesizer-driven music of Kraftwerk, and were jammed with Yella's basic drum beats, Dre's scratching, and rapping from Wreckin' Cru member Cli-N-Tel. It took them forty-five minutes to record "Slice" and Lonzo drove down to Macola, a small pressing plant in Hollywood that pressed small batches of vinyl for a few hundred dollars. Macola allowed artists to retain the publishing rights to their music, and the plant let acts place their own imprint labels on the recordings. Lonzo created a two-sided, twelve-inch single of the dance singles they cut, had it credited as Kru-Cut Records, and sold the records out of the trunk of his Mazda RX-7.

"We sold five thousand of them," Lonzo said. "Five thousand! That's like ghetto gold."

It was the push they all were looking for, and they continued to make the transition from club DJs to recording artists. They followed their first release with the lusty "Surgery," which was written and produced by Dre and marked his debut as a rapper. Dre fashioned a beat with a crawling bass, a synth line that beeped like a heart monitor, and some hard snares. He also dropped in a sample of a voice saying "Fresh" and built it into a scratch solo that featured a robotic voice simply repeating his name "Dr. Dre."

"Dr. Dre," Yella began.

"Yo," Dre responded in a deep husk. "I'm Dr. Dre, gorgeous hunk of a man / Doing tricks on the mix like no others can / The nurses say I'm cute, they say I'm fine / But you betta beware cuz' I'll blow your mind."

"Surgery" was a smash, selling fifty thousand records—ten times as much as their debut single.

Wreckin' Cru found further success with "Juice," a high-energy dance record inspired by Afrika Bambaataa's seminal "Planet Rock," which the track sampled. In 1985 the group decided to put out an album. *World Class* was packed with electronic funk, fast drum beats, and lots of turntable scratching. "Planet" also gleaned its inspiration from "Planet Rock" and its futuristic-sounding synths. Another song, the erotically titled "(Horney) Computer" was a glitchy romp filled with a woman's moans, and "Lovers" found its inspiration in LL Cool J's smooth "I Need Love," with its moody keyboard riffs that recalled Prince. They came with a topical message on "Gang Bang You're Dead," which Cli-N-Tel thought of after a friend was killed by gang violence:

'Cause gang bangin', dope slangin', bad for the head
If you do it too long, you'll end up dead

Dre was really feeling the harder, edgier sounds coming out of New York, but Alonzo scoffed at doing anything with much grit. Instead, he wanted lighter fare that was more romantic. Dre thought it all sounded wack—dated and soft. Even though he had a great deal of control in the studio, it was Lonzo's group and what he said went.

For the cover Lonzo had them in flashy outfits as if they were the Temptations or Soulsonic Force. They were created and designed by Verna and a tailor friend of Alonzo's. Lonzo sported a black-sequined jacket and earrings in the shape of diamonds. Lonzo and Cli-N-Tel donned shiny, purple satin suits. Yella was outfitted with a white lace glove in the vein of Prince, while Cli-N-Tel wore a jacket with black sequins on the lapel, his dress shirt unbuttoned almost to his navel. Dre, with his handsome baby face and thin athletic frame, was dressed in a tailored white-sequined body suit fashioned out of a medical supply store smock, and he had a stethoscope around his neck. Continuing the Prince influence, their faces were touched with powder and eyeliner for the shot in which they were washed in purple light and wafting smoke.

Wreckin' Cru's first show was opening for New Edition at Freemont High School. They made the rounds, playing Dooto's, a Compton club Lonzo started promoting in 1985 after he was forced to close Eve's, as well as the skating rink that opened next door called Skateland. The crowds grew as Macola sold the Cru's records to its network of independent distributors around the country and the group's manager Jerry Heller got them booked.

The Cru toured with Rick James, the Bar-Kays, and Oran "Juice" Jones, and went as far as London's Wembley Arena, playing a hip-hop event called Fresh Fest. "We wanted to put on a show. We didn't want to just come up and DJ," Dre remembered. "I would put on like a shiny doctor's outfit with the stethoscope . . . the whole thing. It haunted me later, but that's what we did then."

While the Cru were on the rise, disharmony was brewing among some its members. Dre and Yella became vocal about their frustrations over money, telling people they went uncompensated for their work and never saw money from the records flying out of Macola. Heller, however, recalled that he deposited numerous checks for Lonzo (since he didn't have a checking account) and had met him near Macola on Santa Monica and Vine in Hollywood when the checks cleared to divvy up the profits. "We'd split up the money right there on the corner, usually $20,000 or $30,000. A few times we had a $100,000 check to split," Heller said. The growing dissension was enough to send Cli-N-Tel packing to pursue a solo career. He was replaced by the group's dancer Barry "Shakespeare" Severe. And then CBS Records came calling. Larkin Arnold, an executive at CBS subsidiary Epic, wanted a meeting. "Larkin was like the black godfather of music. If he said there was a meeting, there was a meeting," Lonzo recalled.

The call from CBS put the strain Yella and Dre were feeling on the back burner. Although he felt the Cru material was dated, Dre and the group went to the meeting—waiting alongside the Dream Team and Bobby Jimmy and the Critters, the same crews they often competed with for nightclub space. The meeting went well. *Very well.* CBS offered them a record deal with a $100,000 advance. Lonzo would take most of the advance, he said, to put toward operating costs like advertising, recording costs, travel, and equipment, much to the chagrin of Dre and Yella.

"From that point on, we had nothing but dissension over money," Lonzo said.

Epic was a vast improvement from their days of pressing at Macola. The label handled recording costs. There was infrastructure to handle publicity and distribution that meant not hustling out of trunks. In January 1986, Epic told the Wreckin' Cru how much they should spend to make the album and gave them complete creative control. Dre and

Yella were done with the electro-dance vibe. What they wanted to do was something harder and edgier. Lonzo wasn't having it, though, and he steered them deeper into R & B balladry.

Maybe to sate Dre's rising profile, or to increase it, Lonzo pushed the young talent to be more central on the record. "He's Bionic" was a bombastic tribute to the rising producer and his prowess behind the boards. The record was filled with snares and computerized chants, and the lyrics described how Dre had two nurses by his side that he kept satisfied, how he was in control sexually, and how was better than all the sucker DJs. "He's bionic! Yes!" the chorus chanted in the song that closely imitated Run-D.M.C.'s blistering "It's Like That." "Love Letter" was another uninspired rap ballad with corny spoken-word lyrics about writing to someone to say "I miss you" on top of subdued synths and gentle drums, while "Mission Possible" continued the album's mission to push Dre to the forefront by letting his voice dominate more tracks. "Your mission, if you decide to accept it, is to take rap music into a new dimension," Dre tells his group members in his best attempt at channeling Mr. Phelps from the *Mission: Impossible* television series.

Wreckin Cru delivered *Rapped in Romance* to Epic in two weeks. Lonzo was handed a $75,000 check and a lashing from Epic executives, pissed the group had recorded on the cheap with drum machines, synthesizers, turntables, and old records—and not with a real band, as they'd hoped. Instructed to record something close to Minneapolis funk guitarist Jesse Johnson's "Free World," the group rushed to produce a recording called "The Fly," which sated the label with its bouncy keyboard riffs, chunky bass, and cowbells. It was enough to get the group the rest of its advance. After Lonzo recouped expenses he handed each member $5,000.

The cover of *Rapped in Romance* took the group's appropriation of Prince even further. Dre stood in the center, with slick Jheri curls, a shiny red suit with padded shoulders, and his white shirt unbuttoned to show off a gold chain. On either side stood Lonzo with his flowing mane of curls falling down a shiny white jacket and Yella with a satiny, patterned gray suit. Shakespeare was perched on a leather couch in front of them, his gold jacket and black pants just as shimmery as his bandmates'. An unidentified woman's hands could be seen in the corner of the portrait caressing a bow.

Rapped in Romance was a flop, and the group was dropped from CBS. The label wasn't about to give the guys another shot, not after Lonzo tried gaming them with skimming on the recording. Dre and Yella were unfazed. After being denied a shot at doing the type of songs they were itching to explore, both men had soured on the Cru.

LA
IS THE PLACE

That South Central became a flash point for the explosion of West Coast hip-hop should come as no surprise. In New York as hip-hop was just beginning to crawl, South Central was in peril. Hip-hop, at its core, has always been reactionary. Emcees use their surroundings as the source for their content. The earliest rap music coming out of the West Coast was largely driven by what was happening in the streets. When President Reagan intensified the War on Drugs, the Los Angeles Police Department responded with the militarization of its force. LAPD chief Daryl F. Gates, who once said casual drug users deserved to be "taken out and shot," pioneered the first SWAT teams with the use of the V-100 Commando, an armored vehicle that resembled a tank, and was once used during the Vietnam War. The Commando was outfitted with a fourteen-foot battering ram instead of a gun, which was designed to smash through suspected crack houses in a matter of seconds. The ram crumbled even the most fortified door. But as the ram gutted the homes of the innocent in search of dealers, the tank became a symbol of oppression for those living in South Central.

Compton DJ Toddy Tee, a disciple of local rap hero Mixmaster Spade, used news footage of a ram bursting through a house to write "Batterram," a tale about the roaming paramilitary vehicle, which he recorded in his bedroom in 1985. Toddy Tee's thing was spinning popular East Coast records into rhymes inspired by the streets. UTFO's "Roxanne, Roxanne" became "Rockman, Rockman" and Whodini's "Freaks Come Out at Night" became "The Clucks Come Out at Night" (a cluck is another term for a crackhead). But it was taking Rappin' Duke's "Rappin' Duke" and flipping it into "Batterram" that catapulted a nineteen-year-old Toddy Tee. His *Batterram* mixtape—recorded to a cassette tape and duplicated on a cheap dubbing deck—was a local sensation, and received heavy rotation on KDAY after Greg Mack discovered the record through promotional events he'd do in area high schools. By the end of the year Toddy rerecorded the song in a legitimate studio over a track produced by funk musician Leon Haywood (his 1975 hit "I Want'a Do Something Freaky to You" was sampled on Dr. Dre's "Nuthin' But a 'G' Thang").

Around this time, Tracy Marrow, a New Jersey native who moved to South Central after the death of his parents when he was younger, took up dancing with the West Coast Locksmiths and later the Radio Crew. He also ran with Crip members he met through his girlfriend, though he never formally joined.

Marrow devoured the work of noir street literature novelists Iceberg Slim and Donald Goines, taking on the name Ice-T as an abbreviation of Iceberg and his own first name. While spitting rhymes to impress the ladies at a beauty parlor called Good Fred—he'd get his hair permed there—Marrow was discovered by producer Willy Strong, who persuaded him to record a single. "The Coldest Rap" was a bubbly, synth-heavy jam where Ice-T detailed the litany of sexual positions he could perform. Jimmy Jam and Terry Lewis played on the record. Released on the short-lived Saturn Records, it became a hit around town, particularly at Radiotron, a youth center in MacArthur Park that served as a safe haven for local break-dancers, graffiti artists, and DJs. Ice-T became a staple at Radiotron. In 1983, he was featured in the documentary about the LA dance scene called *Breakin' 'n' Enterin'* directed by Topper Carew (who went on to cocreate classic ninties sitcom *Martin*). He would also star in the seminal 1984 hip-hop film *Breakin'*, which was inspired by the documentary.

Toddy Tee and Philadelphia rapper Schoolly D influenced the direction Ice would go next with his music. Schoolly D, born Jesse Bonds Weaver Jr., independently financed the release of his self-titled EP in 1985. The six tracks on the record serve as a brash manifesto of rough street life with his witty, profane lyrics, which garnered him far more attention than previous work that wasn't as aggressive. "P.S.K. What Does It Mean?" stood out on the EP. It was dark and menacing with an ominous beat and a title shouting out Schoolly's neighborhood gang, Parkside Killers. "Put my pistol up against his head and said, 'You sucker-ass nigga I should shoot you dead,'" he rapped. The record introduced a new form of hip-hop, one that pulled from the grim realities of those caught up in gangster life. Schoolly D's work was a catalyst for Ice-T, who, as a teenager, wrote poetic rhymes, which he'd later perform. He wanted to capture the strife he was seeing on the streets of South Central and crafted a ghetto noir titled "6 'n the Mornin'" that offered a peek into the life of "a self-made monster of the city streets."

Like "Batterram" before it, "6 'n the Mornin'" is mind-blowing in its vividness. Produced by the Unknown DJ, the record is focused on an antihero on the run from the cops. After police raid his home early in the morning, our protagonist escapes out of the back window of his bathroom and takes to the streets of Los Angeles.

> *Six in the morning, police at my door*
> *Fresh Adidas squeak across the bathroom floor*

Upon its release, "6 'n the Mornin'"—released on the Unknown DJ's Macola-distributed Techno Hop imprint—jolted listeners on both the West and East Coasts. "It shocked people when he said: 'We beat the bitch down in the goddamn street.' Back then, people didn't associate Los

Angeles with 'hood stories,'" said collaborator Afrika Islam. "We thought it was all Hollywood and Malibu Beach."

#

During the first years of hip-hop's infancy, albums from the Sugarhill Gang, Kurtis Blow, Grandmaster Flash and the Furious Five, Run–D.M.C., Beastie Boys, Whodini, and Salt-N-Pepa helped establish the genre. However, for all of its growing success, hip-hop was mostly dismissed as a passing fad and seen as a novelty that major labels, radio stations, critics, and music television barely wanted to touch. This was before hip-hop had even spun out into its many subgenres that would solidify it as a driving force in pop music for decades to come. A handful of hits, however, managed to burst through and chipped away at the glass ceiling that was keeping hip-hop from reaching pop status.

Run-D.M.C.'s banging 1986 collaboration with Aerosmith, "Walk This Way," was one of them. Before its release the trio scored airplay on MTV with its 1984 single "Rock Box," which featured Eddie Martinez on the guitar and the group performing amid black and white dancers at popular nightclub Danceteria, but "Walk This Way," a remake of Aerosmith's 1975 hit, was the song that propelled the group to ubiquity on the network. The video for the single showed Steven Tyler literally smashing through a wall that separated the hard-rock band from the hip-hop group. This melding of different worlds hardly appears innovative by today's genre-blurring standards, but back then it was unparalleled. Run-D.M.C.'s version of "Walk This Way" charted higher on the *Billboard* Hot 100 than the original, peaked at number four, and was one of the first major hip-hop singles to land among the top ten in the UK. The success of Run-D.M.C. brought with it more rotation for hip-hop videos on MTV.

When MTV launched in 1981 with the Buggles' deliciously ironic "Video Killed the Radio Star," its stable of videos was exclusively by white artists. Pat Benatar, Rod Stewart, the Who, Styx, REO Speedwagon, Iron Maiden, and Phil Collins were among the first rotation of musicians featured on the network, and MTV continued to look like this despite the movement happening a few boroughs away from the network's New York City headquarters. *Rolling Stone* observed that during MTV's first eighteen months on the air, of the 750 videos played fewer than two dozen featured black artists.

MTV argued that music from black artists didn't suit the desired format—in other words, the network's mostly young, white audience wouldn't like the music. Rick James was turned down "because the consumer didn't define him as rock," its founder, Bob Pittman, said, while another MTV executive shrugged off the criticism with this curt argument: "You cannot be all things to all people."

"Rock and roll is not a guitar, it's not long hair—that's not rock and roll. It ain't about an instrument, or this or that. The blues is the start of it all," Ice Cube said. "You add some rhythm to that blues and you have all kind of people that's doing rock and roll. And that develops into hip-hop. All of it is a spirit—the spirit of coming outside of the box. If you don't see how N.W.A is rock and roll, then you really don't get what it's all about."

In 1983, while he was promoting his *Let's Dance* album, David Bowie—himself one of the first artists featured on the network—famously took the network to task for its lack of diversity during an interview with original VJ Mark Goodman. "Having watched MTV over the past few months, it's a solid enterprise with a lot going for it. I'm just floored by the fact that there's so few black artists featured on it. Why is that?" Bowie inquired. Goodman nervously explained to an incredulous Bowie how the network was thinking in terms of narrow-casting and were playing what they believed the entire country would like, suggesting Prince "or a string of other black faces" might scare viewers in the Midwest.

MTV was forced to loosen the reins with the arrival of Michael Jackson's *Thriller*. It was an impossible album to ignore as much of the country flocked to record stores to purchase copies. As a visual artist, Jackson was transforming the music-video medium with his innovative work, but by no means did the network view him as a rock artist, much to the chagrin of Walter Yetnikoff, the president of Jackson's record label CBS. Enraged when MTV refused to play Jackson's video for "Billie Jean," Yetnikoff threatened to go public with the network's position on black artists and to pull all videos of CBS acts from rotation. With extra pressure from Quincy Jones, MTV relented and added "Billie Jean" to its playlist. *Thriller* went on to sell an additional ten million copies, and the network's viewership surged.

Michael Jackson's prominence opened MTV up to more R & B, and soon Lionel Richie, Billy Ocean, and Prince became a presence in the network's programming. Rap, however, was a tougher sell. The first time much of MTV's audience got exposed to hip-hop came courtesy of Blondie's shimmering disco jam "Rapture." On the record Debbie Harry raps and name-checks Fab Five Freddy, who appeared in the music video alongside landmark graffiti artists Lee Quiñones and Jean-Michel Basquiat. "Rapture" set the precedent for rock artists to embrace hip-hop and vice-versa, but until more rock-rap hybrids surfaced, MTV was reluctant to showcase the genre. The same went for BET—which launched a year before MTV and catered exclusively to black audiences—until it slowly introduced rap videos in a segment during *Video Vibrations*. Rap videos did have a home on local, syndicated New York shows like *Video Music Box* and *New York Hot Tracks*, as well as on TBS's *Night Tracks*, but were typically rejected by MTV for looking cheaply made—ironic considering labels didn't want to invest more into rap videos *because* MTV refused to play them.

The same year Run-D.M.C. released "Walk this Way," Beastie Boys crossed into rock-rap stardom. Previously a hard-core punk band, the Beastie Boys released their debut *Licensed to Ill*, which became the first rap album to reach number one on the *Billboard* chart. Its breakout single, "(You Gotta) Fight for Your Right (to Party!)," broke them to MTV.

"Walk this Way," "(You Gotta) Fight for Your Right (to Party!)," and "Wipeout"—Brooklyn rap troupe the Fat Boys' remake of the surf rock classic featuring the Beach Boys—got frequent airplay during MTV's early days. It's hard to believe those videos would have gotten the same airtime had there not been a white artist prominently featured on the record that appealed to MTV's core audience. Roxanne Shanté, Kool Moe Dee, and Grandmaster Flash and the Furious Five weren't any more or less relevant to the genre at the time than Run-D.M.C. or the Beastie Boys, but where were they when it came to MTV spins?

As New York rappers began getting wider exposure, the LA hip-hop scene was flourishing with homegrown acts. What helped the West Coast rap scene explode in the mideighties? Much of the credit goes to KDAY, an underground record scene powered by a laid-back vinyl presser and a pair of roller rinks.

KDAY operated out of a windowless redbrick bunker on a grassy hill between Echo Park and Silver Lake. Its six antennas shot a fifty-thousand watt AM signal focused on a narrow path toward downtown and South Central, which gave the station an awfully spotty signal as most of its power was being sent out over the Pacific. KDAY hardly reached many parts of the city during the day, but at night it could be picked up in Hawaii and as far as Japan and Russia. During its prime, personalities like Wolfman Jack, Art Laboe, and Alan Freed called KDAY home, but the station turned its focus on black music since its signal was crystal clear across South LA. KDAY was far past its heyday when an ambitious, enterprising music director arrived to take over. He didn't care that he was headed to a station in the midst of a slump. Twenty-eight and "barely scraping by" in Houston as a radio personality at KMJQ, Greg Mack (a shortened take of Macmillan) saw the KDAY gig as his entry into a massive market— the second biggest in fact. When Greg arrived in LA in 1983, out of the five black stations in the city KDAY was right near the bottom. His first objective was to top another low-rated black AM station, KGFJ.

Living in South Central, it wasn't long before Greg realized the slow

R & B jams the station had in rotation weren't exactly what the kids thought was cool, as the old saying goes. What Greg heard blasting from car stereos and boom boxes, selling in shops and swap meets, were the sounds of East Coast rap. When Greg got hip to LA's party scene, he witnessed Egyptian Lover, Bobcat, and Roger Clayton of Uncle Jamm's Army lure ten thousand kids to the Sports Arena. Scores of Latinos packed Casa Camino Real to get down to freestyle music, a fusion of the syncopated percussion of electro music with synthetic instrumentation. "I had never heard the kind of music they were playing," he recalled of the genre that seeped out of Latin neighborhoods in New York City and Miami in the early 1980s. "I started looking for stuff that sounded like that. That's when I discovered Trinere, Debbie Deb, Lisa Lisa." Greg started adding electro to his playlist and reintroduced rap back into programming whenever he was permitted. Initially he got pushback against adding rap, as it was removed from the station's circulation at the behest of a conservative program director a few years before. But Greg was given the okay to bring it back, with a condition. Rap could only be played during late-night hours. KDAY saw an immediate surge in ratings and by 1986 at least 60 percent of the songs heard on the station were rap.

Records from East Coast rappers like Run-D.M.C., Whodini, and LL Cool J dominated KDAY's programming, but Greg was clamoring to showcase local DJs like the ones he saw in clubs. He figured he could partner with Uncle Jamm's Army with an idea that appeased both parties—the station got the most popular DJs in the collective on its airwaves while Uncle Jamm's got free promotion for its events. During an Uncle Jamm's party, Greg made his way to the stage and introduced himself to the crew's leader Rodger Clayton.

"Does it look like I need fucking radio? We don't need y'all," Clayton barked. He had a point. Uncle Jamm's was packing kids in strictly through word of mouth.

Getting dissed by Rodger Clayton pissed off Greg. "I'll just start my own thing," he thought. Greg named his rival collective the Mack Attack

Marines. He then tried to poach Clayton's DJs. Bobcat passed at the idea when Greg tried to lure him over. The DJ had zero interest in working for free. Bobcat did have some advice for Greg, though, telling him not to bite Clayton's military theme, suggesting instead he call his unit the Mack Attack Mixmasters. Bobcat connected Greg to a young, New York–born Cuban-American DJ that went by Tony G, whom he hired along with DJ personalities Julio G and M. Walk. Greg then made a visit to Dooto's, a new club being promoted by World Class Wreckin' Cru leader Lonzo Williams. Lonzo regularly advertised on KDAY and, unlike Clayton, didn't tell Greg to fuck off. Lonzo suggested he use his DJs Dr. Dre and DJ Yella in exchange for on-air promotion.

"Man, he's damn good," Lonzo promised of Dre.

Greg loved the mixes by Dre and Yella. "They weren't normal mixes, they were actually productions. It was eight-track mixes. You had eight songs playing. I'd never heard anything like it," he recalled.

Dre and Yella were added to his Mixmasters crew and recorded daily blends of R & B and rap for a show Greg dubbed the *Traffic Jam*, a format pretty much every city has now. Because there was no budget to pay them, Lonzo got ten- to fifteen-second commercial spots before and after the show: "*This* Traffic Jam *is brought to you by the World Class Wreckin' Cru. They are live every Friday at Dooto Music Center, located at 135th and Central.*" Greg took tapes of old mixes the station put together and gave them to Dre and Yella to record new ones over. The duo did their mixing in the dinky, four-track studio Lonzo had built in the club. He also had the *Traffic Jam* mixes pressed on twelve-inch vinyl to sell. Greg broadcasted live from high schools, clubs, and popular roller rinks. The Mack Attack Mixmasters also performed at events around the city and Greg, who strongly believed in fostering community, sent his DJs around town to community centers, schools, and shopping centers, "in the places people told us not to go."

Greg's instincts paid off: KDAY beat KGFJ on his first book as music director. He brought the hottest acts to Dooto's, including LL Cool J,

Soulsonic Force, Klymaxx, New Edition, Run-D.M.C., and Big Daddy Kane, and broke a ton of rap records—angering label bosses who wanted the single chosen for its artists played. "Back then record companies didn't want to put out the best song. They wanted that song to stay on the album to sell the album," he said. "I'd always get every album and listen to it and go, 'Oh, there's that song.' That was the key to us being different."

KDAY also played a crucial role in gang relations. Greg built a rapport with the bangers who ruled the streets. He often found himself in gang territory while working clubs and roller rinks and being aware of the different, sometimes volatile crowds was crucial. Dooto's and Skateland were Blood areas. World on Wheels, a popular skating haunt in Mid-City, was Crip territory. Casa Camino Real was neutral. Sherman Square mostly attracted Hispanics while 321 Club in Santa Monica was the spot for the white folks who didn't want to go to any of the other clubs. An admittedly corny, country boy who wore cowboy boots, Greg had the trust of gang members because of his kind disposition and neutrality. "Anytime somebody got smoked I usually got a phone call. I would always tell them, there's a better way to handle it. But these are the streets. The streets have a court system all their own," he said. In the aftermath of the 1986 gang riot that shuttered a Run-D.M.C. concert in Long Beach, KDAY held a Day of Peace where regular programming was suspended and Greg had Run-D.M.C. and soul-funk crooner Barry White, who was a former member of sixties LA gang the Businessmen, on air to promote nonviolence. A cease-fire was called and observed on the Day of Peace and a few weeks later a dozen members from the warring Bloods and the Crips signed a treaty—however, the peace was short-lived.

Despite KDAY's success, complaints were rampant. People were furious over the music Greg was playing. Even though he turned the station around, record labels thought he was "fucking crazy" for playing rap. "They'd call my boss and go off," he said. "Everybody thought it was a novelty." And of course, there was the content of the records. Perhaps more comical, albeit achingly disruptive, was how KDAY's wonky antennas beamed the twenty-four-hour broadcast into the telephones, televisions, stereo players, bedroom walls, and even toilets of residents near the station's headquarters. "It's awful. It's unbelievable. At night it's unbearable," one resident was quoted in the *Los Angeles Times*. "It's even worse in wet weather. You can walk in my yard when it rains and hear the 'rap, rap, rap' music on the chain-link fence."

KDAY's playlist quickly filled with homegrown acts who had discovered Macola Records.

A storefront on a shady strip of Santa Monica Boulevard housed Macola. It was run by a silver-haired Canadian named Don MacMillan. His father had been a "rack jobber"—a wholesaler who merchandises goods on racks in retail stores—for records. When MacMillan moved to Southern California in the 1960s, his dad got him a gig at Cadet, a vinyl manufacturing plant located in South Central. Cadet pressed vinyl for its parent company Kent Records, handling releases from Ike & Tina Turner, B. B. King, and Lowell Fulson. When Kent folded in 1983, MacMillan purchased the small Hollywood plant with twelve manual vinyl presses and shrink-wrapping machines in a bankruptcy sale for $10,000. He named it Macola, an amalgam of MacMillan and Olaug, his Norwegian-born wife.

His timing was impeccable, as the LA rap scene had started to pop. Uncle Jamm's Army DJ Egyptian Lover with his single "Dial a Freak" was one of Macola's first clients. A thousand dollars got five hundred records pressed, which the DJ did for his next single "Egypt, Egypt." He sold the records out of the trunk of his car and peddled them on street corners and swap meets. MacMillan offered to help the Egyptian Lover sell records, pressing additional copies free of charge and shipping them to contacts he had with independent record-store distributors around the country, such as California Record Distributors, Select-O-Hits in Memphis, Schwartz Brothers in Baltimore, and Big State in Texas. MacMillan made a percentage of the profit, taking 15 percent of gross receipts as a distribution fee. If the records didn't sell, though, he'd eat the costs and give artists a chance to come pick them up—lest they wanted them to be recycled and pressed

as something else. MacMillan had the upper hand in this business agreement since he could press additional copies the artist might not know
about in order to boost his profits. Another client was a trio of Riverside
air force reserve men who called themselves 2 Live Crew. Their bouncy,
bass-heavy electro rap single "Revelation" became especially popular in
Miami as did Egyptian Lover's "Egypt, Egypt," and both acts headed to
Florida for promotional appearances. 2 Live Crew ended up relocating
there and aligned with a local promoter named Luther Campbell who
performed under the moniker Luke Skyywalker. Campbell became their
manager and added himself to the group, becoming its lead member. The
group then took on a raunchy, sexually explicit aesthetic and became a
national sensation—to the intense scorn of conservatives.

Macola continued to attract young, enterprising artists. World Class
Wreckin' Cru leader Lonzo Williams launched his Kru-Cut imprint under
Macola, while Unknown DJ called his imprint Techno Hop Records. At
one time or another MC Hammer, Digital Underground, Too $hort, and
Timex Social Club released records through Macola. MacMillan essentially operated the plant like a record label, taking his clients to sales meetings and radio conventions. He called radio stations to work records for
airplay and reached out to retailers to get them stocked.

✳

Despite the arrival of compact discs, vinyl was still quite viable throughout the eighties, as were cassette tapes. Introduced to the United States
in the spring of 1983 after first hitting Japan and Europe six months
prior, the technology of compact discs allowed sound to be reproduced
with remarkable clarity and a dynamic range. Discs lacked the distor-
tion or the *pop* and *hiss* of vinyl and were a significant improvement on
the sound quality of cassette tapes. Throughout 1983 and '84, approxi-
mately four hundred thousand CD players were sold in the United States.
But the players could cost up to $1,000, which, at the time, was far too

steep a price for most Americans. Record players were cheaper, and far more dependable than a new technological advancement. Because vinyl and cassettes were more affordable than compact discs, aspiring musicians were able to record without assuming much financial risk. This all made for a robust scene where independent local acts and mom-and-pop record shops thrived.

An essential cog in the underground record scene was the Roadium, a swap meet on Redondo Beach Boulevard in Torrance, California.

Located on a sprawling patch of beaten asphalt once home to a drive-in movie theater, the dingy open-air flea market was lined with varying wares as far as the eye could see. The Roadium had it all, and for bargain prices. Irregular socks and underwear, secondhand clothes, canned goods and nonperishables that were dangerously close to expiring, toys, rugs, car batteries, radios, and tons of cheap products imported from China and shipped to the Los Angeles Harbor through San Pedro. Every weekend, people poured in from Redondo Beach, Lawndale, Hawthorne, Carson, Gardena, Inglewood, Compton, and as far as Anaheim to peruse the Roadium.

Steve Yano had one of the most popular booths there. Before he was a vendor at the Roadium, Steve worked as a gardener to help pay for classes at California State University, LA, where he was studying psychology. He found part-time work transporting and selling records and tapes at an Orange County swap meet. Within a year, Steve was part owner of a shop with the man who hired him to transport records. The store did okay, but "okay" wasn't enough to pay them both. Steve sold his half of the business to his partner and took payment in merchandise. His plan was to start his own record-selling enterprise. He brought on his wife, Susan, to help sell records at a number of flea markets in Southern California before landing at the Roadium in the early 1980s.

Seeing the rising popularity in electro dance music, the Yanos started hosting weekly disco parties at their house. Steve is likely the last person you'd take for being in the know about the latest jams, but he quit college to focus on his business full-time. His booth, located near the Roadium's entrance, was a hit. Always cramped with music fans, Steve was flush with the hottest vinyl, some of which was procured with the help of Lonzo Williams. Steve had old school R & B, East Coast rap like Grandmaster Flash, Kurtis Blow, and Run-D.M.C., and the dance records percolating throughout the city. He had records no one else had, some of which weren't even officially released and had no labels or packaging.

"Pretty soon Lonzo is coming to me with stuff and I'm carrying one hundred titles. I'm selling one hundred a week of some of them. The DJ craze hits. Now everybody and their mother is a DJ and they all want the latest [music]. So they all come to me. I was selling a lot of twelve-inch vinyl. I mean, a lot," Steve once said. "Pretty soon other dealers are coming to me. I'm meeting these guys outside bowling alleys in parking lots at midnight. It was like we were dealing drugs."

During a visit to Eve's After Dark, Steve caught a practice session between World Class Wreckin' Cru's Dr. Dre and DJ Yella for their KDAY *Traffic Jam* mix. He watched in awe as Dre scratched over a beat Yella programmed on a drum machine.

"Is that how you do it?" Steve inquired.

"You want us to make you a tape?" Yella offered.

Steve took the tape Yella and Dr. Dre cut for him to the Roadium the following weekend and the kids around the booth went wild, asking how they could buy it. The Yanos begun selling Dre's homemade mixtapes Dre crafted in exchange for records. "He'd tell Steve, '*This one* is gonna be a hit,'" Susan Yano said. "And he was usually right." Indeed the mixtapes were a sensation, with titles like *'85 Live!* and *'86 in the Mix* featuring hundreds of songs chopped into a sixty-minute mix with Dre's scratching. Steve sold the records for ten dollars a pop—even though it was quite illegal for them to peddle music they didn't own the rights to.

Dre's mixes piqued the interest of Eric Wright, who frequented the Yanos' stall to sift through the piles of twelve-inch records and stock up on what he liked. Eric was fixated by the special mixes Steve blasted at his stall. After learning the tape was produced by a kid he knew from two streets over, Eric scooped up all the titles Steve had of Dre—taking out the money from his sock to pay. "Tell Dre Eric says, 'Whassup,'" he told Steve. A week later, Eric came back to the stall to drop more money on records—and to snag Dre's number from Steve, who wouldn't budge on giving out the producer's information. Same thing the next weekend. It became enough for Steve to ask Dre if he'd heard of a short fellow with a stoic swagger by the name of Eric. Of course Dre knew of Eric. His candy-painted Suzuki Samurai announced his arrival—flashiness that brought him extra attention wherever he traveled. Most people around the neighborhood knew of Eric. Steve agreed to set up a meeting over the phone. "Next thing I know," he said, "those guys are on a three-way call with me at two in the morning. Eric wants to open a record store. I tell him, 'Don't do it. It's a bad business. I can show you how, but don't do it.'"

What Steve suggested instead was they consider starting a label.

Shortly after Dre and Eric connected, they began recording tapes in a piecemeal studio in Wright's garage. From there a mobile DJ crew was launched. They called it High-Powered Productions (later the name Dre produced N.W.A's music under, alongside DJ Yella) and played house parties and proms all over South LA. Dre was desperate to do music that wasn't the romantic Prince knockoffs Lonzo required of the Wreckin' Cru. Teaming with Eric gave him the opportunity to explore the music that moved him. Eric and Dre couldn't have been more different. Eric was gruff with his mind laser-focused on hustling, and Dre, though he grew up seeing the harsh realities of street life, was the furthest thing from it. Yet both of them wanted the same outcome, something better for themselves. Rap, they realized, was a way out.

I AIN'T THA 1

The World Class Wreckin' Cru was making noise around Los Angeles, and Dre was growing more creatively fulfilled through his side projects with Eric. At the same time, O'Shea Jackson was a high schooler being shuttled from South Central to the San Fernando Valley for class. The youngest of four, O'Shea was raised in an unincorporated portion of LA County wedged between South Central and Inglewood. Both his parents worked at UCLA, his mother, Doris, a custodian and his father, Hosea, a groundskeeper. The Jackson household was a strict one, with a close-knit family structure playing a key role in keeping O'Shea from falling in with the neighborhood Crips ruling his block—besides, his brother Clyde, nine years his senior, had already ventured down that path and cautioned him against it.

Short and well-built from years playing basketball and Pop Warner League football, O'Shea was far more obsessed with rap than any sport. Sugarhill Gang's lightening bolt "Rapper's Delight" captured a then-ten-year-old O'Shea. Nicknamed Ice Cube by his brother, ribbing him for thinking he was "too cool" for his age, O'Shea's infatuation with hip-hop continued through his early teenage years, as acts like Run-D.M.C. and the Beastie Boys started dropping records. "I remember seeing Run-D.M.C. and Public Enemy for the first time," Cube said. "Every time I can see them onstage after that I cherish it because I know its only a moment in time."

"Yo, you ever write a rap before?" O'Shea's classmate Terry "Kiddo" Hayward asked him one day in class. They were bored freshmen in a typing class they got stuck with since neither made it to their counselor in enough time to pick a more intriguing elective course. O'Shea thought Kiddo was one of the coolest kids in school, and their friendship flourished over a shared affinity for rap music.

O'Shea obsessed over rap records—Run-D.M.C.'s landmark song "Sucker M.C.'s" was perhaps his favorite. Writing raps wasn't something he'd yet done and Kiddo insisted they give it a shot.

"You write one and I'll write one, and we'll see which one comes out the best."

O'Shea mulled it over, coming up with a few bars: "*My name is Ice Cube / I want you to know / I'm not Run-D.M.C. / I'm not Kurtis Blow.*" He was just fourteen.

Inspiration took over from there. O'Shea started filling his notebook with rhymes. Pages and pages were covered with lyrics and O'Shea—a great student who got As and Bs and particularly excelled in English classes—would use what was going on around him as source material. And for a teenager growing up in South Central during the early eighties, there was an abundance of inspiration. His neighborhood was infested with gangbanging, crack dealers, and addicts everywhere. "And then you had hip-hop, which was something new, other than what we were doing, which was sports, playing football, basketball, baseball. And I was excited," Cube remembered.

Life in South Central and the Jackson's one-story, midcentury home on Van Wick Street was a far departure from the affluent Valley community of Woodland Hills, with its multimillion-dollar homes and celebrity residents. O'Shea and his homies from the neighborhood were shipped to attend William Howard Taft Charter High School in the Valley as part of a busing program that started in the seventies after the Los Angeles Unified School District had been found guilty of intentionally segregating city schools.

For O'Shea, daily trips to the Valley offered him "a chance to see that the world was bigger than Compton," and he became angered by the bleak circumstances surrounding him. And soon he channeled that rage into lyrics. "Think about how you felt at that age," Cube says. "I was mad at everything. When I went to the schools in the Valley, going through those neighborhoods, seeing how different they were from mine, that angered me. The injustice of it, that's what always got me—the injustice."

When O'Shea would get home from school, he would walk two doors over to his homeboy Anthony Wheaton's house. Wheaton was a break-dancer and an aspiring producer who called himself "Sir Jinx." It was dancing that got him into hip-hop, with "The Return of Captain Rock" being the first rap song he fell in love with. "That cadence, I was drawn to it," he said. Since Jinx's mother didn't tolerate loud music in the house, the garage was converted into a makeshift studio. The two spent hours working, Jinx on a beat machine he acquired from a drug-dealing friend and O'Shea trying to get his skills together as an emcee. "We'd be in there smelling dog shit, stepping over dog shit, rapping in the garage," he recalled of the space they shared with its main tenant, Jinx's dog. Along with their friends Darrell Johnson, who went by K-Dee (aka Kid Disaster), and Barry "Master B" Severe, they formed a group called the Stereo Crew.

The Stereo Crew cut several unpolished demos in ramshackle studio setups, but what the group dreamed of was a shot to work with Dr. Dre, who was making a name for himself in World Class Wreckin' Cru—and who also happened to be Sir Jinx's older cousin.

O'Shea, who briefly rapped under the name Purple Ice, finally got a chance to meet the local hero when Dre moved into Jinx's house. Frustrated her son wasn't in school or working beyond sporadic, low-paying DJ gigs around town, his mother, Verna, put him out.

Initially Dre didn't want to be bothered. He had to promote the Cru's single "Surgery," which had picked up a bit of steam locally. But he relented, agreeing to check out the Stereo Crew in the garage where they worked. O'Shea was eager to impress Dre. He never went anywhere without his notebook—writing in his bedroom, during the long ride to school and in class. O'Shea felt more than ready. And right in that stinky garage, he broke out into a routine. *The kid is good*, Dre thought.

Dre and O'Shea immediately clicked, despite their four-year difference in age. "Next thing I know I'm ditching school to go hang out with Dre. Trying to come up with concepts and songs," he said. They hung out often, picking up girls, cruising around South Central. Dre would also take him to clubs and Lonzo's garage where he worked on tracks in the primitive studio there.

One night Dre bumped into O'Shea at a show at Skateland, the Compton roller rink with an audience more notorious than the Apollo with its penchant for hurling insults, or worse, if you were wack. "The place was rowdy as a motherfucker," Dre recalled. "You had to get up there and get busy." Dre suggested O'Shea get on the mic. He'd never rapped publicly before but he was cocksure and ready to go.

At the time, parody raps were insanely popular. South Central native Weird Al Yankovic had become a sensation for his irreverent dressings of pop and rock hits, and radio jocks routinely transformed popular songs into silly tunes. Lewd, X-rated comedy albums from Richard Pryor and Rudy Ray Moore were tawdry adult fun. O'Shea had discovered the records in his parents' collection next to soul and R & B records. "We used to sneak and listen to that," Sir Jinx said. "It was a secret pleasure. Listening to the curse words and feeling grown. We ran to that."

The craze carried over to hip-hop, and soon enough O'Shea was writing his own filthy parodies. Brooklyn crew UTFO's hit "Roxanne, Roxanne" sparked a flame among emcees looking to one-up each other with their own answer to the insult record about a woman who wouldn't respond to advances—and O'Shea had a version he wanted to do. Dre put on an instrumental of the record and began cutting it up on two turntables. O'Shea unleashed his own raunchy version, which he called "Dianne, Dianne." It was gloriously profane, sending the crowd wild. Ice Cube had officially been born.

Intent to find success outside of the World Class Wreckin' Cru, Dre started working more closely with the Stereo Crew. The Crew had become acquainted with Lonzo, who came on to manage them and scored them a one-song deal with Epic Records. Lonzo and Dre coproduced the group's 1986 single, "She's a Skag." The nearly seven-minute recording was clunky, stuffed with cowbells and synths ringing over a throbbing breakbeat. On the record Cube bashes a "freak" for refusing his advances, labeling her as a skag—a hilarious, albeit sophomoric, amalgam of skank and hag:

> I said "I'm Ice Cube from the Stereo Crew"
> She looked at her friend, and they both said "Who?"

The record was mostly forgettable, but the Stereo Crew was shocked to hear it in Michael Jackson's music video for 1987's "Bad," a short film directed by Martin Scorsese and partly inspired by *West Side Story*. Lonzo never told them about the placement, nor did they ever receive any payment. "He robbed us. We don't know what happened. To hear your shit on TV, and we didn't know how it got there. Lonzo could have been the Russell Simmons of the West Coast if he wasn't so fucking greedy. Look at all the people that came from Dr. Dre, Lonzo could have had those people. So it all went downhill from there. We were just making music and didn't even know we were supposed to get paid." Although it wasn't ideal, the experience gave Cube a taste of working in the record business. "We didn't like the label situation with the Stereo Crew. But everything else to us was positive," Cube later said. "We was getting a chance to hang out with Dr. Dre, and we learned with him. We were all trying to figure out what was gonna work."

After "She's a Skag," both Dre and Cube's groups would see personnel changes. Cli-N-Tel dipped out of the Wreckin' Cru to pursue a solo career ahead of *Rapped in Romance*. He would be replaced by Barry Severe, who would go by "Shakespeare, the Poet of Love" in place of his more street moniker, Master B. With Barry out of the Stereo Crew, the remaining members rechristened themselves C.I.A.—Criminals in Action, until they decided to soften it to Cru in Action. Cube and C.I.A. doubled down on the parody raps. Run-D.M.C.'s "My Adidas" flipped to "My Penis." Salt-N-Pepa's "I'll Take Your Man" was "I'll Fuck Your Friend" and Joeski Love's "Pee-Wee's Dance" became "VD Sermon." "With C.I.A., it was the same guys, but our content changed," Jinx said. "We were starting to do harder music, finding our niche."

C.I.A. signed to Lonzo's Kru-Cut label and recorded tracks that tapped into the braggadocio style of their idols, Run-D.M.C. and LL Cool J. Dre produced tracks mimicking the work New York producer Rick Rubin did on the Beastie Boy's disruptive, groundbreaking debut *License to Ill*. The beats were big, the scratching frantic, the samples varied, and the lyrics as irreverent as they were profane. "My Posse," "Ill-Legal," and "Just 4 the Cash" were hard, brimming with arrogant swagger and profoundly inspired by the Beastie Boys, a trio of Jewish boys from New York City. In 1987, Kru-Cut Records issued *Cru' in Action!*, a three-song EP that made some waves locally. At Dre's suggestion, the group opened for Wreckin' Cru during shows at Eve's After Dark and Skateland.

✳

Skateland USA was one of two roller rinks pivotal to hip-hop flourishing in LA during the 1980s. The other, World on Wheels, was anchored in Mid-City. Skateland, like World on Wheels, started its life as a bowling alley. In 1962, Woodley Carl Lewis Jr., one of the first black players in the NFL, invested in a 36-lane alley with an attached restaurant and cocktail lounge. The Compton native used money he earned as a defensive back for the Los Angeles Rams and opened the Woodley Lewis Sportsman Bowl. Next door to the alley was Dooto Music Center, an entertainment complex. Dooto's, which boasted a recording studio, production facility, and small auditorium, was opened by Walter "Dootsie" Williams, a record producer who crafted the doo-wop classic "Earth Angel" by the Penguins and released comedy albums by Redd Foxx and Rudy Ray Moore through his Dooto label.

Before Lewis and Williams founded their establishments, black businesses owners in Compton were nonexistent. "It is unlikely that any Negro-owned center of this kind is to be found anywhere else in America," the *Los Angeles Sentinel* wrote of Williams's complex in 1963. Neither business, however, would hold up for long after the 1965 Watts riots decimated parts of South Central, both physically and psychologically. After Lewis was arrested for bookmaking in 1970, a suspicious fire scorched the inside of the Sportsman Bowl. Dootsie cut town, leaving World Class Wreckin' Cru frontman Lonzo Williams (they weren't related) to take over Dooto's, which he turned into a nightclub. Before Craig Schweisinger and his father, Fred, purchased the Sportsman Bowl for dirt cheap, the forty-thousand-square-foot property sat vacant for more than a decade. Craig convinced his father they should turn the place into a roller rink since it would be fairly simple to transform the space. The Sportsman Bowl needed serious rehabbing when the Schweisingers purchased it. The building was stripped of its copper wiring and plumbing by thieves and had holes in the ceiling and a warped floor due to flooding. First Schweisinger had to persuade the neighborhood to embrace the idea of opening an establishment catering to teens and young adults, and likely to attract a mixed crowd. "Majority of them said, 'Fuck no.' They didn't want a skating rink there because the gangbangers would be all over it." After guaranteeing residents that their kids would be safe, and shelling out for extra security as required by the city, the neighborhood eased on its resistance—especially after he pointed out how Skateland, with its enclosed lot, would be a much safer destination than World on Wheels.

Skateland opened its doors on November 16, 1984, a Saturday night. Its North Central Avenue location was a block over from West Piru Street, the nucleus of Blood territory. Although a sign reading "NO CAPS—NO COLORS" was posted at the door, the crowd typically featured a sea of red pants and hats. Security wasn't lax, as Schweisinger hired his own enforcement composed of neutral guys from the neighborhood, and everyone passed through a pair of airport-style metal detectors. Guns, box cutters, surgical scissors, and nail files often landed in collection. A giant safe that would barely budge with the help of a forklift protected the money and was kept behind a bulletproof wall. And Schweisinger had a room sealed off with an exit directly outside that he used to bring in performers—when it wasn't used as a green room, the space doubled for an aerobics class taught during the day. Because it was deep within Blood territory, Skateland wasn't as subjected to turf wars the way World of Wheels was, given its proximity to three rival Crip sets. Still, that didn't make filing into Skateland on a Saturday night any less jarring, considering there were 212 gang-related murders in Los Angeles County the year it opened.

Schweisinger smartly aligned with two of the area's most well-known purveyors of local hip-hop: His neighbor at Dooto's, Lonzo Williams, and KDAY's Greg Mack. "He was all over me like stink on shit," Schweisinger said of Lonzo.

Lonzo's World Class Wreckin' Cru performed during Skateland's grand opening. The spot was packed wall to wall. There was a huge line outside, due to promotion on KDAY and posters and fliers Schweisinger had printed up. For opening night, he splurged on bright searchlights he placed out front, and business was so good his dad spent much of the night in the cashier's room counting piles and piles of single dollar bills. Mack, KDAY's star on-air personality, paid to install a line so he could broadcast from the rink the way he did at World on Wheels. "They came in with their Wreckin' Cru attitude," Schweisinger said of the night's headliners. "We had a good night, trouble free. The Cru rocked the house."

It didn't take long for Skateland, Compton's first roller rink, to become the hottest hip-hop venue in the city. When Schweisinger wasn't booking acts, he was beefing up business by hosting dances for Centennial High School, where he kicked back the school's service clubs a small profit for having their events there. "I wasn't a hard-core skating rink owner," Schweisinger laughed. Local celebrities like Mixmaster Spade, Toddy Tee, and Uncle Jamm's Army performed at Skateland, as did East Coast stars EPMD, Queen Latifah, and the Real Roxanne. An early indicator of Skateland's popularity came during a January 1987 show for Long Island duo Eric B. & Rakim, where the rink nearly doubled its 1,720 capacity. The fire and police departments were pissed. "When Run-D.M.C. came in they were scared to fucking death. They said, 'Look at all these fucking gangsters out here.' I said, 'Hey I can get you out safe, not to worry,'" Schweisinger said.

And soon a group with a ton of attitude would take to Skateland to make its debut, and change everything.

THE BOYZ-N-THE-HOOD

When the Wreckin' Cru got the last bit of their advance for *Rapped in Romance*, Lonzo bought himself a house and a BMW—much to the ire of Dre and Yella, whose pockets weren't as flush with cash despite their work on the album. A consolation of sorts, Lonzo handed Dre the keys to his old Mazda under one condition: Dre would cosign for the car, and Lonzo would handle the payment himself using Dre's stipend from the CBS payout. The Mazda had seen better days. It was old and beat up. But the problems Dre would face with the car weren't related to its performance. He racked up numerous tickets, which he ignored. Some crook broke into the car, smashed the back window, and yanked out the radio. With his shattered window, he'd make the hour-long drive to Rialto to see his girlfriend, Anna Cash, who rapped as Lady Anna in a female rap group calling themselves J. J. Fad.

Dre's crap luck with his car continued when someone stole it. He scraped up the money to get it out of an impound lot, but ignored the moving violations that piled, even though he'd received terse notices in the mail that announced the fines had doubled and tripled. He kept pushing his luck until it simply ran out. When cops pulled him over one day, they saw he owed $500 in tickets, impounded the car, and tossed him in a cell. Lonzo paid to have him freed in the chance the Cru landed a weekend gig.

A few months later Dre found himself in the same predicament, in a cell because of another stack of warrants. The bail was $900. Again, Lonzo got a call. But this time he wasn't as accommodating. He had his own car to worry about paying.

"You know what? I'm gonna let your butt sit in jail for a while," Lonzo told Dre. "Maybe you'll learn something."

Dre turned to his buddy Eric, realizing that if anyone had the money, it would be him. "Sure, I'll post your bail," he told him. "But you got to do something for me." Eric had warmed to Steve Yano's idea to launch a record label, and he wanted Dre to help get it off the ground. Dre and Eazy were particularly turned on by the hard, street-centered hip-hop of Ice-T and Schoolly D. "They were saying things that we could relate to," Dre recalled in the essential hip-hop documentary *Rhyme & Reason*.

Eager to craft music like that, Dre began to tinker on his own productions at Lonzo's small home studio. He'd bring along Cube, introducing him to Eric, and the three of them bonded over a shared love for brash raps. One day, Dre played Cube and Eric a beat he'd crafted. It was a monster from the first listen—sparse and menacing with its heavy 808 bass, hard snares, horn blasts, and high-pitched keyboard riffs.

Cube, the scribe of the group, was tasked with writing to Dre's beat. Cube tapped into the stories he'd heard from around the neighborhood, along with the drama of violent mob films like *Scarface* and *The Godfather* he caught at the drive-in, to write a gritty, profane street noir he called "The Boyz-n-the-Hood."

"Boyz-n-the-Hood" is the story of a young thug's harrowing day—an afternoon filled with sleazy deeds. Cube weaved the lyrics with visceral details that today still feel like the script for a gangster flick by Francis Ford Coppola. Cube's hood protagonist cruises around town in his '64 Cadillac, searches for girls, snuffs a crack addict, catches a friend trying to steal his car stereo, gets drunk off malt liquor, smacks his girlfriend, and beats down her father. He wrote it while bored in English class one day and recorded a demo of himself performing it over Dre's production.

Eric never had much interest in rapping; he was strictly supposed to be an investor and benefactor to this foray into hip-hop. Dre brought him a group they could launch. Originally from Brooklyn, the group called themselves H.B.O., aka Home Boys Only. H.B.O. were living in Orange County when they met Dre in 1986. It was decided H.B.O. would cut Cube's "Boyz-n-the-Hood," and Eric booked time in Lonzo's studio.

But when Dre played the record for the group, they were confused and turned off by Cube's lyrics that spoke exclusively to a South Central experience, with the language to boot.

"This ain't us. We can't do this. This is West Coast lyrics . . . we don't even know how to say half this stuff," Dre remembered the group saying.

"What is a 'six-four'?" one member asked.

The talk of drive-bys, gats, O.G.s, and slapping bones was enough to send H.B.O. packing. Dre and Eric weren't sure what to do next. The studio time was paid for already. Dre came up with an idea, suggesting Eric tackle the song. It made sense, he thought, as Cube was locked down with the C.I.A. and Dre was committed to the World Class Wreckin' Cru. Eric, however, was not a fan of the suggestion.

"Man, I don't know how to rap," Eric miffed. "I never did this before. This ain't what I'm here to do."

Dre wasn't having it. He kept nagging Eric until he relented. Of all of them, Eric's life was closest to the street thug depicted on the record. "Might as well give it a shot," Dre told him.

"Put your glasses on, cut the lights down," Dre instructed an understandably timid Eric, embarrassed to be pushed outside of his comfort zone. "Just do it."

Eric gave it a go, reading Cube's lyric into the microphone. It was terrible. The man had no type of rhythm in his delivery, and his timing was far off the mark. To ease his nerves, Dre opted to "punch in" every single line of every verse—having Eric rap a tiny bit before piecing together the best take of each line.

"*Cruising down the street in my '64.*" Again.

"*Jockin the freaks clocking the dough.*" Again. And again.

It was a test of both Dre's patience and genius. After eight or nine hours, there was something worth playing.

Over a beat sounding like an ice-cream-truck jingle on acid, Eric rapped a raw, hard-core tale. It was a celebratory gangster anthem—simultaneously bouncy and jarring—that was especially captivating under Eric's unique voice, squeaky and laughably high-pitched.

"I was like, damn. I looked at Dre in amazement, like: 'You turned this dude into a rapper,'" said Cube.

And with that, a Gangsta rapper was born.

✳

Eric settled on Eazy-E as his rap name, though no one can agree on how he landed on the moniker. He quickly took the record down to Macola to get copies pressed, where he used the profits he made from slinging dope. He spent $7,000 to get five thousand twelve-inch singles of "Boyz-n-the-Hood," crediting the record to an imprint named Ruthless Records and listing his family home on South Muriel Drive as its address. It was packaged with "Fat Girl," a ribald number where Eazy hurled juvenile insults at a girl's figure, and "LA Is the Place"—both songs featured Eazy's homeboy Ron-De-Vu and were written by Cube.

Record in hand, Eazy went down to Steve Yano at the Roadium where he knew the single would be a hot seller. A T-shirt guy at Yano's booth personalizing T-shirts with spray paint sketched what became Ruthless's logo. Eric recruited friends, gangbangers, and whoever wanted to make some cash on the side to take the single to record stores and swap meets. Eazy called them "snipers" and the practice, known as "street teams," would become rap industry standard. Free cassettes of the single were handed out to neighborhood tastemakers: leaders of popular cliques, dudes running gang sets, and kids who flocked to Crenshaw Boulevard on the weekend to show off their lowriders.

One night Dre took Eazy to downtown nightclub Casa Camino Real to meet KDAY's Greg Mack, who was hosting an event that night. The three went out to Greg's car where Eazy and Dre played the single. "I wasn't crazy about it, to be honest," Greg recalled. "I listened again and I started to like it. But then I said, 'Here's what y'all gotta do. You gotta clean it up.' There was a lot of cussing. The next day they had it, and I put it on. It was our number-one most requested record, right away."

It's not entirely clear how many copies of "The Boyz-n-the-Hood" were moved during those first months—Macola did a terrible job at book-keeping—but some figures have stated more than five hundred thousand copies were sold throughout South Central. What can't be denied is the song was a certified hit with constant rotation on KDAY.

With "Boyz-n-the-Hood" now an underground sensation, Eazy thought about the next move. What he wanted was a "supergroup," a gang of dudes everybody rocked with that would put out records together. He already had an alliance with Dre, whose reputation as a producer was unmatched on the local tip, and Cube, a wordsmith who had notebooks bursting with raps just as edgy and raw as "Boyz." Having become a fix-ture at the shows the Wreckin' Cru performed, particularly at Eve's, DJ Yella also received an invitation from Eric, who like Dre was growing tired of the Cru. "We all was in some weak groups," Yella once joked. Eazy also tapped his running buddy from the neighborhood, MC Ren, to fill out the ranks.

MC Ren, born Lorenzo Patterson, grew up in Compton with his

parents, two brothers, and one sister. He joined a Crip gang and earned pocket change through petty drug sales. During junior high Patterson began calling himself Master Ren. While attending Dominguez High School he and a beatboxing friend named Chip created a group, Awesome Crew 2. The duo even got a shot performing at the Roxy, one of the famed venues on the Sunset Strip. Ren considered enrolling in the army as an option after high school, but *Full Metal Jacket* scared him out of that dream. Music was his true passion. Ren would let Eazy hear the demos of raps he recorded whenever Eazy, who lived two blocks over, stopped by the house to hang with Ren's older brother. Eazy also recruited techno-rap writer Kim Nazel, who went by the name Arabian Prince. Raised in Compton and Inglewood, Nazel, who inverted his given name to Mik Lezan, created the same type of electro dance records Dre produced for the Wreckin Cru' and C.I.A. Eventually the two crossed paths on the area DJ circuit and began hanging together, to scoop records at the Roadium or drive down to Rialto to visit J.J. Fad, as both were dating members of the group. Dre was seeing Lady Anna and Arabian Prince was dating Juana Burns, who rapped under the moniker MC J.B.

As 1987 wore on, the end of World Class Wreckin' Cru seemed imminent. Having parted ways with Epic Records, they returned to Macola. Dre's relationship with Lonzo continued to weaken. The Cru booked gigs here and there but they weren't earning much. Lonzo thought the group could remedy its slump by getting back in the studio. When Lonzo saw that Dre's side work with Eazy seemed promising, he further loosened the strings and ceded more creative control to Dre when the Cru went into the studio to cut its first post-Epic record.

At Dre's behest, Ice Cube joined the Wreckin' Cru in the studio to help pen new material. On "House Calls," which Cube wrote with Dre and Yella, the Cru ventured away from their typical dance fair. "*Hello, this is Dr. Dre, I'm not in right now,*" he said in a breathy lilt, mimicking an answering machine. After the sound of a beep, a female voice inquires if Dre could make a "house call" since her man was out. It was another record that leaned heavily on "Planet Rock" but Dre loaded it with samples and old-school breakbeats, much to his pleasure. "Cabbage Patch" also followed a similar sonic arrangement. Written by Cube, Dre, and Lonzo, it was essentially a take on Run-D.M.C.'s "My Adidas." A sample of Billy Squier's "The Big Beat" was used along with a horn Jam Master Jay employed on a few D.M.C. songs and a record UTFO had already worn down. It was a hard party record that bit off the growing craze of the Cabbage Patch dance, which became popular after Gucci Crew II's "Cabbage Patch" took off. The Cru put its own spin on the dance in a bid to create its own signature move: "Move your left shoulder up and the right one down, and if you wanna get ill try to turn it around." And there was "Must be the Music," a funky dance number that showcased female vocalist Monalisa Young. Dre, ever the frontman, dropped in at the end for a quick verse.

Whatever optimism Dre and Yella felt after cutting the new records with Lonzo's Cru were wiped away when Lonzo informed his members that the group owed the Macola plant $65,000, meaning no royalty payments were coming anytime soon. One night, Eazy called a meeting at his house and assembled Dre, Yella, Cube, and Arabian Prince and made his pitch for this supergroup he envisioned. "We were broke, we had no money, and we were getting ripped off by the people we were producing for. We had hit records, but we weren't making any money at the time. And Eazy had flashy cars and he always said he wanted to rap," Arabian Prince recalled. "He says, 'I'll fund you guys, I don't want to do the whole drug thing anymore, I want to stop.' And we were like, 'Okay, you want to go legitimate, we want to continue making records.' So we said we'd do the song and just start this new group and go from there."

The group had a singular vision to represent the streets they were from, the same way New York rappers put on for their boroughs, and Schoolly D repped Philadelphia. They needed a name, though. While brainstorming at Arabian Prince's house in Inglewood, he suggested From Compton with Love as a play on James Bond—picturing an album cover where they would all be toting guns as if they were spies. It didn't play well with everyone.

Eazy leaned forward with another suggestion. "How 'bout N.W.A— Niggaz With Attitude?"

NIGGAZ . . . WITH ATTITUDE

Nigger. Is there a word more divisive in the American lexicon than these six letters, traceable to the sixteenth century? Is there a word that's uglier or filled with more vile or attached to such deep hatred for a group of people? The N-word isn't the only pejorative term to be hurled at a race, but no other slur has infiltrated the zeitgeist and defined a musical genre the way it has.

When Eazy suggested his "supergroup" call itself Niggaz With Attitude, he knew the name would turn heads. Though the N-word's colloquial variant, "nigga," was adopted by blacks as an attempt to snatch back the power of the term, or, as Cube said, "Using it instead of getting abused by it," its mere utterance was most often met with contempt. There's not a single black person in this country who has escaped the pain of having the N-word hurled in their face or cringed when they heard it casually dropped by someone— black or white. There are centuries of discourse on our relationship with this six-letter word, and Eazy absolutely knew the use of it would raise eyebrows.

Across the country in hip-hop's New York epicenter, acts like Public Enemy and KRS-One used white fear, and the opposition toward the genre born out of that fragility, to fight back with radicalized lyrics driven by black pride. But the men of N.W.A had a different plan. Calling themselves Niggaz With Attitude was a direct exploitation of that fear. The thought was flippant and simple: You think we are niggas, we will be the niggas you fear. "I wanted to go all the way left, everybody trying to do this black power and shit, so I was like let's give 'em an alternative," Dre once said. "'Nigger niggernigger, niggernigger fuck this fuck that bitch bitch bitch bitch bitch suck my dick,' all this kind of shit."

It was as provoking of a group name as you could get, inciting discomfort in white America and disdain among blacks who abhorred the term. And that was the point.

Most of the hip-hop records coming out of LA at the time were buoyed by the quick turnaround of Macola. With "Boyz-n-the-Hood," Eazy's savvy as a dealer proved a worthwhile skillset for getting the record into people's hands. He would often drop by the plant's Hollywood headquarters and make small talk with whoever was at the front desk. "Yeah, yeah, how my record doing?" Eazy would ask. He certainly cared, but he was really just biding time before he could slip into the back room, snatch a few boxes, take them out the back door and load them into his jeep to sell them—by any means necessary. "I used to make people buy records," he gloated to a reporter, who then dared to ask how he did it. "With a gun," Eazy casually responded, his face straight and scowling.

N.W.A's collective of talents went to Audio Achievements, where the Wreckin' Cru recorded its tracks, and got to work on more records that would cement its hard-core image. Dre and Cube came up with "8 Ball," a laid-back joint with lyrics written by Cube, celebrating Olde English 800—a malt liquor that was especially popular in urban neighborhoods due to its cheapness and potency, despite its horrid taste. Dre produced the track, which built in pieces of Beastie Boys and Marvin Gaye. Eazy slipped into his role as gangster antihero with ease. "*Police on my drawers, I have to pause, forty ounce in my lap and it's freezing my balls,*" he rapped.

Cube penned "Dope Man," which, like "Boyz," was a precursor to what was to come from N.W.A in terms of image and sonics. The bouncy jam, which included the first example of Dre's employment of the Ohio

Players' "Funky Worm" (the high-pitched whine of the Moog synthesizer is a staple of hip-hop sampling), sees Cube starkly detailing the day-to-day hustle of selling crack. The lyrics both celebrate and condemn the dealer. It was a ferocious look at a life that had, until then, really only played out in the scope of late-night news footage:

> It was once said by a man who couldn't quit
> "Dopeman, please can I have another hit?"

It was Arabian Prince who drafted "Panic Zone," an electro-groove number that felt like a Wreckin' Cru outtake, save for its lyrics, which spoke of the grimness of their hood. "*It's called the panic zone . . . Some people call it torture, but it's what we call home,*" the lyrics went. Cowritten by Arabian Prince, Dre, and Mexican-American rapper Krazy Dee, a friend of Eazy's who became a dope dealer, "Panic Zone" was N.W.A's first single, despite only including a tiny fraction of the group, and was a minor hit locally.

As the group worked on material at Audio Achievements, Eazy asked Lonzo Williams to introduce him to the Cru's manager, Jerry Heller. Prior to the request, Eazy had known about Heller from conversations he'd had with Dre. Eazy owed Lonzo $500 for studio time from sessions with Dre and offered an extra $250 when he settled his bill if Lonzo agreed to expedite the meeting.

Jerry and Lonzo have detailed the arrangement in their respective memoirs, and while neither seem to agree on much about it, they both acknowledge it took Lonzo quite some time to convince Jerry to take the meeting. Jerry eventually caved after much pressure and agreed. On the morning of March 3, 1987, Eazy and MC Ren rolled up to Macola in Eazy's Suzuki Samurai.

"Hey, Jerry, this is Eric Wright," Lonzo said, introducing both Eazy and Ren to Jerry.

Eazy didn't say anything at first, instead reaching down to retrieve a wad of money from his striped white crew sock and peeling off what he owed Lonzo. Right there on the spot. Jerry was equally amused and intrigued.

"The music business and I were made for each other," Jerry wrote in his 2006 memoir, *Ruthless*. A bombastic statement, yes, but Jerry had already made and lost a fortune in the industry before he even met Eazy-E.

✳

Jerry Heller grew up in a Jewish household in Shaker Heights, a well-to-do suburb of Cleveland. His father owned a scrap-metal business and a young Jerry would hang out with the Jewish mob, he says, and gamble on sports. After high school, he headed west to study business at the University of Southern California. Jerry went on to business school and soon after found employment as an agent and promoter in the early sixties, working stints at Coast Artists, Associated Booking, and Chartwell before branching out on his own. His Beverly Hills–based Heller-Fischel Agency booked tours for the Who, Grand Funk Railroad, Black Sabbath, Humble Pie, Black Oak Arkansas, Carly Simon, Van Morrison, and Cat Stevens. Jerry's agency grossed nearly $2 million during its first year of operation—and by year four it had done $7 million in business.

In the sixties and seventies, Jerry was considered one of the most influential managers in the business. Marvin Gaye and Creedence Clearwater Revival were clients, and he mentored legendary manager Irving Azoff. He promoted Kraftwerk's first US tour and booked Elton John's first shows in America at the tiny Troubadour nightclub in West Hollywood. Jerry hit the skids, though, falling deep into cocaine and alcohol. His vices, plus a nasty divorce, devastated him, and by 1985, a forty-five-year-old Jerry was sleeping on his parents' couch in Encino.

As luck would have it, Jerry was tight with Morey Alexander, a manager who learned about the boon of dance and hip-hop artists doing business with Macola. The two friends formed an alliance and Jerry met with Macola's owner Don MacMillan. The idea was they could cherry-pick Macola's best acts, using their respective connections to get them deals at reputable labels and sharing the commission. For example: Jerry begins managing Macola act LA Dream Team; Alexander reaches out to Jheryl Busby, head of black music for MCA Records, and he signs the group; Busby cuts the advance check and Alexander passes half the commission to Jerry and pays a small tribute to MacMillan on the condition he relinquishes the right to release future records by them. Alexander and Heller then scoop up Egyptian Lover, Bobby Jimmy and the Critters' Russ Parr, and Lonzo's Wreckin' Cru.

And now Jerry, a washed-up rock manager, was face to face with Eazy-E, a former dope dealer. The men didn't have much in common except that they were opportunists looking to catch a break.

Jerry says Eazy later told him of their early encounters that he was the first white guy he had ever really talked to who wasn't trying to collect rent—or arrest him.

Eazy made his pitch: He wanted to start a label.

Jerry, an admittedly arrogant, puff-out-your-chest kinda guy, suppressed the desire to tell Eazy he was just one of many knocking at his door trying to do business with him.

"You want to play me something?" he asked instead.

Eazy fished out a tape from his jacket and put it into the conference-room deck and pressed play: "*Cruisin' down the street in my six-four, Jockin the freaks clocking the dough.*" Jerry was blown away. "This was the Rolling Stones, the Black Panthers, Gil Scott-Heron; this was music that would change everything," he wrote in his memoir. "No apologies, no excuses, just the straight undistilled street telling me things I had never heard before, yet that I understood instantly."

"Who is that?" Jerry asked. "Was that you?"

Eazy didn't answer, but he played the record again after Jerry asked him to. He then played "8 Ball." And then "Dope Man."

"The label you want to start—it have a name?"

"Ruthless Records," Eazy told him.

"And the group? What do you call them?"

"N.W.A," he said.

"N.W.A?" Jerry pried. "What's that mean, 'No Whites Allowed'?"

It made Eazy laugh. "Close enough."

Their first meeting lasted three hours. Jerry pressed Eazy on whether or not he was the "dope man" as depicted in the record, something Eazy shrugged off. He was mysterious. Jerry was intrigued. According to his account of their business agreement, which was hastily agreed upon the same day, Eazy told Jerry he wanted to do a fifty-fifty partnership because it would make the math simple. Jerry rebuffed the idea, insisting he only take a 20 percent fee.

"Every dollar comes into Ruthless, I take twenty cents. That's industry standard for a manager of my caliber. I take twenty, you take eighty percent," Jerry told him. "I am responsible for my expenses, and you're responsible for yours. You own the company. I work for you."

"Total black ownership, one hundred percent," Jerry assured. "It doesn't make any sense any other way." The deal was sealed with a handshake.

The next afternoon, Jerry, accompanied by Eazy, met in the back room of Hollywood Italian eatery Martoni's, a favorite haunt of music industry types. Jerry's partner Morey Alexander and the Macola artists they were working with were also there: Rudy Pardee, Rodney-O & Joe Cooley, Arabian Prince, Egyptian Lover, Lonzo Williams, and the Unknown DJ (who Jerry wasn't even working with). There's conflict about what happened in the room. Jerry says he announced to everyone that he'd signed on as general manager of Eazy's nascent Ruthless Records. Anyone who didn't want to sign with Ruthless would need to secure other representation, he informed them. The other version of the story is that the Macola acts gave Jerry an ultimatum—it was either them or Eazy.

Either way, Jerry and his clients split ways and he switched his focus to Eazy and Ruthless.

Their bond confounded those who were around Jerry and Eazy at the time. What did a guy from the hood, who made his own from peddling drugs and evading jail, want with someone who had already fried his career on booze and blow? What could they possibly have in common? But their relationship was one that went far beyond the professional to what some might consider a father-and-son bond. Jerry was of great influence to Eazy. He helped him set up his first bank account and taught him how to manage his money, but they also spent time having heart-to-heart conversations about anything and everything. "My uncle told us, Jerry loved your dad like his son, and your dad loved Jerry like a second father," Eazy's daughter Erica said.

"They had a great dynamic," said Tracy Jernagin, an ex-girlfriend of Eazy's. "Jerry was stern, but him and Eric—with his jokester ways—they had a playful and quirky relationship."

Still, it ruffled those around Eazy, almost immediately, to see him running with Jerry.

The concern was understandable, considering Jerry was managing artists and the label to which they were signed—a dizzying conflict no matter how you cut it. And there too was the matter of race. Business dealings between black and white men in the music industry has historically been cause for great debate. For many, the image of a black artist being managed by a white executive conjures negative thoughts of control and duplicity that stem from the systematic oppression of blacks in this country in the centuries after slavery. The chatter bothered Eazy tremendously. "People callin' me, askin' me, 'Why you got a white man as your manager?'" he said. "It's like, when I was lookin' for a manager, I closed my fuckin' eyes and I said, 'I want the best.' Jerry happened to be the best."

. . . AND THE POSSE

As "Boyz-n-the-Hood" and their other recordings, "Dope Man" and "8 Ball," continued to pick up steam around Los Angeles, Eazy decided to issue a five-song EP anchored by his all-star collective.

Dre and Cube teamed together on "A Bitch Iz a Bitch." It's a brutal indictment against women where Cube explains what it takes to be called a "bitch." Between narrations by a man speaking in a straitlaced tone, Cube details the infractions worthy of branding a woman with the five-letter word: Conniving women, those who use men for money, those who gossip, those who wear scandalous clothes. *"Now the title bitch don't apply to all women, but all women have a little bitch in 'em. It's like a disease that plagues their character, taking the women of America,"* Cube raps between shrill retorts from a female voice. It's an early glimpse at the vicious misogyny that would come to define their music. Eazy recorded "Fat Girl," and there was the dancey Arabian Prince–produced number, "Panic Zone."

Eazy assembled the group and its network of affiliates for a portrait on a graffiti-covered alleyway near Macola's Hollywood headquarters. Dre was in the center, rocking a badass black jacket. Ice Cube hoisted a forty ounce bottle of Olde English. Eazy and Ren are in plain, white T-shirts, Eazy wearing a blue Dodgers cap, Ren in a black cap, both in blue khakis. Sir Jinx is in all black wearing a Flavor Flav–style clock, and Arabian Prince's curly, shoulder length locks wins for best hair of them all. C.I.A. member Kid Disaster is in the picture, so is DJ Train, Candyman, Krazy Dee, MC Chip, and DJ Scratch. The portrait would become rap legend after Macola used it for an album called *N.W.A and the Posse,* a collection of cobbled-together tracks produced by Dre featuring the earliest, still-developing N.W.A roster and recordings from other acts.

Around the same time, Dre also found another recruit to bring into the Ruthless fold. During a trip to Texas for a DJ gig, Dre linked up with Dr. Rock, an early member of the Wreckin' Cru who'd gained local fame as the only pop-locking DJ in LA. Rock was spinning records for a local Dallas radio station and had an amateur group called the Fila Fresh Crew. Rock wanted to get the Crew some studio time with Dre, who was happy to help. During the sessions, Dre couldn't help but be drawn to member Doc-T. He hadn't heard many people rap like him before. Agile and quick-witted, Doc's flow was one of the best Dre had heard.

Growing up in Dallas, Doc-T, born Tracy Curry, was inspired by East Coast staples Run-D.M.C., Fat Boys, LL Cool J, Rakim, and Slick Rick. Like Cube, Doc was a ferocious wordsmith—inheriting a love of words from reading to his grandmother. Dre saw a potential solo star in the making, but also saw a formidable songwriter who could beef up their records, something they'd need when Cube would leave LA to study architectural drafting at the Phoenix Institute of Technology.

Dre's pitch to Doc was straightforward: "Nigga, you the shit. If you come out to the West Coast, I guarantee you we will be rich." The timing worked out perfectly for Doc. His mother was pressuring him to enlist in the army and he was looking "to get the fuck away," so he reached out to his friend Andre "LA Dre" Bolton. LA Dre connected Doc to his brother who let him crash in his spot behind Centennial High School in Compton. When Dr. Dre pulled together enough money to get a spot with DJ Yella in Paramount, a city just east of Compton, Doc crashed on their floor.

As soon as Doc had arrived in California, Dre recruited him to the Ruthless team to become a sort of unofficial member of N.W.A—Doc actually thought Dre was going to be his DJ since they had discussed it. At Audio Achievements, Doc met MC Ren, DJ Yella, and Eazy. Doc still didn't quite understand why he wasn't being made a member, considering how much he contributed. "They just didn't want me in the group, I guess. I don't know. Maybe because I wasn't from California," he said. Doc's first task was writing lyrics for a solo number for Eazy—and in fifteen minutes he banged out "We Want Eazy" with help from Ren. Doc, who later started calling himself the D.O.C. (adding the periods to connect himself to the group he was working for), wanted to write lyrics for Eazy that were more palatable for radio, rhymes where every other word wasn't "bitch" or "motherfucker." "I've always known how to talk to white people. I knew if you made it funny and clever, it would be less threatening," Doc said. "You could say whatever you wanted as long as you let 'em know it's a joke. 'Don't take it to heart; I'm not really going to cut your heart out.' But I might."

Before Dre could completely focus on Eazy's project, he reluctantly agreed to join the Wreckin' Cru in the studio in August 1987 to record R & B ballad "Turn Off the Lights." Lonzo had written the song in the parking lot at the Compton Swap Meet one afternoon, and it took persuading to get the guys on board. Neither Dre nor Yella was feeling the song, but agreed to do it because they wanted to make some cash. Dre wanted to show off his improving production skills, so he crafted a harder beat more in tune with the music he was most passionate about. It wasn't a complete departure, though, as Dre incorporated some of the piano lines from the Cru's ballad "Lovers" and the Prince-like synths that were the Cru's hallmark.

For the lead vocal, Lonzo tapped an R & B singer from South Central named Michel'le Toussaint. Like so many R & B singers before her, Toussaint grew up singing in a Baptist church. She'd often sing during her shift at May Company at the Fox Hills Mall, where she met an aspiring rapper who persuaded her to come to an audition he had with Lonzo. Toussaint blew everyone away with her powerful, throaty vocal, which, given her unusually high-pitched speaking voice—she naturally talks over her larynx—came as a surprise to those who heard her. "[Lonzo] called me back the next day and asked if I wanted to do some songs and I thought, 'Oh, yeah, okay.' The next thing I knew I was there, and we were writing and trying to put together some songs," she recalled. Since the Cru's regular female vocalist, Monalisa Young, was in Connecticut working with star R & B producer Kashif, Lonzo asked Toussaint to record the track in her absence. Though the song is a sensual tête-à-tête between her and Dre, she says the two "didn't say anything other than hello" on their first encounter. Afterward, however, he started pursuing her, and in late 1987 the two began dating.

"Turn Off the Lights," however, would turn out to be the final straw for Dre and Yella's involvement with the Cru. Both felt like Lonzo was swindling them. When the men saw Lonzo receive a $1,000 check from Macola, they inquired about royalties, to which he told them the money was a refund for money he spent on recording expenses—not a royalty payment. They felt played, again. And it was no longer worth it for them. With the Wreckin' Cru, Dre and Yella felt stuck creatively and continuously cheated. By the time "Turn Off the Lights" became a hit on urban and pop charts in 1988, the World Class Wreckin' Cru was finished. "I wanted to get up outta that shit. Money wasn't right . . . I just felt like I wanted to be in control of my shit," Dre admitted. "I was just sitting in the studio knowing what I can do. I didn't have no input on a lot of that shit that came out."

RADIO

One of the first moves Eazy made for Ruthless was to sign J. J. Fad. He got hip to the Inland Empire–based female rap group, as Arabian Prince and Dre were both dating members.

Originally a quintet, J. J. Fad was an acronym of the group members' given names: Juana "MC J. B." Burns, Juanita "Crazy J." Lee, Fatima "O. G. Rocker" Shaheed, Anna "Lady Anna" Cash, and Dania "Baby-D" Birks. The ladies wanted to make a record with Dre, but the lighter, dance-heavy side of hip-hop was a sound he was desperate to escape. In 1987, Arabian produced a single for the group, the cheekily titled "Anotha Ho" along with its deliciously infectious B-side, "Supersonic," which J. J. Fad released through Dream Team Records. The single was distributed by West Coast Records, which was established by Egyptian Lover, Lonzo Williams, Rudy Pardee, and Unknown DJ, and became a hit around LA after KDAY started spinning it. J. J. Fad's first single sold four hundred thousand copies. But after a beef over management and money sent Cash, Shaheed, and Lee packing, the group then became a trio when Michelle "Sassy C." Franklin joined. The group then changed its acronym to now mean Just, Jammin', Fresh, and Def.

Eazy was impressed with J. J. Fad when he saw them perform at

Casa Camino Real. Ruthless didn't have a female rap act on the label and there needed to be one, Eric thought, especially since pioneering New York group Salt-N-Pepa blew up with "Push It." With J. J. Fad now under Ruthless, Dre, Arabian Prince, and DJ Yella worked together to rework "Supersonic," and the ladies recorded this remixed version. "The cool thing about Eazy was he was about motivating you to do you. He was never the person to say do it this or that way," said rapper-producer Gregory "Cold 187um" Hutchinson, whose group Above the Law signed to Ruthless in 1989. "He never played like he knew any more than what he knew already."

J. J. Fad have long been written off as a one-hit wonder, but the reality is "Supersonic" was a monster hit that really established Ruthless. From the success of that record, the burgeoning label secured the group a distribution deal with Atlantic Records's subsidiary Atco.

The group's debut album, *Supersonic*, released in July 1988, was the first release for Ruthless. It was a huge success, selling hundreds of thousands of copies and being certified gold. "Supersonic" went on to be nominated for the first Grammy awarded for Best Rap Performance in 1989, alongside Salt-N-Pepa, DJ Jazzy Jeff & the Fresh Prince, LL Cool J, and Kool Moe Dee. J. J. Fad showed up, but since the show opted to not televise the award announcement, most of the other nominees boycotted the Grammys, including the winners, DJ Jazzy Jeff & the Fresh Prince. "If they don't want us, we don't want them," Salt-N-Pepa said in a statement.

J. J. Fad gave Ruthless its first successful album, but the bright pop confections the group put out are mostly forgotten—lost in the shadows of the fiery brand of risqué rhymes that came to define Ruthless. Even to this day, J. J. Fad is often overlooked in the conversation of Ruthless's legacy.

With the Wreckin' Cru behind him, Dre focused on a solo record for Eazy, aptly titled, *Eazy-Duz-It*. "Boyz" was still in constant rotation on KDAY, with the single selling thousands of copies each week. In Cube's absence, MC Ren stepped up. Ren and D.O.C. pushed Eazy toward the brash gangsta archetype that would make him infamous. Eazy, the exaggerated persona of Eric Wright, only gave a fuck about pussy, money, and gangbanging and that's it. D.O.C. penned breezy jams like the hit "We Want Eazy." Ren wrote the album's title track, "Ruthless Villain," and "Radio," which featured KDAY's Greg Mack on the song's intro. "What you heard is one take. Matter of fact I never got a penny off that record," Mack laughed. "We just helped each other like that."

The lyrics crafted for Eazy were stellar, but he was deeply insecure about becoming the frontman—not because he lacked confidence, but he hated his voice and lacked rhythm, constantly struggling to pick up on the twisty flows that were written for him. Dre would sit behind the board with a sheet of paper and every time Eazy missed a take, he'd jot down a mark on the page. *Notch. Notch. Notch.* Hundreds of marks filled the page.

"He sounded and looked like a little kid. That's why we pushed him out front—he was the image," said Yella, with his group members reassuring him by saying how commercial his voice was and encouraging him to continue.

During a session for "Ruthless Villain," Ren spent hours attempting to teach Eazy how to recite the lyrics for one particular verse to no luck. The beat was faster-paced than "Boyz" and Eazy kept stumbling over the words. He couldn't grasp the wordplay. Ren would repeat the lines, and Eazy would try—and fail—to get it. Again. And again. And again. Dre finally got frustrated enough to tell Ren to just perform the verse.

Sessions for *Eazy-Duz-It* were progressing when Jerry booked the group its first tour. He knew they needed serious promotion and a distribution deal to really get to the next level. N.W.A had ironically opened for Lonzo's new, revamped version of World Class Wreckin' Cru and in November 1987, the group landed a slot on the West Coast dates of the Salt-N-Pepa tour, as Jerry went looking for a partner to distribute the music.

N.W.A was touring on the strength of a few of its early singles while Cube was away at school. He had gone to Arizona to study drafting as a fallback plan because he was unsure if anyone outside of South Central would care about what they were talking about. But the music was starting to pick up, and although Cube didn't regret his decision to pursue a degree, he felt left out of the action. "I'd get calls from them, 'We're about to go to Chicago, then we fly to Atlanta.' And I'm asking, 'How much you all making?' 'They're gonna give us $10,000 a show.' And here I have six months of school left! That was the worst year of my life," he said. "My dreams were leaving me behind." When Cube finished, the nineteen-year-old fell right back into the groove, getting to work creating verses for Eazy.

"Panic Zone," "Dope Man," and "8-Ball" comprised N.W.A's first EP. To capitalize on the group's budding popularity, Macola took the EP and fused it with an assortment of tracks Dre produced for other artists, including Eazy and the D.O.C.'s Film Fresh Crew, and packaged it as an album. "That shit was like some wack shit," Ren said. The unauthorized bootleg, *N.W.A and the Posse*, was released on November 6, 1987, and sold very well, staying on the *Billboard* black album charts for a chunk of a year. The group was incensed as many of the tracks—high-energy party cuts mostly mirroring the work Dre did with the Wreckin' Cru—weren't supposed to be released. In early interviews the group even declined to discuss the album. "They ganked us, man, straight fucked us with no grease," a miffed Eazy later said.

GANGSTA GANGSTA

"Oh, fuck, here we go," Eazy said, seeing the black-and-white cop car creep to a stop. Eazy, Dre, Yella, and Jerry were in front of Audio Achievements, catching some air in between studio sessions when the cruiser pulled up to the curb. The Torrance recording studio was base camp for N.W.A in the fall of 1987 as the collective worked on *Eazy-Duz-It*. They were quite familiar with the studio, especially Dre and Yella, who'd recorded there with the Wreckin' Cru before and were most often the first ones to arrive and the last to leave.

Two officers emerged from the squad car, their right hands cautiously hovering over their pistols.

"On your knees, hands behind your neck," one commanded, approaching Yella. The same directive was given to Eazy and Dre by the other cop, albeit a little more forcefully.

"What's going on?" Jerry asked, befuddled at the casual stop-and-frisk happening in front of his eyes.

Eazy felt his legs kicked apart as he was pinned up against the stucco facade of the studio, while Yella was forced to kneel. The officers dug into the men's pockets, withdrawing their wallets, checking their IDs, and tossing them on the pavement before retreating to the squad car and pulling away.

"What the hell was that?" Jerry asked, distraught by the event and the casual response he received from the guys.

"Day in the life," Dre told him, as they filed back into the studio, shrugging off the incident. Indeed they were all used to this, feeling like targets to a police force that saw their black bodies as a threat. Shoved up against walls, slung over the hood of squad cars, laid out on the concrete—it was all the same. The LAPD's reputation was especially notorious among blacks in South Central: there was a good chance a cop would fuck with you if they saw you on the street. For many, it felt like a daily way of life, and change wasn't coming. There wasn't a single young black man growing up in South Central during the 1980s who wasn't fed up. N.W.A decided to channel that.

"The world was changing from 'Parents Just Don't Understand' to kids just don't give a fuck," D.O.C. said about the feelings he and the members of N.W.A felt at the time.

Nearly a decade had passed since Sugarhill Gang's "Rapper's Delight" arrived to soundtrack a movement brewing on the streets of New York, establishing a genre that would permeate pop music and become the most influential sound in American music since the birth of rock two decades before. But in 1988 as Jerry Heller worked to get a distribution deal for Ruthless and N.W.A, hip-hop was still mostly viewed as a blip.

Pop audiences embraced "Rapper's Delight," but many dismissed the ubiquitous tune as a novelty and a reminder of the glittery days of disco. All the while, rap continued to innovate with seemingly every release. A sweep of 1987 alone yields Eric B. & Rakim's *Paid in Full*, *Criminal Minded* by Boogie Down Productions, LL Cool J's *Bigger and Deffer*, Ice-T's gangster-fied *Rhyme Pays*, and Public Enemy's siren of a debut, *Yo! Bum Rush the Show*—a wide sampling of how radically diverse the genre was, almost from infancy. It was the emergence of the politically and racially charged Public Enemy that showed hip-hop could be more than party starting, chasing girls, and bragging on material possessions. Public Enemy's brand was about celebrating blackness. Their music was uplifting and empowering, while giving voice to the anger and frustration that comes with being black in America. Confrontation was a major through line of Public Enemy's lyrics, which often provided a biting critique of societal ills. Ever provocative, their logo was a silhouette of a young black man in a rifle's crosshairs. But while Public Enemy provided a lightening bolt to the earliest days of mainstream hip-hop, a storm was brewing out West.

Finding a major-label distributor for N.W.A, however, wasn't as easy as Jerry imagined. He greatly prided himself on his robust Rolodex, always bragging how he knew everybody who was *anybody* in the industry. Jerry thought N.W.A was a surefire thing and it was only a matter of time before he procured a deal given his deep connects. He went to Capitol, believing it aspired to become a presence in rap, given Columbia's deal with Russell Simmons and Rick Rubin's Def Jam Records was a game-changer. Jerry said he tried to play "Boyz-n-the-Hood" and "Dopeman" for famed label head Joe Smith and got stopped right on the spot. "What makes you think anyone is going to buy this garbage? Who's going to listen? Tell me who is going to play it? No radio station in the world," Smith lectured. He did, however, offer to buy the rights to the Ruthless name.

Elektra was a no. Columbia passed. Same for Atlantic. Jerry was indignant. His pride was on the line, and rejection doesn't bode well for a man like Jerry. He was, after all, *the* guy, or so he thought. Pride aside, Jerry really believed in the music and felt it was among the most important rap records he'd ever heard. Jerry knew N.W.A could change the face of pop music, if they just had the shot.

*

While Jerry struggled to secure a deal, N.W.A continued to get busy in the studio. Dre worked for hours at a time, going as long as twelve hours behind the board—starting sessions at noon and keeping things moving as to not waste studio time. He was the group's main ear, telling them what worked and what didn't as they cut material. "He'd tell you, 'Try to make it like this.' You'd do it. He'd be like, 'Cool.' Or, 'That's terrible.' Dre'd look at you like, you dumb mother . . ." Ren remembered. "We'd go in there, lock the doors, then just start working."

At the mixing board Dre would work on beats, Yella would work on the recorder, board, drum machines, and other equipment. Dre would stack 808s, synths, and an E-mu SP-1200 sampler, and he'd get session musicians to cover old riffs, turning to the original records if he didn't like the sound. As Dre programmed beats, MC Ren and Cube served as the group's lyricists with some assistance from D.O.C. Cube would also offer ideas for records to scratch. It got incredibly competitive in the studio among the guys. "Everybody in the room had great music minds. Great writing minds. There was always major competition among the ranks. Everybody had that kinda edge—Cube, Ren, Dre, Yella, everybody," remembered Cold 187um. "Everybody was trying to showcase their wares and do their best," D.O.C. added. "That's why the shit was so good. It was about making great songs."

The competition was healthy, and there was just as much playtime going on between sessions, as they joked and bagged on each other. "They were having a ball, being young dudes just having fun," CPO Boss Hogg said. "When the transformation came was when it was time to work. Everybody went into their mode."

One day, at Dre's apartment, Cube brought up an idea for a chorus. After hearing the words "Fuck tha police," Dre skims the lyrics and passes.

"What else you got?" Dre asks Cube, initially dismissing the song because it isn't something you can drink and party to. Dre's attitude about the song changed when he and Eazy got busted by some cops for shooting paintballs at people and the officers put guns put to their heads.

Cube initially wanted "Fuck tha Police" to be a solo number, but both Dre and Ren believed it should include the whole group, and so they all gathered with pen and paper to flesh out the song, with lyrics inspired by old-time radio courtroom dramas.

Dre surveyed the milk crates housing his stacked record collection. Flipping through breakbeats he got from Steve Yano's booth at the Roadium, Dre started pulling out records.

The beats Dre was producing for N.W.A varied differently than what he did with the Wreckin' Cru. No more dancey techno. Soul and funk samples collided with sirens and gunshots. He wanted to craft productions that sounded as dark and ominous as the streets often felt. Dre built around James Brown's "Funky President (People It's Bad)" and "Funky Drummer" (both are some of the most-sampled rhythmic breaks in hip-hop), Marva Whitney's "It's My Thing," Roy Ayers's "Boogie Back," and Fancy's "Feel Good." The beat was aggressive, ferocious, and in-your-face, and when paired with the words Cube and Ren penned, "Fuck tha Police" was a fire-starter that played like an episode of a juicy prime-time drama.

The scene is an easy one to imagine playing out:

~~~~~~~~~~~~~~~~~~~~~~~~~~~~~~~~~~~~

INT. COMPTON COURTHOUSE-ROOM 603-AFTERNOON

We track backward through a wood-paneled courtroom to reveal a jury box filled with young black and Latino men. The gallery is split—on one side, there are rows of red-faced and seething police officers of varying races and on the other, black and Latino men, some of whom antagonize the officers by throwing up gang signs; a few even cradle Olde English bottles in their hand. Next to the jury box, a panel of lawyers are hastily scribbling on yellow legal pads at one table. They are huddled around a white police officer (voiced by the D.O.C.). Seated at the opposing table, DJ Yella, MC Ren, Arabian Prince, Ice Cube, and Eazy-E are dressed in suits, sunglasses and black ball caps. The entire room stands as Dr. Dre, dressed in a black silk robe, enters and sits at the bench.

JUDGE DRE

Right about now, N.W.A court is in full effect, Judge Dre presiding in the case of N.W.A versus the Police Department. Prosecuting attorneys are MC Ren, Ice Cube, and Eazy-motherfucking-E. *Order, order, order!* Ice Cube, take the motherfucking stand. Do you swear to tell the truth, the whole truth, and nothing but the truth to help your black ass?

Cube approaches the stand. He pushes away the Bible the bailiff is holding and takes a seat, the white officer rolls his eyes and mutters what sounds like the N-word under his breath. Cube is seething with anger.

ICE CUBE

You goddamn right!

JUDGE DRE

Well, won't you tell everybody what the fuck you gotta say?

ICE CUBE

Fuck the police coming straight from the underground, a young nigga got it bad cause I'm brown. And not the other color so police think they have the authority to kill a minority.

The camera pans across the jury box to show the men whooping and hollering in agreement. Some of the spectators raise middle fingers to the cops, all of whom sit their with their mouths agape as Cube continues his rant.

~~~~~~~~~~~~~~~~~~~~~~~~~~~~~

Cube's indictment is a fierce, audacious one. In just that one verse, he details the abusive cops that frequent his hood, racial profiling, police brutality, blasts black officers as more violent in a bid to impress their white counterparts, and threatens violent retribution. Ren continues the takedown, with an even angrier verse calling "the so-called law" weak before there's a vignette with Eazy on the receiving end of harassment from a squad of officers.

"What did I do?" Eazy pleads with the officers.

"Just shut the fuck up—and get your motherfucking ass on the floor."

Eazy was just as acidic with his verse. "Yeah, I'm a gangsta, but still I got flavor," he brags before dismissing cops as weak and dumb. "Without a gun and a badge, what do you got?"

The scene concludes with Judge Dre finding the white cop guilty of his crime—"bein' a redneck, white-bread, chickenshit motherfucker." D.O.C., voicing the offending cop, shouts movie-worthy dramatics.

"I want justice!"

"Fuck you, you black motherfuckers!"

"Fuck tha Police" was one of the first songs the group put together. And it was a spark in their early recording sessions. "We were trying to see how far we could push the envelope," Dre said. They continued to push, crafting startling vivid tales of inner-city life—from streets ravished by gang warfare and crack to beef with police. Liquor store holdups, bank robberies, drive-by shootings—the nightmares of urban life were brought to reality. Their words were piercing. The beats were menacing. And the message clear: We don't give a fuck.

"Do I look like a muthafuckin' role model?" Cube proclaimed on "Gangsta Gangsta," a track that opens with a woman being robbed of her purse before the sounds of gunfire silence her pleas. "To a kid lookin' up to me: Life ain't nothing but bitches and money."

Sessions continued like this. Cube, Ren, and the D.O.C. churned out vivid ghetto noir, both brash and profane. Dre was like a Dr. Frankenstein of sorts in the studio, piecing together songs by assembling a complex weave of obscure records and breakbeats. He found funk records by Funkadelic, the Isley Brothers, and the Ohio Players. A recording of Ronnie Hudson saying "In the city of Compton" got plugged in on one track, as did the Jimmy Castor Bunch, Bob James, the Honeydrippers, Kool and the Gang, Jimi Hendrix, Public Enemy, a guitar lick from Steve Arrington's "Weak at the Knees," and Richard Pryor's routine "Prison." Yella assisted him, programming the drum machine and splicing together songs. Particularly close attention was paid to *how* the record sounded, especially in the car. This was crucial to Dre. Since LA is a sprawling maze of highways and freeways, riding with the radio blaring was a way of life, and he wanted the music to be perfectly primed for those rides.

RUTHLESS VILLAIN

In March 1988, at the familiar Skateland, N.W.A performed for the first time. "Just as they were getting ready to go out, Eazy walked up to me and said, 'Man can you believe it, N.W.A at Skateland USA? This shit is epic,'" Skateland owner Craig Schweisinger recalled. "And I put my hand on his shoulder and said, 'Eric this is truly going to be an epic night.' He was a little guy, his stature wasn't that dominant. But once he got on stage that guy was ten feet tall."

N.W.A's aesthetic was no frills. All black was the look—black jeans, black jackets, and LA Raiders caps were the choice accessory. It was the most identifiable thing they wore.

"Eazy was a hard-core little Crip. They brought him a Kings jacket and a Raiders hat and that's how they performed when they were there not with Lonzo. They would come in anytime we were open, stay until we closed, and then they'd go in the DJ booth and start working with the mixing board while we're cleaning up," Skateland owner Craig Schweisinger remembered. "They'd be in the snack bar writing lyrics. They would roll an 808 in and cut and sample tracks."

"We just knew the image—that pirate, the silver and black— represented what we were all about more than any other team in Los Angeles," Cube said. "We saw groups that was wearing Troop suits and we knew that wasn't us. We had to kinda be in some way uniform and look like a group so we all decided whatever you do just come in black. And then we started putting on Raiders gear on top of that because the black matched so good."

MC Ren said the guys just wanted to represent where they were from, and it didn't hurt that the Raiders' colors were far less flashy and gaudy as the Lakers. "N.W.A in purple and gold? That wouldn't have looked good on us," he said. There was also the practicality of wearing all black—it kept them neutral among the sea of Crips and Bloods who were constantly at war.

Before the Raiders moved to LA, the Oakland players were seen as the bad boys of football. They played rough and dirty, often finding themselves among the league's lead in penalties for their unsportsman-like behavior. A reputation of being nasty and mean, paired with their black-and-silver insignia, got them labeled the black sheep of the league. They were seen as thugs on the field, and it seemed like a football was the only thing that kept them from being considered an actual gang. The team's menacing presence was enough to win over a young Cube, who worshipped them and called their move to LA in 1982 the happiest day of his life. He wasn't alone. All throughout South Central, dudes represented the team, with its hard-edge appeal.

Countless rappers have made their hometown teams part of their official look, but the marriage of N.W.A's nihilistic music with a natu-rally violent sport and its toughest team was the perfect synergy. N.W.A, before one of their concerts, went to the team's marketing director and persuaded him to give them jerseys and paraphernalia to wear onstage. Their request was gladly accommodated without the director knowing he was handing merchandise over to Gangsta rappers—not that he would have minded, considering how much the stuff was flying off the shelves as the group wore it everywhere.

Uptick in merchandise aside—the LA Kings hockey team even adopted a black-and-silver motif to cash in on the popularity—the Raid-ers' association with N.W.A became bad optics when violence erupted at games and gang members co-opted their colors. Things got so bad players stopped allowing their families to come to games, and the league hired a crisis PR firm to diffuse the negative press. In 1994 the team left LA to

return to Oakland, but still to this day, the LA Raiders insignia is as synonymous with N.W.A as it is football. "N.W.A made the Raiders more
official to LA than the Raiders while they were there," Chuck D said.

✳

During the summer of 1988 as N.W.A worked on its debut, Public
Enemy's sophomore album, *It Takes a Nation of Millions to Hold Us Back*
dropped. It was the Long Island group's attempt to make the hip-hop
equivalent to Marvin Gaye's *What's Going On*, the soul crooner's searing
meditation on the conditions blacks faced in America. *It Takes a Nation*
was instantly hailed for its production and the socially and politically
charged lyrics, and would be named the best album of 1988 by the *Village
Voice*. Three thousand miles away from Public Enemy, N.W.A, though
obviously inspired by the group's bombastic sonic, took a radically different approach to their record.

While Public Enemy tapped into black rage and political revolt, the
tracks N.W.A were recording were steeped in celebrating the hedonism
of the streets. There was rage, but it was directed at "bitches and hos"
and gave voice to the flippant street thug. N.W.A was political—even if
they argued they weren't—posturing as violent maniacs that needed to
be feared. It was an image that had already been projected on black men
for decades by white America so they figured, why not *show* the world
what that nightmare actually looked and sounded like? It's what made
their record *Straight Outta Compton* feel like such a bold, potent assault.
"You are now about to witness the strength of street knowledge," Dre
announced. It was a mission statement: We are punk rock personified
through a gang of rap dudes looking to put our hood on. "It went right
to the point. Wasn't no sugarcoating. Nothing," Yella said. "This is where
we from. This is how it is."

It took just six weeks and cost $8,000 to make what would be N.W.A's
first album, also titled *Straight Outta Compton*. Grim, gritty, profane, and

unflinchingly obscene, the bulk of the album was dedicated to capturing the ruthlessness of the streets. Much of the album's laurels rest upon its opening salvo of tracks—the album's title track, "Gangsta Gangsta" and "Fuck tha Police"—which are still among the most disruptive entries in rap history. Much of the album played out in that vein. There were harsh rhymes and biting polemics against women, police, and whoever else they damn-well pleased. "One day Ren said they'd finished the album and asked if I wanted to hear it," said CPO Boss Hogg, remembering the days Ren would hang and rap on the corner with his brother and their friend. "I sat on the corner with them and listened to this cassette tape that was *Straight Outta Compton*. It was bomb. The thing is, at that time the East Coast was still the big thing, so I didn't see this coming into anything. Next thing I knew they were one of the biggest things out because of 'Fuck tha Police.'"

Each member except Yella and Arabian Prince recorded a solo track: MC Ren on "If It Ain't Ruff" and "Quiet on tha Set," Ice Cube on "I Ain't tha 1," Eazy on a remixed version of "8 Ball" from the *N.W.A and the Posse* bootleg, and Dr. Dre on "Express Yourself," the beat of which was a carbon copy of South Central soul group Charles Wright & the Watts 103rd Street Rhythm Band's 1970 hit of the same name. Oddly enough the album is capped off with "Something 2 Dance 2," a bouncy electro record that owes a great debt to Sly & the Family Stone.

"Something 2 Dance 2" features the lone appearance of Arabian Prince, a member whose contributions have all but been erased from the legacy of the group. There have been conflicting stories about what drove Arabian Prince to exit N.W.A during the recording of *Straight Outta Compton*. It's often speculated his style that leaned toward electro and disco was too much for the group, with members feeling the sound was lighter than what they were trying to do and thus an ill fit for the group. "It was like . . . we wasn't doing that type of shit," Ren said. Jerry Heller wrote in his memoir that the "Supersonic" producer simply dropped out of sight without any bad blood and speculated Arabian didn't need the money since his father, Joseph Nazel, was in the publishing business. But Arabian Prince has pointed to finances as the motivator for his exit, taking issue with the way Jerry and Eazy conducted their business. "I was a solo artist first, so I knew what royalty statements were. I knew that when you sell this many records, every quarter you get a statement, you look at that statement, you see how much money came in, and you share the money," he said. "That wasn't happening."

And so after posing with the group for the album cover—all six of them staring toward the ground of an LA alley as Eazy points a handgun directly at the camera or, better yet, the mark who was about to get smoked—Arabian Prince bounced, leaving Dre, Eazy, Cube, Ren, and Yella as N.W.A's most famous lineup, even though that roster never actually created an album together.

＊

Jerry Heller's luck changed when he made a last-ditch pitch to Bryan Turner and Mark Cerami of Priority Records.

Turner and Cerami were former executives at K-Tel International, a Winnipeg-based company known as the original "As Seen On TV" peddler of goods. At K-Tel, Turner licensed old hits for compilation albums advertised in the late hours of the night to insomniac impulse buyers. *Roots of Soul, Motown Love Collection, Funky Super Hits, Hooked on Swing*— the list goes on. After K-Tel went bankrupt in 1984, Turner relocated to Los Angeles and founded Priority Records with Cerami, who was the son of K-Tel's head of sales, and Steve Drath. They didn't attempt to reinvent the wheel at first, opting to keep the compilation formula. Turner had great relationships with executives Cory Robbins, Fred Munao, and Barry Weiss, who cut him licensing deals without asking him to pay in advance, as well as a distribution deal with Capitol-EMI's distribution arm, CEMA.

Priority's first compilation, *Kings of Rap*, was released in 1985, sold 300,000 copies, and subsequent releases like 1986's *Rap's Greatest Hits* did well. After a commercial featuring claymation anthropomorphized raisins performing a groovy rendition of Marvin Gaye's "I Heard It Through the Grapevine" became wildly popular, Turner approached the California Raisin Advisory Board about licensing the name and likeness of the "California Raisins." He then tracked down Buddy Miles, the former Jimi Hendrix bandmate who sang the vocal in the commercial, and booked studio time with him. More commercials were produced, and the fictional R & B group of dried grapes released the first of four albums, *The California Raisins Sing the Hit Songs*, in 1987. It sold a staggering two million copies. Emmy-nominated prime-time specials, a Saturday morning cartoon, and copious amounts of branded merchandise followed.

Priority had zero cache in the rap world, and almost no familiarity with the genre outside of the cash-grab compilations they put out, but Jerry was desperate as 1988 was winding down. He'd been rejected everywhere, including Capitol, whose independent distribution company CEMA disseminated Priority releases. Jerry knew Turner and Cerami back during the K-Tel days, as their offices in the fifteen-story Cahuenga Sunset Building were close to each other and he was able to secure a meeting with Turner, Cerami, and the Priority staff. Prior to the meeting Turner received a call from a distributor who raved about how "Boyz-n-the-Hood" was still moving thousands of units on the regular.

A hell of a first impression was delivered in that conference room. Eazy propped his Air Jordans up on a desk and was distracted by the pager on his belt. Ren scowled. And then there was the music. Dre inserted a cassette containing the first three tracks of *Straight Outta Compton*—records that are astonishingly obscene and vivid in its depictions of street life.

Straight outta Compton, crazy motherfucker named Ice Cube
From the gang called Niggaz Wit Attitudes

The music was startling. Turner admits he didn't get it at first. He was sold when Jerry brought him to an N.W.A gig at Sherman Square Roller

Rink in Reseda (Jerry taking him through the stage door so he wouldn't get a glimpse of the weapons folks tossed before going through metal detectors). The label head was dumbstruck seeing the crowd chant "Fuck tha Police"—the most controversial of the three recordings he had previewed. The song could be found on a free mixtape Eazy had his "snipers" spread across LA. A week after the concert, Turner and Cerami agreed to finance and distribute *Straight Outta Compton* and *Eazy-Duz-It* through Priority via Eazy's Ruthless Records. The members of N.W.A were also given "airtight" artist contracts, with each signing inducement letters agreeing that regardless of what happened with Ruthless or between one another, they had to honor their obligations to Priority.

"It was the best of both worlds: major-label clout with effective indie distribution," Heller said.

PARENTAL DISCRETION
IZ ADVISED

In the liner notes for *Straight Outta Compton*, N.W.A thanked "all the gangsters, dope dealers, criminals, thieves, vandals, villains, thugs, hoodlums, killers, hunters, base heads, hypes, winos, bums, arsonists, police, maniacs and badass kids" that listened to their shit. In the years since its August 1988 release, *Straight Outta Compton* has been heralded as a landmark debut, one of the most important hip-hop works of all time and an album that helped launch West Coast rap, ushered a new movement for the genre, and shifted pop culture. All those things are true, yes, but when it was originally released the album was met with little fanfare outside of their neighborhood.

There was hardly any radio play. Critics ignored it. The media wrung their hands over the album's explosive lyrics and the group's provocative name, with N.W.A members even coercing reporters into saying "nigga" when mentioning the group by name. "If you rose to the bait, you were a racist . . . There was no middle ground," journalist Jonathan Gold once wrote. Despite this, sales of the album soared, with the record performing extremely well in mom-and-pop record shops unafraid to carry rap.

N.W.A's appeal broadened into white suburban communities as the media coverage of the group ramped up. The music was "illicit, forbidden fruit" as one *Los Angeles Times* report would say. Junior high students across the country couldn't get enough of this foreign land called Compton where drugs, gangs, and the police wreaked havoc on its denizens. Some of that appeal quickly turned into obsessive imitation as white boys widely appropriated Gangsta-rap aesthetics—adopting the language, dressing the way they saw rappers on BET and MTV, and quoting the lyrics as gospel. Fascination with black culture wasn't a new idea, it went back decades from "the white negro" during the jazz and swing eras of the 1920s and '30s, the hipster and beatnik movements, and the blue-eyed soul that started popping up in the 1970s. The adoption of hip-hop by whites almost rarely felt authentic given the genre's percolation through black and Latino communities. Whites who pulled from hip-hop culture—the music, the dancing, the art, and, especially, the fashion—were often dismissed as "wiggers" (a portmanteau of "white" and "nigger") or "wankstas." Today, those attitudes have barely changed. There are few white artists who have sustained long, successful careers in hip-hop outside of Eminem—and he had Dre as a cosigner. Much of it boiled down to posturing versus authenticity. Paul Mooney said it best on *Chappelle's Show*: "Everybody wants to be a nigga, but *nobody* wants to be a nigga."

The term "Gangsta rappers" was lobbed upon N.W.A after their missive "Gangsta Gangsta." At first it annoyed the group. They considered their music "Reality Rap" because the lyrics were pulled from what they observed and something only black folks could truly understand.

In six weeks, *Straight Outta Compton* sold half a million copies—and that was without a hit single or a video on MTV. Not that they didn't try. A visual for "Straight Outta Compton" was filmed. In it they strutted down Compton streets with their hardest scowls on their faces and re-created an LAPD gang sweep. The video's director, Rupert Wainwright, originally wanted the story to play like a revolution on the streets of Compton—until he listened to how ferocious the record was. "I realized this could actually cause a riot. So I flipped the idea on its head, and we shot a police sweep, where N.W.A look like the victims of police brutality."

MTV refused to play the clip, claiming its policy was to "prohibit videos that glorify violence and/or show gratuitous violence."

During its first years on air, MTV had received much criticism for its reluctance to embrace black artists, and was even more hesitant to feature rap artists on air before Run-D.M.C. exploded in 1986 with "Walk This Way." It never mattered that N.W.A were rapping fictional tales, nor did it matter that the video for "Straight Outta Compton" didn't actually depict the group engaging in violence. Ultimately, news of the MTV ban added to the group's illicitness and translated to more sales. N.W.A was being talked about as if they were nefarious thugs hell-bent on destroying the moral fiber of America, and the ban solidified that reputation. Controversy is good for business, and they learned to embrace it, but the group was incensed by MTV's stance. The network had a huge audience and now that it was showcasing rap videos it was that type of visibility that could propel them.

"On MTV they play heavy-metal music, they show people worshipping the devil and all this, but when we bring our video telling the truth of how it is on the streets to show everybody so that they could be aware of this, they don't want to play it saying we are promoting violence, promoting drugs—I disagree with that," said Ren, who felt like there was more violence shown on kiddie cartoons such as *G.I. Joe* than their video.

The release of *Straight Outta Compton* came at a time when rap had gotten far too loud to ignore by MTV. In August 1988, the network aired the pilot for its first hip-hop show, *Yo! MTV Raps*, a mix of rap videos, interviews, and in-studio performances. The first episodes appeared on Saturday nights and were hosted by Fab 5 Freddy, a visual artist and rapper who'd emerged in New York's graffiti scene during the dawn of hip-hop. Within a few months the channel cleared its schedule for a weeknight edition hosted by Ed Lover and Doctor Dré (not to be confused with N.W.A's Dre). *Yo! MTV Raps*, became wildly popular and successful in its attempt to market what Freddy called "the cutting edge of black culture."

By 1989, other networks followed MTV's lead: Fox debuted *Pump It*

Up, hosted by Dee Barnes, half of Delicious Vinyl's girl group Body & Soul; comedian Arsenio Hall debuted his talkshow that routinely showcased rap artists; and BET rolled out *Rap City*, a direct response to *Yo! MTV Raps*.

A month after *Straight Outta Compton* was released, Ruthless and Priority issued *Eazy-Duz-It*. Like *Straight Outta Compton*, Dre and Yella produced while Ren, Cube, and the D.O.C. wrote its lyrics from top to bottom.

The group joined Eazy in promoting his solo album. He was nervous about playing at the Apollo in Harlem—and for good reason, the East Coast was still fairly cool on anything coming out of the West. He got booed, and even worse, the audience tossed things. But Eazy and N.W.A were becoming a national sensation. With Ruthless Records, Eazy cemented his legacy in hip-hop as the first rapper to own a nationally successful record company.

Where N.W.A's album was grim, Eazy's took an almost cartoonish approach in the vein of the Rudy Ray Moore records the men grew up listening to. The bulk of *Eazy-Duz-It* is dedicated to ribald humor, with lewd songs about being well-endowed, his voracious appetite for women and, far more problematically, violence against them. "I might be a woman beater, but I'm not a pussy eater," he boasts on "Still Talkin'." And on "Nobody Move" Eazy attempts to rape a woman before discovering his target is a transexual. He raps about shooting their genitalia because it was "one faggot that I had to hurt."

Eazy-Duz-It outsold most of the albums coming out of New York, and would go on to sell 2.5 million copies, with *Straight Outta Compton* eventually selling 3 million records. As the group got popular, so did the outcry over their lyrics. Mainstream radio shunned them, while some major retailers refused to carry the album. Journalists who landed interviews with Eazy or N.W.A took them to task, especially for their diatribes against women. "We're not putting down women," Eazy told one reporter. "It's just street talk. Women understand that. They like us. They buy our records. They don't think of us as bad guys. . . . That's just how you talk about women." A number of black college radio DJs in the Bay Area decided to ban the music altogether because they felt N.W.A's image promoted negative racial stereotypes, the same reason many black leaders abhorred them.

"Words like bitch and nigger may be shocking for somebody who is white, but that's not why we use them," Ice Cube explained. "It's everyday language of people around my neighborhood. When they refer to a girl, they might say 'bitch,' or when referring to a guy, they might say, 'that nigger over there.' It's not used by us the way (bigots) used to use it."

No groups were more furious of N.W.A's building mainstream presence than conservatives and law enforcement. In the spring of 1989, *Straight Outta Compton* was on its way to hitting the one million sales mark, and attempts to censor the group were firing up. N.W.A filmed a video for its next single, "Express Yourself." The recording was devoid of cursing and its message wasn't one of violent revelry—instead, it was an empowering message celebrating the freedom of self-expression. Dre even boasts about how he doesn't smoke weed, ironic given the rest of the album's content. The direct sample of Charles Wright & the Watts 103 Street Rhythm Band's funky hit of the same name boosted the record's radio-friendly appeal.

The video for "Express Yourself," however, took on a more provocative message. It opened with slaves toiling on a plantation field before a master strikes a child with his whip, before a shot of the group—dressed head to toe in black and wearing thick gold chains—bursting through a banner inscribed with "I Have a Dream" (the words are blurred in some versions). Again the group is being antagonized by police officers. There are shots of them rapping from behind bars near the child slave from the opening scene, linking the continued persecution of black men to slavery and showing how it's cyclical. In other scenes, Dre plays the role of the president and parodies John F. Kennedy's assassination. The video ends with Dre in an electric chair ready for execution. More envelope-pushing than the clip for "Straight Outta Compton," yet MTV approved it for air. And because the tune was radio friendly *and* absent of curse words and violent lyrics, radio DJs were permitted to play it. For many, "Express Yourself" was their first taste of N.W.A thanks to radio play, and it soon raced up the rap charts higher than the group's previous singles. By the summer of 1989 N.W.A was the most popular rap group in the country.

The group's popularity was in part boosted by the opposition it faced from religious watchdog groups and law enforcement in response to its lyrics—and the opposition was growing louder by the minute. As N.W.A prepped a forty-date national tour, the 203,000-member Fraternal Order of Police declared a boycott of any musical group that they believed advocated violence against police officers, voting not to provide security services at their concerts (off-duty cops staff most concert security teams). Although Tipper Gore's Parents Music Resource Center, a committee established to keep explicit music away from kids, got major labels to start placing parental warning stickers on profane music years prior, law enforcement intensified its efforts to repress acts they deemed indecent— which was anyone who swore, engaged in erotic posturing, or had violent lyrics.

Cities like Columbus, Georgia; Cincinnati and Toledo, Ohio; Johnstown and Erie, Pennsylvania; and Poughkeepsie and Syracuse, New York, were particularly stringent when it came to policing acts who performed there. Bobby Brown, Skid Row's Sebastian Bach, LL Cool J, and Gene Simmons all saw themselves arrested for indecency because of their performances during this time. "Basically, I got arrested for humping a couch. I was simulating making love to a girl . . . *on the couch*. And they just felt like they didn't need a black man humpin' a couch in Georgia," LL Cool J said with a laugh. None of it made much sense, really. For instance, rock band GWAR was restricted from cursing at a concert in Toledo but allowed to decapitate mannequins onstage.

N.W.A's first national tour opened in Nashville in the spring of 1989, just after Memorial Day, headlining a bill with Salt-N-Pepa, Kid 'n Play, and Too $hort. A few dates on the tour would be coheadlined by LL Cool J. The group had a flashy set engineered for the tour inspired by the landscape of their hood: Yella's DJ stand was behind trash cans, and there were street lamps and yellow police-line tape across the front of the stage.

Drama followed the tour from the very beginning. There was an incident on the group's first flight, when an argument with a flight attendant forced the plane to land at Phoenix's Sky Harbor Airport so the twenty-nine person crew could be escorted off. Jerry Heller had to splurge on another round of airline tickets.

Law enforcement and local community leaders targeting the group added extra scrutiny to the tour. An article in Reverend James C. Dobson's magazine *Focus on the Family Citizen* brought attention, and outrage, to N.W.A's music. The headline alone was startling: "Rap Group N.W.A Says 'Kill Police.'" "Alert local police to the dangers they may face in the wake of this record release," the article stated in response to the group's "Fuck tha Police." Police departments were notified by the magazine's Christian readers and the song's lyrics were disseminated via fax among police departments.

N.W.A agreed not to perform the song on the road, but there was mounting pressure to cancel shows on the tour. Washington, DC; Milwaukee; Chattanooga; and Tyler, Texas, gave in, nixing the group's tour stops out of fear of riots. Nothing ever happened, though.

In Cincinnati, federal agents conducted a drug search on them and asked if they were gang members using the tour as a front for a crack business, and the show only went on after Bengal linebacker and city councilman Reggie Williams, along with several of his teammates, spoke up in support of the group.

In Toledo, N.W.A performed only after Reverend Floyd E. Rose went public about police who were pressuring local black clergymen. "Rightly or wrongly, the perception in our community is that the 'police think they have the authority to kill a minority,'" Rose wrote to the police chief, quoting the song, "and that [police] think that every black teenager who is wearing a gold bracelet and driving a nice car is 'selling narcotics.' . . . I must say that while I do not like the music and abhor the vulgar language, I will not be used to stifle legitimate anger and understandable resentment."

And when the group hit Kansas City, the city's acting mayor, Emanuel Cleaver, tried to stop their concert, imploring the group to "Take your trash back to LA." At the end of the show, Cube told the crowd, "We just showed your City Council that blacks, whites, Mexicans, and Orientals can get together for a concert without killing each other." As concerts went on, N.W.A noticed something peculiar: More white kids were in the crowd singing the words to all their songs. Cube would later surmise that 30 to 40 percent of the group's audience and record buyers were white.

"These people aren't doing anything but capitalizing off of death and violence, and it's something that we should not want to promote or tolerate," Lieutenant Harry Taylor of the Compton Police said of N.W.A during a newscast covering the controversy.

Cube had emerged as the group's de facto spokesperson, defending their right to say what they wanted to say on record in interviews throughout the tour. "We're not talking about all police. But there are some police that just don't give a fuck. They figure they got a gun and a badge and they can treat you any kind of way," he said. "Just because a kid hears a song, that don't mean he's going to take action. A song is a song. Just like if I made a song called, uh, 'Fuck Your Mother.' You think the kids are gonna go out and beat up their mother? For a rap song?"

✳

As the backlash against N.W.A intensified, tragedy befell Dre and his family early into the tour. Late on the night of June 25, 1989, his mother, Verna, was awakened by her stepson, Warren, informing her that two men were in the living room wanting to speak to her regarding Tyree.

Verna raced to the door. There stood Tyree's best friend, Jerry, along with two men in suits carrying briefcases.

"What happened to Tyree?"

The two men, homicide detectives it turned out, came with bad news. Tyree was dead.

Tyree, who was twenty-one with his own son and had just lost his own father three weeks prior, was with three friends when he was confronted by a gang member. Things turned physical. In the throngs of blows between the two, Tyree's opponent grabbed his head and jerked hard. He fell, striking his head on the concrete, and never regained consciousness. "Neck got broke and all kind'a shit," Dre said.

With their tour bus traveling through mountains, the repeated 911 dispatches to his pager failed to get through to Dre. At a truck stop he jumped to call home and fell to his knees when he heard. Dre cried for days, returning home to help his mother plan the funeral. The last words Tyree heard while alive, Dre later said, was "Fuck tha Police" blaring from a nearby radio. "So it kinda fucked with me. My brother was my best friend," said Dre, who admitted Tyree's death pushed him to drinking.

And trouble continued. A July tour stop in Birmingham, Alabama, would later bring serious trouble to MC Ren. According to a lawsuit filed in November 1990, a woman named Sheila Davis alleged Ren lured her aboard the group's tour bus at a post-concert party and raped her. Davis, who was sixteen at the time of the alleged assault, said the incident resulted in a baby.

No criminal charges were filed against Ren, then twenty, who denied the two ever had sex. Davis sued Ren, along with Eazy, Yella, and Dre (she didn't name Cube in the suit). Her lawyer, Gusty Yearout, stated that a blood test established a 99.8 percent probability that Ren was the biological father; however, Jerry Heller maintained no proof of paternity was presented and that Ren passed a polygraph test.

The case originally went to trial in August 1992 and was settled for

$350,000, but the group refused to pay. One of their lawyers at the time, Louis Sirkin, offered a sworn statement saying his clients never approved the settlement, which prompted a circuit judge to impose $16 million in penalties that the group had to pay Davis because it violated the settlement. The decision was then reversed, and the case was set for a retrial before being resolved out of court the following year. Davis, who is now deceased, was awarded $2 million. Years later Yearout recalled having to take the group's depositions and described everyone except Eazy as calm and polite. "Eazy-E was kind of a smart-ass during the deposition," Yearout said. "He said things like . . . Ren would never rape anybody without wearing a prophylactic."

There was trouble in-house too.

As the tour went on, Cube grew weary of the financial split between members. Unlike the rest of his N.W.A brothers, Cube still lived at home with his parents, despite the group's success. Cube was annoyed by the profits he got from *Eazy-Duz-It*, an album he considered an N.W.A project given they all greatly shaped its creation. Combined, *Straight Outta Compton*, of which he'd cowritten a great deal, and *Eazy-Duz-It* accounted for more than five million records sold. Cube only earned $32,700 in album royalties, and of the $650,000 the group went on to gross on tour, he took home $23,000, as Jerry collected $130,000. "Eazy's royalty statement came in. So I just know that this money is about to be broke up five ways, and everybody's gonna get paid," Cube said. "And dude was like, 'Nah, this is Eazy-E money, we getting N.W.A money. I'm like, 'Eazy-E and N.W.A's the same thing!'"

Between shows Cube had seen people selling merchandise with the group's name and likeness on them and was brushed aside when he inquired about profits. He was irate when the group declined an offer to go on Jesse Jackson's *Voices of America* for an episode about controversial music simply because the appearance wouldn't be paid. After a Columbus, Ohio, date, Cube went to Eazy about his grievances with Jerry. He told him that it wasn't working with Jerry. "It's either him or me," Cube told

Eazy. Not one to be pushed into a corner Eazy shrugged off Cube's ultimatum and told him, "N.W.A is me, Dre, Yella . . . and Jerry Heller; here's
your plane ticket home."

"Jerry Heller lives in a half-million-dollar house in Westlake, and I'm
still living at home with my mother. Jerry's driving a Corvette and a
Mercedes Benz and I've got a Suzuki Sidekick," he groused to a reporter.
"Jerry's making all the money, and I'm not. Jerry has no creative input
into the group: he just makes all the fucked-up decisions and gets all the
fucking money."

"There was no money. When he did 'Dopeman,' '8-Ball,' and all
those other songs, there was no payment. It was Eric saying, 'You want
a car? You want something?' Stuff like that," Sir Jinx recalled. "There
was a little money when they started doing shows. But by the time that
happened, Cube was a star already and he knew a little bit about the
business and it was like something ain't right. He started saying he wasn't
comfortable."

While on the road, Cube privately consulted the group's publicist,
Pat Charbonnet, who advised him to get a lawyer. Things came to a head
when Priority Records staff met the group in Arizona to present them
with plaques to commemorate a million copies sold of *Straight Outta
Compton*—and checks for $75,000 each. The money was payment for
previous works and an advance on their next album, but it came with a
catch: they'd have to sign a contract since their previous agreement was
nothing more than a handshake.

Cube was pissed. This was money he was entitled to and he shouldn't
have to sign a contract in order to get it. Cube at least wanted to show
the paperwork to his lawyer before accepting the deal. "Jerry told me
that lawyers were made to cause trouble," he said. "But lawyers only
cause trouble if there's trouble to cause." Cube and his lawyer attempted
to negotiate with Ruthless because outside of this he had no qualms.
"Not even with Eazy or anybody in the group," he said. With no plans
to sign, Cube implored his bandmates to do the same. Ultimately every-

body *except* Cube signed on the dotted line and were baffled to learn he didn't.

"It was kinda like, why didn't you sign the contract. $75,000. Broke as we been?" Yella said.

NO ONE CAN DO IT BETTER

As N.W.A forged on amid controversy and success, Ruthless Records was growing. J. J. Fad's "Supersonic" was a Grammy-nominated hit, and Eazy's sensational debut was topped by *Straight Outta Compton*, a record that catapulted N.W.A into infamy as the most controversial group in the country.

The label was just getting started.

Since arriving from Dallas, D.O.C. had delivered on his potential by contributing to both Eazy and N.W.A's albums. Ever loyal, he instantly became Dre's go-to guy and a sturdy behind-the-scenes utility player, penning lyrics and helping shape records. While on tour with N.W.A, the D.O.C. stepped into the spotlight as a solo artist with his own opening slot on the show.

At first D.O.C. played just eight minutes, but the crowd ate him up—his complex rhymes and dexterous flow made him a beast on the mic. Gradually his set grew. A few extra minutes in Kansas City. Twelve in Houston. By August, he was doing a thirty-minute set. It felt good, especially since he felt marginalized by the group he was working for. "I couldn't really attach myself to the N.W.A thing, the way I wanted to. I always got, 'You're not in the group.' And that stung," D.O.C. admitted. "From my perspective we were all together in this. I didn't want to separate us and compete because that was the nature of hip-hop in those days, but I took on that attitude: Let me show you guys how this thing supposed to go."

Dre made D.O.C.'s debut, *No One Can Do It Better*, his next priority.

He pulled out all his favorite funk jams and breakbeats for the record: "Impeach the President," "Hook and Sling," "Funky Drummer," "Chocolate City," and obscure picks from Heatwave, Sly & the Family Stone, B. T. Express, Lou Donaldson, Yellow Sunshine, and Teddy Pendergrass. D.O.C. wasn't interested much in tough-guy posturing, instead opting for braggadocio rhymes about his prowess as an emcee.

After a bidding war between Atlantic and Warner, Ruthless inked a deal with Atlantic to distribute the album. Radio picked up on "It's Funky Enough," a Dre production with way more commercial reach than, say, "Fuck tha Police." One of the album's most lauded tracks, "The Formula," came to Dre in a daydream as he was coming home late at night with girlfriend Michel'le. "It was me and you bustin' a song called 'The Formula' to a Marvin Gaye beat," Dre told D.O.C., who was living at Dre's spot and asleep on the floor. Dre rushed to grab a tape of Gaye's socially conscious anthem "Inner City Blues (Makes Me Wanna Holler)" and played it for D.O.C. before passing out for the night. D.O.C. stayed up through the night working out lyrics.

No One Can Do It Better, released while N.W.A and D.O.C. were finishing their tour, went gold in three months. By the fall of 1989, D.O.C. was a certified rap star. In November of that year he simultaneously filmed two music videos, "Beautiful But Deadly" and "The Formula." For "The Formula" Dre plays a Dr. Frankenstein working to build the perfect rapper, with D.O.C. as the monster creation. The days were brutal. D.O.C. boozed and smoked weed to get through the arduous eighteen-hour shoot. He celebrated the completion of the videos by partying with girls late into the morning. "I was going from chick to chick's house high on ecstasy and liquor," he said.

D.O.C. was on the way home from Beverly Hills around three-thirty in the morning when, intoxicated and high, he ran a red light. A cop flashed his lights to pull him over but he kept going. "I actually tried to outrun the fucking Beverly Hills Police, hitting a couple corners, and then shut the car off and laid down in the seat as if they weren't going to remember what car it was." He laughed. "They came and tapped on the window real politely." When they caught up with him, a wasted D.O.C. cracked jokes with the officers. He's got his gold and platinum records in the back and the cops laugh the whole thing off, even posing for photos with him and his plaques. "They gave me a ticket for running a red light and let me go—and I'm high as a kite. Thirty minutes later, I was close to death." Racing down the Ventura Freeway, he fell asleep at the wheel. D.O.C.'s Honda Prelude barreled into a concrete divider, sending him flying through his back window—he hadn't been wearing a seat belt—and face-first into a tree. Cops had to pry his teeth out of the tree bark.

When the medics arrived, it was a struggle to sedate him. Heavily inebriated, D.O.C. resisted as emergency responders tried to intubate him—causing the breathing tube to damage his larynx. At Cedars-Sinai he underwent more than twenty hours of reconstructive surgery and spent three weeks in the hospital. Eazy, Dre, and Michel'le were the first to arrive at his bedside. The extent of D.O.C.'s injuries was so severe that, his haircut was the only way his friends could recognize him.

D.O.C. fully recovered from the incident, but his voice would never rebound from the damage sustained by the breathing tube—damage he said was multiplied after a doctor removed too much scar tissue in an operation meant to expedite the healing process for his vocals, which are still marked by a rough grit. "It was never even possible for it to ever heal like it once was," he admitted. "That dream was dead after that point."

Like Cube, D.O.C. had issues with the compensation he received at Ruthless. He got a $25,000 advance for his debut album, but never signed a proper contract. "That was my first piece of loot, and even that was a fuck job because they were taking the publishing from that too. I didn't get any real money," he said. "They were doing me dirty." Eazy and Dre fronted the bill for his living expenses. Jerry Heller said Eazy took care of D.O.C.'s hospital bill, paying more than $60,000 "out of his own pocket," and that he himself spent $72,000 to take care of the down payment on a house for the injured rapper in Westlake Village, near where Eazy and Dre lived.

Even more disconcerting is the fact the D.O.C. owns very little of the publishing from the records he wrote and performed on during his time at Ruthless. One anecdote is when the group were shopping for thick gold chains ahead of promotional appearances, D.O.C. wanted in on the bling and Eazy took advantage by getting him a gold chain with a diamond-encrusted nameplate, a watch, and a ring in exchange for the royalty rights to a number of songs. D.O.C. was a nineteen-year-old kid from Dallas. He had no clue what publishing was or how it worked. He ended up taking about five thousand dollars in jewelry and forked over, at his estimation, about a million dollars worth of publishing. "I didn't know anything about the business. I was just happy to be making really great music. I was happy to be involved," D.O.C. admitted. "I didn't think of money. I was just a team player willing to do whatever it took to make the team win because I figured if I gave all I could to those guys, sooner or later they'd give all they could to me.

"Before Eric bought that gold chain, they had already taken the publishing. *We Want Eazy* was already out and certified gold—before he gave me any fucking thing" D.O.C. said, seething at the memory. "I'm sure that he knew and Jerry knew that what they were doing was kinda dirty. Sooner or later everybody found out at the label that they were getting screwed."

NO MORE LIES

Shortly after the arrival of the D.O.C.'s debut, Ruthless introduced its first nonrap act with the release of R & B songstress Michel'le's self-titled album. The South Central singer, born Michelle Toussaint, was an early Ruthless recruit because of her relationship with Dre. A few years earlier she had gotten her feet wet in the music industry when Lonzo tapped her to record "Turn Off the Lights."

Michel'le blew away anyone who heard her sing. She had a hearty and powerful vocal, which stood in stark contrast to her speaking voice that sounded like a child that inhaled helium, the result of naturally talking over her larynx. She was paired with Larry "Laylaw" Goodman to develop her material. Laylaw was a local drug dealer (he actually used to give Eazy dope on consignment) turned writer/producer who even cut a few Macola-distributed recordings, including 1985's Halloween-themed "Monster Rapping," produced by Dre and Lonzo. Because of the squeaky tone of Michel'le's voice, Laylaw decided her stage name should be Baby.

"Laylaw got this pacifier and put it around my neck on this chain. It sounds crazy," Michel'le said, laughing at the memory. "I was Baby for about two weeks. Dre said it was wack."

She decided to pay homage to her Creole heritage and Frenchified her given name by inserting an apostrophe.

Eazy was looking to push an act that wasn't hard core. "We can't only have all this rap shit on Ruthless. We have to have an R & B thing going," he told Jerry.

Michel'le wasn't looking to be the next Whitney Houston, whose polished R & B–pop was marketed to the masses. Instead, she wanted to go street. It's what she knew, and who she was. Dre and Yella collaborated to produce hard-knocking hip-hop and dance-pop beats for an album that became a seminal entry in the new jack swing movement transforming R & B in the late eighties. Though she's not always given her props, the arrival of Michel'le laid the foundation for hip-hop-flavored R & B and soul music that later launched Mary J. Blige and Faith Evans to fame. A novice in the studio, aside from the one song she did with the Cru, Michel'le was insecure about working with Dre, given his experience. Neither were sure they'd gel given their varying styles, but together they stumbled upon a sound.

"I knew nothing about hip-hop, because I grew up with big bands. I had just gotten into hip-hop a little bit and loved it," Michel'le said. "We didn't get in there with no plan. Dre worked around what I could do, and I worked around what he could do."

Michel'le's self-titled album, released in October 1989, went gold in five weeks. The record was crammed with banging new jack grooves like "No More Lies," a gold-certified hit, "Nicety," "Keep Watchin'," and the jazzy ballad "Something in My Heart," which has become her signature tune.

Despite their musical synergy, Michel'le's union with Dre was rocky from the very beginning.

They started dating following work on "Turn Off the Lights." At first Dre was seeing her *and* J. J. Fad's MC J. B. simultaneously, before Michel'le busted him. He also fathered a child with another woman while they were together. The couple eventually got serious. Dre proposed and bought a lavish troubadour-style home for them in Calabasas. Michel'le got pregnant in 1990, finding out while touring with MC Hammer. She decided to pause her career to raise their son, Marcel.

Michel'le is candid when disclosing the physical abuse she claims to have endured throughout her relationship with Dre.

"I do remember when he first hit me, when he gave me my very first black eye," she said in a radio interview in 2015. "We laid in the bed and he cried. He was crying. I was crying because I was in shock and hurt and in pain. I don't know why he was crying, but he said, 'I'm really sorry'—I think that's the only time he said he was sorry—and he said, 'I'll never hit you in that eye again, okay?' And I was like, 'Yeah, okay.' And we fell asleep."

It wouldn't be the last time he struck her, she said. Michel'le alleges Dre punched her with a closed fist on several occasions and that he gave her black eyes on at least five occasions—bruises she had to cover up with makeup in order to film her music videos. She said he also broke her nose—which required plastic surgery—left her with a cracked rib, and pulled out a gun and shot at her during a heated argument.

"It just never stopped. It became commonplace," Michel'le confessed. "It became so bad, it got to the point where people around us was like, 'Okay, I'm leaving, I gotta go.' No one helped—other than D.O.C. He would say, 'Hey, Dre, man, stop, you don't have to do this.' He was one of the *only* people to my memory. There may have been others [but] he was the main force that would be like, 'Dre, what are you doing?'" D.O.C. respectfully declined to discuss the matter.

When asked if Eazy ever stepped in, Michel'le giggles. "Not putting his business in the streets, but I don't think he could have helped," she said, noting the vast size difference between the two.

Michel'le was so accustomed to the abuse, she said, that she grew weary whenever too much time passed between incidents. It's a feeling she admits sounds ridiculous, but facing a man's fist just came with love, or so she believed. People in her life, like her grandmother, told her it was normal and so it was something she accepted. "At the time it felt like if he didn't hit me, I felt like something was wrong," she said. "It's almost like a child, if they get As they get a gift. In my mind, if a man beat you it was like 'Okay, he cares.' I couldn't believe I was actually that girl."

Michel'le documented her abusive relationship with Dre in a 2016 Lifetime biopic, *Surviving Compton*. Dre, through a statement given to his attorney and included in the film's ending credits, denied abusing Michel'le and "challenges her credibility."

F**K THA POLICE

The backlash against N.W.A, and specifically the controversial song "Fuck tha Police," came to a head on August 1, 1989, when Priority Records president Bryan Turner scanned his mail.

There was a letter, printed on Department of Justice stationery. It was just three paragraphs:

> *A song recorded by the rap group N.W.A on their album entitled* Straight Outta Compton *encourages violence against and disrespect for the law enforcement officer and has been brought to my attention. I under-*

stand your company recorded and distributed this album, and I am writing
to share my thoughts and concerns with you.

Advocating violence and assault is wrong, and we in the law enforce-
ment community take exception to such action. Violent crime, a major prob-
lem in our country, reached an unprecedented high in 1988. Seventy-eight
law enforcement officers were feloniously slain in the line of duty during
1988, four more than in 1987. Law enforcement officers dedicated their
lives to the protection of our citizens, and recordings such as the one from
N.W.A are both discouraging and degrading to these brave, dedicated officers.

Music plays a significant role in society, and I wanted you to be aware
of the FBI's position relative to this song and its message. I believe my views
reflect the opinion of the entire law enforcement community.

The letter was signed by Milt Ahlerich, the assistant director of the
bureau's office of public affairs.

It was the first time an FBI official had offered a position on a recording, book, film, or any other kind of artwork in the bureau's entire history.
No specific recording was referenced in the letter, but given the furor from
law enforcement throughout the country, there was little question that it
was about "Fuck tha Police." The assistant director hadn't actually heard
the song himself. He was reacting to lyrics sent to him by "concerned law
enforcement officials." Ahlerich's missive didn't actually accuse the group
of committing a crime—there wasn't an offense to break considering the
right to free speech extends to music—nor did the letter threaten any
consequence, as anything of the sort would have been unconstitutional.

"What are they gonna do? Put us in jail for making a record?" Eazy
wondered.

Turner, however, was terrified. "You kidding? It was the FBI. I'm just
a kid from Canada, what do I know?" he said.

Jerry Heller showed the letter to lawyers, who confirmed what he
already knew: there wasn't actually anything the FBI could do. The group
found the entire ordeal comical—"Oh, I didn't know they were buying

our records, too!" Cube snarked. Ruthless decided not to make the letter public.

The label did, however, give a copy to Phyllis Pollack, executive director of the anti-censorship organization Music in Action. Pollack had long been a supporter of N.W.A and shared the letter with New York rock journalist Dave Marsh, her partner in Music in Action. Pollack, who later joined Ruthless as a publicist, and Marsh investigated Ahlerich's letter and the government's involvement in censorship for a bombshell *Village Voice* cover story. "The FBI Hates This Band," was printed in bold red letters over a portrait of the group in black hats and thick gold chains, Yella with a handsome smirk plastered across his face. *Billboard* and the *Hollywood Reporter* did their own versions of the story, and Oprah Winfrey displayed the front page of the article on an episode dedicated to the outcry over lyrics from N.W.A, Ice-T, and Guns N' Roses.

Ultimately Ahlerich's three-paragraph "warning" became a boon for business. There was a backlash from the media, furious that the government attempted to censor or intimidate musicians, and reporters tripped over themselves to call out law enforcement agencies while first-amendment activists, and even a member of Congress, publicly blasted the FBI for Ahlerich's actions—ironic given how critical the press was of their music.

US congressman Don Edwards, chairman of the House Judiciary Committee's Subcommittee on Civil and Constitutional Rights, penned a terse rebuttal to the FBI, admonishing them for crossing a line.

"The FBI has developed an official 'position' on a rap song by the group N.W.A and has conveyed that position to the group's record publisher, Priority Records. I am afraid this smacks of intimidation. Officials of the FBI should not be music or art critics," Edwards wrote. "I do not believe that it is appropriate for the FBI to single out a particular song or film or book and write to its distributor. The only credible purpose of such an exercise is to encourage the distributor to drop its promotion of the work or the performer, and that would seem to be censorship."

The American Civil Liberties Union insisted the letter had the potential to do more harm than good in decreasing violence against police. "It reinforces the notion among minorities that the government is against them," an ACLU chairman told the *Los Angeles Times.* "Rap is one of the most positive role models, a positive way for poor people using their energies, making art and poetry out of their social dilemma. They should be applauded by the police."

While the fiasco delivered a wealth of publicity to N.W.A and boosted sales for *Straight Outta Compton,* one can't help but wonder how many more records the group would have sold if it was more widely available to purchase or if mainstream radio had shown support. Ahlerich's letter now sits on display at the Rock & Roll Hall of Fame in Cleveland as a testimony to the great length the government went in an attempt to censor rap.

"That letter wasn't for N.W.A," D.O.C. theorized. "It was for the public at large. It was a sign to America to not like them. The United States government says this is no good, so everybody says this is no good—the preachers, the teachers that are listening to the words and not listening to the message. 'Fuck tha Police' was a really poignant record. That was actually the best record to tell you what the possibilities of that group was. Eazy just wanted to say, 'Suck my dick, kiss my ass, shoot a bitch, stab a ho.' Eazy didn't give a shit. But Cube and Ren? Both of those guys were very mindful of the fucked-up conditions young blacks were exposed to in California. None of those other guys felt like that. If it was just a Cube and Ren [album] the records would have been a lot more Public Enemy, and a lot less Eazy-E."

✳

A few days after Priority received the FBI notice, N.W.A approached the final date of its tour. All summer, along various tour stops, police departments attempted to stop the group from performing.

For the entirety of the tour, N.W.A abstained from performing its most controversial recording. Still, it wasn't enough to curb fears from law enforcement that the group would incite violence against them. Washington, DC, Milwaukee, and Chattanooga were some of the cities that caved to pressure and pulled the plug on their shows.

When N.W.A arrived at Detroit's Joe Louis Arena on August 6, 1989, they didn't encounter a police boycott—instead they were met with a beefed-up law-enforcement presence, including members of the force's undercover gang squad. "There were close to two hundred of us," retired Detroit police sergeant Larry Courts remembered. "We were strategically placed . . . we didn't think there was going to be a riot. But we had our marching orders. We were told that under no circumstance that they were to perform that song."

The show had just gotten some bad press a few days prior, when its stop at the San Diego Sports Arena ended with a melee between members of two rival gangs and security guards. Three guards were injured in the fracas, two suffering black eyes and the third a broken wrist. Jerry and the brass at Priority were on edge for Detroit.

Twenty-thousand fans filed into Joe Louis Arena for the show. The evening was part of LL Cool J's Nitro Tour, which had Eazy and N.W.A billed as special guests alongside Slick Rick, De La Soul, and Big Daddy Kane. N.W.A was the second act to hit the stage. The group "absolutely, categorically, unconditionally guaranteed it would not perform" its controversial police kiss-off, Jerry wrote in his book.

"You down with the way it's going to go tonight?" Jerry asked Eazy by phone ahead of the show.

"Sure, Jerry," Eazy answered.

"Skip over it," Jerry implored.

"I got to go."

Throughout the day fans who spotted them at their hotel asked them if they planned on performing the insidious recording and they told them no. "Oh man, y'all shouldn'ta come if y'all wasn't gonna do that," one fan sniped. Backstage before the show, the group discussed whether or not they would perform it. Granted they agreed not to, but it was the last date on the tour and it had been so long since they last performed in Detroit. The guys couldn't come to consensus, so Cube assumed it wasn't going to happen on this night either.

MC Ren, Dre, and Yella hit the stage first. And then Cube emerged. After they performed "Gangsta Gangsta," the crowd was chanting: "*Fuck tha police! Fuck tha police! Fuck tha police!*"

They performed "A Bitch Iz a Bitch." Same thing afterward.

"*Fuck tha police! Fuck tha police! Fuck tha police!*"

And then "Straight Outta Compton." Again, the crowd was rapturous in its request.

"*Fuck tha police! Fuck tha police! Fuck tha police!*"

During "I Ain't tha 1," Cube noticed Dre and Ren talking near the turntables. Before Cube unleashed "Dopeman," Ren moved to the front of the stage.

"Wait a minute," Ren said, "Everybody say, 'Fuck the police!'"

"*Fuck tha police!*" the twenty-thousand-strong audience roared back.

Dre, from the turntables, gave Cube an instruction: "Come in on two."

He counted down, and Cube got down to business: "*Fuck the police! Comin' straight from the underground . . .*"

"The place went stupid," Cube recalled. "Then we see about twenty motherfuckers from the back trying to bum-rush the front. Undercover police. They're in the back of the arena, but they're throwing chairs out the way to get to the front of the arena. Nobody knows they're police, not even me."

The officers rushed the stage, climbing the barricade and going for the amplifiers, unplugging them quickly. Security guards tussled with the plainclothes officers since they didn't know they were police.

Jerry was on the phone with N.W.A's production manager, Gary Ballen, when the surge happened. "The cops are charging us!" Ballen screamed.

"Get 'em outta there!" Jerry ordered.

Pop! Pop! Two loud bangs rang out from the audience. Cube and Ren fled the stage, thinking the cops were shooting at them. In actuality someone had set off M-80 firecrackers.

The cops pushed their way backstage, charging through LL Cool J's dressing room by mistake. N.W.A's road manager, Atron Gregory, pushed them into a van and told them to go to the hotel and pack their shit. "The police goin' crazy . . . We're going to Canada."

The group packed and when they popped up in the lobby later in the night, cops were waiting on them. Eazy, Dre, Cube, Ren, and Yella were detained, but not charged with anything. "We just wanted to show the kids that you can't say 'fuck the police' in Detroit," an officer told the *Hollywood Reporter*. Cube offered to help the cops produce a diss response called "Fuck N.W.A"; the officers weren't at all amused.

N.W.A took the next flight back to LA. The tour was over. "It was a trip. Niggas broke the fuck out," D.O.C. remembered. "The other cities we made it across the county line on the tour buses. In Detroit we didn't. It was great. The kids loved it. The adults or anybody in a position of power hated it—they didn't understand it, they didn't get it."

AMERIKKKA'S MOST WANTED

N.W.A was the most popular rap group in the country. But the group's breakout success was complicated by Cube's frustrations with the group's finances. The way Cube saw it, Jerry was taking them all for a ride—and coaxing Eazy into making decisions. "It wasn't like Jerry was all the brains and Eazy was aloof or just a frontman of this label and all this stuff people think," said Tracy Jernagin, an ex-girlfriend of Eazy's. "Jerry really did follow Eazy's lead."

After failing to convince his group members not to sign the contracts Jerry demanded in order to get paid, Cube felt betrayed that his friends didn't take his concerns more seriously.

"Man, I ain't got no money. I ain't got nothing," Ren told Cube. "Nigga, I been rappin' for nothing this long, and nigga fittin' to give me seventy Gs?"

There was an attempt to squash the financial dispute between Cube, who really wanted to continue with the group, and Ruthless—but his lawyer said it was impossible. "[The] other guys' positions as far as business was concerned? Ren and Dre were *fiercely* loyal to Eric," D.O.C. noted. Their "Straight Outta Compton" video director, Rupert Wainwright, put it more plainly: "Nobody in N.W.A fucking coughed or farted without

Eazy's permission. He'd made a decision and bang, that was it. There was no dispute."

"We tried to settle this dispute diligently," his lawyer, Michael Ashburn, told *Spin*. "We bent over backward to try and make a financial agreement that was acceptable to both sides. I was surprised how indifferent they were when it came to settling this dispute. It was like Jerry Heller didn't care whether Ice Cube—someone who unarguably had made a major contribution to the group—left or stayed. Ice Cube would still be with N.W.A if our very reasonable financial demands had been met. They gave us a statement showing that Ice Cube had been advanced $32,700. He's owed at least another $120,000, plus his publishing royalties, which he hasn't received a cent on so far."

Cube felt pushed into a corner. He went to Public Enemy's Chuck D for advice. Cube looked up to him tremendously, and Chuck D was a friend to the group. "Stay with the group, man," Chuck advised. "The group is the thing." Eazy was indifferent to Cube's feelings of strife. He already knew where he stood—Jerry was staying, like it or not. In fact, he suggested D.O.C. as a replacement, a peculiar suggestion considering his voice had yet to return to its former tone and likely never would. "Go out and be a flop like Arabian Prince," Eazy said, brushing Cube off.

Jerry was the most upset. He saw Cube as an irrational brat. And he didn't think Cube was operating on his own accord, insisting folks like Priority head Bryan Turner and the group's label publicist, Pat Charbonnet were in his ear.

In his memoir, Jerry insists Eazy had scheduled a Cube solo project as the label's next release following N.W.A's 1989 tour, but Cube was pissed off after Jerry told him the album would have to wait until the debut of Ruthless's newest signee, a troupe from Pomona who called themselves Above the Law, along with releases from Eazy *and* N.W.A—both of which Cube would be expected to write for. "We're putting a lot of trust in you, man," Jerry told him. "Don't fuck it up."

One afternoon Dre convened the group to his home in Calabasas. He had a studio in an upstairs bedroom that was far more sophisticated than Audio Achievements. The crew had a routine, they'd hang out watch TV and maybe crack open a forty ounce before retreating to work. When the guys started heading upstairs, Cube stayed put on the couch. "I was like, 'Aw, shit.' I knew something was going on," Dre said.

Sure enough, Cube called Dre later and broke it down for his homeboy. To Cube, the math simply didn't add up. If they worked on two albums that sold millions of copies and they played to sold-out arenas across the country, shouldn't there be more money in their pockets? Royalties. Publishing. Merchandise. Ain't no way they were getting back everything they should, he told Dre.

Cube tried to level with Dre, friend to friend, during the hours-long chat. "Is your money right for sure?" he inquired.

"Nah, man, my shit is kinda shaky too," Dre confessed.

A meeting between members without Jerry was proposed by Cube, but it didn't happen. And with that he was done with N.W.A.

"From the inside looking out, there was this feeling of you shouldn't have left," Cold 187um said of Cube's abrupt departure. "We were all really young, we're all kinda somewhat becoming successful and now Cube is leaving? Everybody felt it was a selfish thing of him to do. Don't abandon us. We're a team. But he was like, 'If y'all wanna continue to get fucked over, I already know whats up, I'm outta here.' We were like, 'You're just being selfish.'"

After Cube left in December 1989, Priority immediately signed him to a solo deal. He reached out to Dre to see if he would work on his solo record. Cube didn't have any beef with anyone in the group—though he was a bit hurt that Eazy didn't push back against Jerry. "He was with it," Cube recalled. "Then we heard that Jerry Heller and Eazy-E vetoed that."

In January 1990 Cube headed to New York on a one-way ticket, determined to record his album on the East Coast. Cube traveled to Def Jam's New York headquarters to meet with Sam Sever, a producer he admired for his work with 3rd Bass, but Sever never showed. On his way out of the building Cube bumped into Chuck D, who invited him to a Public Enemy session later that night at Greene Street Studios in Lower Manhattan. Public Enemy was working on their *Fear of a Black Planet* album and were going in to record a track with Big Daddy Kane. "You wanna jump on there," Chuck asked him. "That'll let everybody know you about to come out solo."

It was an obvious yes for Cube, who was clamoring to work with the Bomb Squad, the production team responsible for Public Enemy's sound. That session birthed "Burn Hollywood Burn," and after the recording was cut Cube told the production team that people laughed at him for coming to New York to do his album. An East Coast producer touching a West Coast rapper? "Not ever going to happen," Cube told the team he repeatedly got as a reaction. The Bomb Squad's Hank Shocklee took it as a challenge. They were on board, but under one condition—they produce the entire album. "I don't like to do *pieces* of records," Shocklee told Cube. "It wouldn't be worth bringing the Bomb Squad to the table unless we were doing a full album."

"I was like, 'Word? Damn, okay.' Dre's a genius, but these dudes are mad scientists when it came to sampling . . . [and] making it sound totally unique and *not* a sample," Cube said.

At Chuck D's behest, Cube grabbed a notebook and started jotting down ideas. "I realized this could be a really good project when Ice Cube showed me six or eight composition books full of rhymes. And they weren't the ninety-page ones, they were two hundred pages, filled up," Chuck remembered.

Cube and Sir Jinx, who he brought on to coproduce the project, bunkered down for two weeks at the Bomb Squad's preproduction lair in Hempstead, New York. The producers told Cube to dig through the crates of records as a starting point for building the sound. "Go find your album," they instructed. He stayed for days, sleeping on the floor of the studio, thumbing through each and every record. Cube spent all hours of the day setting aside funk records from Slave, Betty Davis, and Con Funk Shun.

"When I went out there I had my ears closed and my mouth open, and they said do it the other way: Close your mouth, open your ears," Sir Jinx said of working with the Bomb Squad. "I was kind of the mediator, keeping the record West Coast as well as having that East Coast edge. I taught them a lot, and they taught me a lot. We never left the studio. From ten o'clock at night to ten o'clock in the morning we worked—everyday. I slept in the studio."

Jinx would prove key to connecting Bomb Squad's pastiche with the West Coast flavor Cube wanted. "Jinx was the gatekeeper, so to speak, to make sure that the sound wasn't going too far left and that the West Coast flavor was still present on the album," Cube said. "That's why the album has a cool balance of East Coast and West Coast production mixed together. The Bomb Squad and Jinx worked great together."

Cube had full autonomy over the project, something he hadn't experienced before: "With Dre, it was like, 'Here's the sound, I'm gonna do this beat and we're gonna like it together.' He's open to ideas, but he's gotta like 'em. If he don't like it, then it's a bad idea," Cube said. "But with Bomb Squad, it was like, 'We can't go to the real studio until we fill these two crates up with records that *you* like.'"

AmeriKKKa's Most Wanted was recorded in about four weeks at Greene Street Studios. Its title was a nod toward Fox's hit fugitive series *America's Most Wanted*—which, like *Cops*, capitalized on the nation's fascination with crime—with the spelling a reference to the Ku Klux Klan. Cube said he was aiming for something "that kinda represents the America we were dealing with [during] Reaganomics" and he didn't want the album, which was heavily political, to be dismissed as a Gangsta record.

Cube made one hell of a statement on the album, right out of the gate with its gut punching opener "The Nigga Ya Love to Hate." He originally working for Tom Kline, a sports agent who was itching to get into the music industry—this was his chance, Suge convinced him. The three of them launched Funky Enough Records, its name taken from D.O.C.'s hit. Suge started auditioning rappers out of Kline's Beverly Hills office, recruiting rising rapper-producer DJ Quik, 2nd II None, and Penthouse Players Clique to the Funky Enough team.

Suge's greatest asset was his power of persuasion. "By any means necessary," Dre once said of him.

Though his nickname, a derivative of "sugar bear," denotes sweetness, Suge's behavior over the years has been anything but. The image of the burly, cigar-puffing gangster who got what he wanted, from whoever he wanted, whenever he wanted it, became his lore. And Suge amassed a lengthy rap sheet filled with nefarious behavior to solidify his status as one of rap's most notorious thugs. He's been tied to dozens of savage beatings and was at the center of multiple shoot-outs, and was accused of breaking a guy's jaw with a loaded pistol and forcing another man to drink a glass of urine. In early 2018 Suge will stand trial for the most serious of his crimes after he allegedly mowed down two men with his Ford F-150 Raptor truck, leaving one dead.

That "by any means necessary" approach to business dealings was famously put to action for the first time, while Suge was managing Mario Johnson, a rapper who went by the name "Chocolate." Johnson told Suge he contributed greatly to Vanilla Ice's debut, *To the Extreme*. Chocolate claimed to have written a number of records for the album, including "Ice Ice Baby."

To the Extreme catapulted Vanilla Ice to pop stardom when "Ice Ice Baby," which incorporated samples from Queen and David Bowie, became the first rap record to hit number one on the *Billboard* Hot 100, the album selling an astounding seven million copies. Chocolate said he never got paid, and Ice's label, EMI, wouldn't return phone calls. As hip-hop legend would tell it, the next thing that happened was Suge and some cronies pulled up on Vanilla Ice at his hotel, dangling him by the ankles over the balcony.

Eazy-E and MC Ren, 1989.

Tammy Lechner/*Los Angeles Times*.

Dr. Dre, MC Ren, Eazy-E, and DJ Yella posing for a photo shoot after Ice Cube left the group, 1991.

Tony Barnard/ *Los Angeles Times*.

Dale's D

defining

Th

de

Eazy-E and Dr. Dre posing for a photo shoot to promote *Efil4zaggin*, 1991.

Tony Barnard/ *Los Angeles Times*.

An essential cog in the underground record machine was the Roadium, a swap meet on Redondo Beach Boulevard in Torrance, California.

Andres Tardio.

N.W.A's first performance took place at Skateland USA on March 11, 1988.

Craig and Todd Schweisinger.

One of two roller rinks that were pivotal to hip-hop's flourishing in LA during the 1980s.

Andres Tardio.

Audio Achievements, where the World Class Wreckin' Cru recorded its early work. N.W.A's *Straight Outta Compton* was recorded there as well.

Andres Tardio.

Eazy-E, circa the early 1990s.

Lori Shepler/*Los Angeles Times*.

Dr. Dre and Snoop Dogg in the studio during the final recording sessions of Snoop's debut album, *Doggystyle*.

Patrick Downs/*Los Angeles Times*.

MC Ren performing as part of the Up in Smoke Tour in 2000.

Ken Hively/*Los Angeles Times*.

Ice Cube standing in front of his childhood home in Inglewood, 2004.

Genaro Molina/*Los Angeles Times*.

Jerry Heller, photographed in 2006 to promote his N.W.A tell-all, *Ruthless: A Memoir.*

Bryan Chan/*Los Angeles Times*.

Jimmy Iovine (*left*) and Dr. Dre (*right*) with Erica Muhl (*far left*) at Interscope's Santa Monica headquarters to announce that they were giving $70 million to create the USC Jimmy Iovine and Andre Young Academy for Arts, Technology, and the Business of Innovation, May 2013.

Mel Melcon/*Los Angeles Times*.

Eazy-E, in holographic form (*left*), shares the stage with Wish Bone of Bone Thugs-N-Harmony at the Rock the Bells festival in Los Angeles, 2013.

Lawrence K. Ho.

Ice Cube, Dr. Dre, MC Ren, and DJ Yella reunite at the 2016 Coachella Valley Music and Arts Festival.

Jay L. Clendon/*Los Angeles Times*.

It's a story that's been passed around for decades, and what really happened is just as harrowing. Actually, Suge reached out to Dick Griffey, an older friend of his, to seek counsel on the matter. Griffey was an industry legend in his own right. He founded SOLAR Records (Sound of Los Angeles) to much success in the seventies by signing acts like the Whispers, Shalamar, Klymaxx, Midnight Star, and the Deele. The label had amassed enough hits that the *Los Angeles Times* pegged him as "the most promising new black music executive" in 1980.

Griffey gave Suge the contact information for an attorney in New York, and Chocolate produced handwritten lyrics for records including "Ice Ice Baby," explaining that he and Vanilla Ice had worked together at a Texas club, and that a girlfriend of his was present when he wrote them. Ice's label didn't budge, telling Suge, "'Look, we'll give you a couple of dollars if you'll let bygones be bygones.' I wouldn't go for it," Suge said. One night Suge and his crew crashed Ice's dinner at West Hollywood steakhouse the Palm and tried to put pressure on him by physically intimidating him. When that didn't move the needle, Suge tracked Ice down to his Beverly Hills hotel with a half dozen goons. Everyone came strapped.

"When we went to the hotel that day, it was strictly for conversation," Chocolate said. "Nobody got pushed—nobody argued, no shoving—nothing."

Ice said Suge's entourage roughed up his security guys and then led him onto the balcony of the fifteenth-floor suite he was staying in, demanding he sign away a percentage of royalties to his biggest hit, "Ice Ice Baby."

"He had me look over the edge, showing me how high I was up there," Ice said. "I needed to wear a diaper on that day. I was very scared."

Ice conceded and signed over $4 million worth of royalties, though he insists Chocolate had nothing to do with the record. "He had us out powered and outnumbered. I signed . . . and walked away alive."

It was Suge's first substantial payout. And his propensity for doing things his way, as unsavory of methods they may be, earned him a wealth of credibility (and fear) within the industry. This was how Suge got down, and he *never* changed—no matter how much trouble it brought him.

"You're talking about many, many years of how [he] dealt with things," said Nina Bhadreshwar, who worked as Suge's assistant. "It's where he's from. It's his history. He's not someone who makes himself vulnerable to people. He's gotta be the protector and provider of people, when actually he needed some mentoring . . . but nobody did because everybody feared him."

The settlement lined Suge's pockets nicely, and he took care of D.O.C., particularly to ease the burden left by his unwise decision to sell his publishing rights to Eazy.

Meanwhile, Dre was now growing frustrated with the dealings at Ruthless. He was feeling treated as an employee for a company he helped establish. And after Cube left, Dre thought more about money, and his share of it. He definitely didn't feel he was being paid as someone whose music built the hottest rap label since Def Jam, with his name on a hand-ful of platinum records.

Dre became distant. A studio rat by nature—it's his favorite place to be—he wanted more control creatively. Jerry Heller said he and Eazy were working on establishing an imprint for Dre, claiming it was one of the rare times they shook hands about something. But the producer was already reconsidering his allegiance to Ruthless and Eazy, especially after figuring out he wasn't fifty-fifty partners with Eazy as he had believed. Learning that D.O.C. was having Suge look into his Ruthless contract, Dre put in a request that would soon unleash a stunning chain of events.

"While you checkin' the D.O.C.'s shit," Dre said, "check on my shit too."

And Suge did, showing up to Ruthless lawyer's office unannounced and snatching all the documents he could get a hold of, including Dre's contract—which, he claimed, Ruthless wouldn't produce when Dre asked for it. "I got a hold of one on my own. We found out that Cube was right. Ruthless was taking Dre for a ride. And not just Dre—every other artist on the roster too."

Suge never copped to *how* he obtained the documents, but he informed Dre, Michel'le, and D.O.C. that they had deals that paid them significantly less than the industry-standard royalty rate. With Dre's permission, Suge acted on his behalf as a manger, bypassing Jerry. He went to Ruthless's distributor, Priority Records, to negotiate a deal that upgraded Dre's terms with Priority—delivering a quarter of a million dollars for back payments and a new album—and left Ruthless in the dark, which angered Jerry and Eazy, who believed the offer of the sublabel would have been enough to placate Dre if not for Suge being in his ear.

"They had the worst contracts I had ever seen in the history of the record business," Dick Griffey admitted. "The contracts that Ruthless and Jerry Heller had with N.W.A and Dre . . . if I said draconian, that would be a kind word."

Dre was honest with Eazy. Before the fame and platinum records, they were boys from the same hood. Dre went to him and was straight up with his grievance. "Look, man, I'm not dealing with Jerry Heller anymore," he told him. "If I'm gonna stay, he has to go. Which one of the two?"

Eazy told him, the same way he told Cube earlier, that he had no plans of ditching Jerry. "He played the divide-and-conquer game," Dre said of Jerry. "He picked one nigga to take care of, instead of taking care of everybody, and that was Eazy. And Eazy was just, like, 'Well, shit, I'm taken care of, so fuck it.'"

Dre agreed to join D.O.C., Griffey, and Suge as a partner in a new venture born in the ashes of Funky Enough, which Kline had decided to back away from. The new label was originally called Future Shock, after an old Curtis Mayfield single, before they came to its permanent moniker: Death Row Records.

The plan was for Griffey to deal with the major labels. D.O.C. would pen lyrics and help groom artists. Suge would be the point man for day-to-day business. And Dre would focus on being a studio wizard, producing the types of records *he* wanted with full autonomy. The company would be split four ways, with Dre and D.O.C. each receiving a 35 percent cut and Suge and Griffey both taking 15 percent.

But there was a major crack in Dre's exit plan: he was still under contract with Ruthless.

✳

On a late Tuesday night in April of 1991, Eazy got a call from Dre asking to meet up and discuss their business differences.

"Hey, yo, you know we got to work this shit out," Dre told him.

They planned to meet at Galaxy, the upstairs studio at SOLAR's Hollywood headquarters. But when Eazy arrived, there was no Dre in sight.

Suge, however, was there as Eazy got off the elevator. Alongside him were a couple of guys, and, depending on who's telling the story, they were brandishing baseball bats or lead pipes and may or may not have been carrying firearms.

Eazy was about to find out what Vanilla Ice now knew: Suge gets what he wants, and does so by any means necessary.

"Where Dre at?" Eazy asks.

"I heard you was trying to get me killed, Blood," Suge says. Eazy plays it cool, knowing he's outnumbered.

Suge presented him with paperwork, documents that would release Dre, D.O.C., and Michel'le from Ruthless. Eazy wasn't easily intimidated, so Suge raised the stakes.

"You see a white van parked down there on the street?" Suge asks him. "We got Jerry Heller tied up in back of that van, gun to his head."

He then tells Eazy he would bring his mother into the situation if he didn't sign.

"I figured he *did* know where my mother lived," Eazy concluded. "I figured either I'd sign the papers, get my ass kicked, or fight them. So I signed the papers."

"It was like *The Godfather*," noted Ruthless Records's lawyer Michael Bourbeau, who said that immediately after Eazy signed the documents Suge faxed them over to Hank Caldwell and David Glew, executives at Sony's Epic subsidiary, with a notice that Dre was "available for all production work." The notice also asked for $125,000 in advance.

Because Eazy had signed under duress, the releases weren't considered valid. He sent letters to all the major record companies to warn them about Suge, who continued to intimidate Ruthless brass.

Eazy and Jerry would have Ruthless lawyers file suit against Suge, Dre, and others, claiming they had violated the Racketeer Influenced Corrupt Organizations Act (RICO), a federal law designed to combat organized crime. The multimillion-dollar lawsuit charged various incidents of racketeering, extortion, and money laundering.

"[It's] a simple dispute between an artist and his label. Dre became unhappy with Ruthless—it's that simple. Dre decided he didn't want to work for Eazy-E," a lawyer for Sony said.

Furthermore, Dre's contract with Ruthless, Sony argued, allowed him to write, sell, and publish music separate and apart from Ruthless, which only held the rights to the music he does for that label.

The RICO lawsuit was eventually dismissed, as was another suit the following year. But the mood at Ruthless had already been decimated, especially given the weight of Suge's tactics to frighten his Ruthless adversaries throughout 1991. He'd made himself an unwelcome presence during the recording of *Efil4Zaggin*, popped up at Eazy's crib once with a squad of thugs demanding the master recordings of Dre's Ruthless work, and Jerry claimed his house was burgled—"Payback's a motherfucker, Jerry" scrawled in Magic Marker across the bedroom mirror and his Corvette missing. It spooked Jerry to the point where he started taking different routes home, stashed loaded guns all over the house (a .380 Beretta rested under his pillow) and installed a $75,000 security system.

"[People] like Suge Knight are just takers," Jerry said. "They make no legitimate contribution to the music business. They just extort people out of the fruits of their labor."

Security at Ruthless was beefed up too, with Jerry hiring an acquaintance, Israeli-born Mike Klein as security director. Klein had ties to both the Jewish Defense League—a group the FBI classified as a "right-wing extremist group"—and the Nation of Islam. He tapped the group to provide security, and soon armed bodyguards populated the halls of Ruthless. Klein also helped to ease the situation between Suge and Ruthless, and assisted with negotiating Dre's exit. He was later named Ruthless's head of business affairs (a deal that wasn't put on paper) after he invested money into the label. "That Mike Klein deal brought a lot of confusion to Ruthless. Everybody in the business knows you don't want to tick off Mike. He's the kindest, sweetest, most unassuming guy—but you know it's like don't [cross him]," Greg Mack said.

Jerry was desperate to try to salvage the label's relationship with Dre. He claimed he brokered a $20 million deal with Irving Azoff, his former protégé, at Warner. The deal would have paid Dre a $2 million advance. But, Jerry said, the label was wary of the national outcry against hip-hop not having quieted and dropped negotiations.

It didn't matter, though. There was no persuading Dre to stick around. *Efil4Zaggin* and an album from experimental rock-funk musician Jimmy Z released in late 1991 were Dre's last projects for Ruthless. The terms of his departure, like everything else with this label, has become hip-hop legend. After Jimmy Iovine's nascent Interscope agreed to distribute Death Row in 1992, lawyers for Eazy, Heller, Dre, and Suge, along with Klein, gathered to strike a deal. Ruthless would receive publishing royalties from Dre's Death Row projects, either as a producer or performer, with Interscope paying Eazy's company 10 percent of all monies he gained from producing, 15 percent from his solo records, *and* a "huge" cash payout. "Eric felt bad for Dre, feeling like he'd done him wrong," Cold 187um said. "He would say, 'He got me wrong. I didn't do this shit. I didn't do

Dre wrong.' But he wasn't busted and disgusted over it. He stood on what he believed in as far as trusting Jerry Heller to the fullest that it meant he thought everybody was against him because he was out in front. Ruthless Records was never sued. The contracts weren't friendly to an artist early in the days, but who knew it was gonna blow up like that? After it blows up they should have renegotiated but that's not what they wanted to do. No one got fucked—you signed what you agreed to sign for. Was it right? Probably not. Was it in your favor? Probably not."

ALWAYZ INTO SOMETHIN'

While the creation of *Efil4Zaggin* was marred by constant tension, it's hard to sense that from a production standpoint. The D.O.C. stepped up considerably in Cube's absence. After the car accident ravaged his voice he was urged to retire, and once again became a key utility player, penning lyrics for a quarter of the record, including "Appetite for Destruction" and "Alwayz into Somethin'." In the studio, Dre decided to venture away from his trusty drum loops and drum machines (sampling—a common practice with somewhat murky guidelines—was now at the center of multimillion-dollar lawsuits). Instead, he gathered musicians to replicate the grooves and licks from old funk and R & B records he listened to for hours growing up.

The album is Dre at his most ambitious, and a vast sonic departure from *Straight Outta Compton*. Where N.W.A's debut was a pastiche of sounds, *Efil4Zaggin* was a tightly focused effort. The recordings were dark, with Dre crafting macabre beats built around the eerie, high-pitched whine of the Moog synthesizer he loved.

"The motherfucking saga continues," Dre declares on album intro, "Prelude."

The 1990s saw a heavy emergence of politically and socially conscious hip-hop that was Afrocentric and sonically eclectic and inventive.

The same year *Efil4Zaggin* was released, Public Enemy issued *Apocalypse 91. . . The Enemy Strikes Black*, another radical collection from hip-hop's "prophets of rage." De La Soul and Black Sheep brilliantly sniped at Gangsta rap on their records, while A Tribe Called Quest dropped their jazz-informed debut, *People's Instinctive Travels and the Paths of Rhythm*. Poor Righteous Teachers added to the growing movement of emcees looking to only spread positive messages and images with their music.

Political and social messaging, however, was of no interest to N.W.A on *Efil4Zaggin*. Cube penned unflinching, profane yarns commenting on the perils of the hood, but he was gone. If N.W.A's critics thought they were obscene before, they couldn't have been prepared for how filthy the rhymes were this go-round. "When Cube left, you really didn't miss anything but his essence of him being Cube," Cold 187um insisted. "At Ruthless we had a high volume of cats that could do things on a next level so Eric had enough people around writing. We all just kinda stepped up—me, Kokane, Laylaw—to help Ren and D.O.C. with the writing. But there was definitely a void. We hated when Cube left and it turned into animosity."

Without Cube's social commentary, deviant sex and extreme violence was the driving force of the group's lyrics.

MC Ren shockingly brags about a fourteen-year-old who "sucks dick like a specialized pro" on "She Swallowed It," a sequel to *100 Miles and Runnin's* ribald "Just Don't Bite It." Eazy lauds himself as "the mothafuckin' pussy-beater" on "Findum, Fuckum & Flee" and flips Bootsy Collins's love groove "I'd Rather Be with You" into "I'd Rather Fuck You," a record that sees him doing his best R & B croon. There's talk of gang rape, forced oral sex, and murdering prostitutes. The cops get a tongue-lashing on "Real Niggaz Don't Die," and the group confronts their rampant usage of the N-word on "Niggaz 4 Life":

Why do I call myself a nigga you ask me?
Well it's because motherfuckers wanna blast me
. . . and label me as a dope dealer yo and say that I'm no good

There are also digs at Cube. On "Alwayz Into Something" Ren labels Cube a "bitch," and a skit dusts off the Benedict Arnold motif. "No matter how hard you try to be," Dre warns him, "Here's what they think about you." Answering messages from "fans" calling in to make disparaging remarks about Cube follows.

Released in May 1991, *Efil4zaggin* was another flash point of controversy. In the United Kingdom, thousands of copies were confiscated by British police under the Obscene Publications Act—a first—before officials ruled the recording didn't break any laws. Seattle libraries later came under fire after a board of trustees voted to ban the album. Critics aggressively panned the record with the *New York Times* calling the album a cheap attempt at shock value—"[T]he equivalent of a slapdash sequel to a first-rate horror film"—and a betrayal of the band. *Rolling Stone* said "listening to it is like hearing the loudest guys at a neighborhood barbecue strut, brag, wolf-whistle, and lie about sex."

But like *Straight Outta Compton*, the lack of radio airplay didn't matter, nor did the fact that national retailers like Kmart, Walmart, and Sears refused to stock the album at a time when department stores accounted for 15 percent of annual record sales. *Efil4zaggin* sold nearly a million copies in its first seven days and opened at number two, the highest entry since Michael Jackson's *Bad* made its debut at number one in 1987. The next week it upended Paula Abdul's *Spellbound* to become the first Gangsta rap album to hold the top spot.

A switch to the computerized SoundScan sales-tracking system greatly boosted the performance of *Efil4zaggin*. Before SoundScan was implemented, *Billboard* essentially relied on an honor system, by asking record stores and DJs to self-report what was popular. It was a method that at best was haphazard and at worst corrupted by label executives. The new system eliminated any chance of error or impropriety by using point-of-sales data from cash registers, and with radio airplay now monitored through a third party, SoundScan revolutionized the way charts had been determined since *Billboard* started publishing a chart of the top albums in 1945.

Efil4zaggin's swift ascent to number one decimated the myths of detractors who abhorred rap and considered its appeal to be limited. Danceable, pop-leaning acts such as MC Hammer and Vanilla Ice had ruled the charts and made rap history, but this was the first time a hardcore rap album sat atop the pop charts. Gangsta rap had officially crossed over, with 1991 marking the most significant revolution in the history of modern pop music. According to researchers in the United Kingdom, who studied the chord structure and sounds of seventeen thousand songs written in the last half-century, the rise of rap and hip-hop was "the single most important event that has shaped the musical structure of the American charts."

Less than a month after *Efil4zaggin* hit number one, N.W.A's former chief lyricist, Ice Cube, made his film debut in *Boyz n the Hood*. Set in South Central during the 1980s, the film—the directorial and screenwriting debut of John Singleton—is a gritty drama about a group of friends coming of age surrounded by drugs, gangs, and violence. Starring alongside Ice Cube were Cuba Gooding Jr., Morris Chestnut, Laurence Fishburne, Nia Long, and Angela Bassett. Cube was Singleton's first choice for the role of Doughboy, whose short life is marked by jail and gang violence, and his performance is masterful, as the inexperienced actor deftly humanizes the type of tragic figure he and N.W.A had, in essence, gotten famous for glorifying. *Boyz n the Hood* was met with acclaim, with Singleton becoming the youngest person, and the first African American, to be nominated for the Best Director Oscar, and in 2002 the film was selected for preservation in the National Film Registry by the United States Library of Congress. "From doing 'Boyz-n-the-Hood,' the song, to doing *Boyz n the Hood*, the movie—the song created the group, and that created the movie," Cube said.

The success of *Boyz n the Hood* wasn't without controversy. Though the film had a strong antigang message, violence between rival gangs marred opening screenings of the film in LA. Nearly two dozen people were injured in incidents from Seattle to Minneapolis to Long Island, and a man was murdered at a midnight showing near Chicago. A subgenre of films closely informed by experiences of inner-city youth was born in its wake, with films like *Juice*, *Menace II Society*, *Above the Rim*, *Poetic Justice*, *Fresh*, and *South Central* debuting shortly after.

*

Rap's foray into the mainstream was a complicated one. The opposition to the genre is especially fascinating considering how widely it was embraced by whites, and not just on the consumer level—two of the genre's most influential entities, rap publication the *Source* and Def Jam Records, were founded by white college students. The relationship between rap music and its white fanbases has often been a point of contention. "Rap's appeal to whites rested in its evocation of an age-old image of blackness: a foreign, sexually charged, and criminal underworld against which the norms of white society are defined, and, by extension, through which they may be defied," David Samuels wrote in 1991 issue of *The New Republic*. And it was seemingly true: rap artists who were promoted as violent thugs were far more popular among white audiences than, say, Afrocentric-minded acts like A Tribe Called Quest.

No one toyed with that perception more than Eazy. His story of drug dealer gone straight leading a crew of hard "niggas" with attitude made him a superstar. It's an image that's much tougher to sell after you've gone multiplatinum, toured the world, and enjoyed the fruits of building a successful independent rap empire that upended hip-hop and pissed off the FBI, and much of America for that matter. Yet Eazy, after success, doubled down on the image of the menacing thug, taking it to outlandish extremes during the promo campaign for *Efil4zaggin*—he showed up to the *Arsenio Hall Show* wearing a straitjacket and a hockey mask.

The image of Eazy as a demented thug made his presence at the White House in 1991, at a republican luncheon no less, all the more confounding—and that was exactly what he was going for.

Having made a substantial donation (about $25,000) to the City of Hope charity, Eazy's name landed on a Republican Party mailing list. Although Eazy was extraordinarily charitable, he kept it out of the spotlight as to not curtail his hard image, Greg Mack noted.

An invitation from Texas senator Phil Gramm arrived: "You are invited to an exclusive Republican Senatorial Inner Circle luncheon," it read. President George H. W. Bush would be on hand to address the Inner Circle, a group reserved exclusively for donors who contributed between $1,000 to $5,000. In a follow-up letter, Senate Republican leader Bob Dole noted that Arnold Schwarzenegger and Estée Lauder were members. For $2,460, Eazy could have two seats at an event called "Salute to the Commander-in-Chief."

The event was set for March 18, 1991, two months before N.W.A's *Efil4zaggin* was set to drop. It was too easy of an opportunity to pass up. The purveyor of Gangsta rap, who drew the ire of the FBI and law enforcement agencies over a profane song, invited to a fancy lunch at the White House? You couldn't make it up if you wanted to. "He was real sharp about the business of show business—how you look, the image," said Cold 187um. "He was really sharp when it came to that."

"I paid $2,500 for a million dollars' worth of publicity. I'm not a Republican or Democrat," Eazy later gloated. "I don't give a fuck. I don't even vote."

Jerry Heller, who would be Eazy's plus-one to the shindig, tipped off CBS News reporter Bob Schieffer, who showed up at DC's National Airport, cameras in tow, and interviewed fans, Eazy, and Jerry about the visit. "Do you think . . . the other members of the Republican Inner Circle know who Eric is and what he does?" Schieffer asks Jerry.

"No, no . . . I think that probably they would be shocked to find out who he really is. But as for us, we're happy to be here," Jerry smiled, his excitement over the press attention beaming through the camera.

Eazy and Jerry sat amid 1,400 Republicans at the Omni Shoreham Hotel, grazing on poached salmon and roast beef as television personality

Willard Scott emceed. Eazy stuck out in his LA Kings cap, black leather suit, and white T-shirt. He also wore a flashy gold bracelet encrusted in diamonds that had his name engraved on it. Jerry wrote in his memoir that Eazy sat next to a woman who, he surmised, had never socialized with a person of color before and didn't even notice Eazy was stoned out of his mind.

President Bush spoke then made his exit. Regardless of the warm invitation, Eazy never got to meet the president.

Eazy's inclination that the media would eat up his appearance was correct, with outlets across the country covering his appearance. "Rap's Bad Boy to Get Lunch with the Prez," a headline in the *Los Angeles Times* read. "Guess Who's Coming to Lunch," the *Washington Post* wrote, making a play on the classic Sidney Poitier and Katharine Hepburn film about interracial marriage. The National Republican Senatorial Committee praised itself when asked to comment—though anything less would have made them look awful.

"This is clear and convincing evidence of the success of our new Rap-Outreach program," a statement from the Republican Hill committee read. "Democrats, eat your hearts out."

SA
PRIZE

"Here's what they think about you." When Ice Cube first uttered those words—on 1990's "Turn Off the Radio," lifted from his debut solo record—he was chiding black people who went to great lengths to assimilate into white culture by reminding them of the litany of foul stereotypes whites have denigrated them with, sampling a montage from *Do the Right Thing*, Spike Lee's searing 1989 exploration of racial tension. A year later Dre used Cube's line to mock him in a skit that collected voicemails from "fans" dissing his former group member. In the war of words between N.W.A and Ice Cube in the early 1990s, the group fired the first shot, but nothing was as venomous as Cube's "No Vaseline," which closed his second album, *Death Certificate*. He'd heard Dre mock him on the "Message to B.A." interlude from N.W.A's *Efil4zaggin* album. Considering the album sold nearly a million copies in its first seven days and made history as the first Gangsta rap album to go number one, it was tough to ignore the diss.

Inspired by the time-honored art form of insult game "the dozens"—depending on what hood you were from, it might be called "capping," "roasting," clowning," "joning," "checkin'," or "snapping"—that serves as the foundation of rap battling, Cube unleashed a verbal attack that is one of the greatest diss tracks to ever land on wax. He took that "here's what they think about you" line that Dre had turned against him and threw it right back at them, sampling N.W.A's insults toward him and capping back—and that's just the intro. "That first line, 'Goddamn, I'm glad y'all set it off,' Cube actually had that rap when he left the group and he just sat on it for a year," Sir Jinx said. Indeed, after hearing his former group members blast him on their latest album, Cube went to the studio the next day, he said. He hadn't found the track he wanted to use as his response until he heard the song "Dazz" from Brick and remembered how Dana Dane had sampled it on "Cinderfella Dana Dane." "Once I found that track, I knew I was doing the song," Cube said. "They dissed me on *Niggaz4Life* and went in, [so] that was my plan."

When the bright, bouncy beat kicks in, Cube growls through verses that cut like razors set ablaze.

"Cube really came out to stand up as an artist," Jinx said. "When we were working on *AmeriKKKa's Most Wanted*, *Kill At Will*, and all those songs, we had the utmost respect for Eric, the utmost respect for Dr. Dre. Cube said, 'I don't want to say anything.' It would be just shitting on your people. That's why there's no funny lines—'Short motherfucker I could kill you' or 'You not a doctor.' When they started doing records it was 'Benedict Arnold' and 'Ice Cube's a bitch' and all this shit. They took it to heart. We took a jab at them on 'Jackin' for Beats,'" but nobody got it. That's why 'No Vaseline' was such a Mike Tyson uppercut."

N.W.A fired the first shot, but "No Vaseline" was Cube taking out an AK-47 and going for the kill.

> I started off with too much cargo, dropped four niggas now I'm making
>   all the dough
> White man just ruling . . . the Niggaz With Attitudes? Who ya foolin'?

Cube rips Eazy over his publicity stunt with the president, says the group is jealous of him, dismisses Yella as a loser, implies that Ren is a slave for the label, accuses Eazy of fucking Dre (anal sex as a metaphor for financial exploitation is quite the thread here), and blasts him for letting a "white Jew" break up the crew, referencing Jerry Heller—whom he saved the bulk of his vitriol for. Cube calls Jerry a devil and instructs his former friends to put a bullet in the manager's temple.

"No Vaseline" is as brutal an indictment as it gets. Ren was so pissed, while at a party where the record was played, he demanded it be cut off. "I was ready to mash. Like 'Oh, this nigga wanna do it like this,'" he said. "I was mad. That was the greatest sneak attack ever." Yella, who got the least of the brunt—though arguably the fact that Cube barely acknowledged Yella said a lot about how he saw him—admitted the entire group knew Cube had won the battle when they heard the record.

"When the song was done, there was a lot of debate in the studio over whether I was going to put it out," Cube said. "People were coming in and out of the studio and asking me to play it. 'Play that "No Vaseline." Play that N.W.A diss.' I was trying to make a concept record and not worry about a diss record, but that was one that I felt like I had to do."

To this day Dre and Cube have never discussed the record, and he actually completed about a verse and a half of a second diss track he was going to release after "No Vaseline," but he decided against it. Jerry Heller spent the rest of his life condemning his former client over it: "I think it's one of the most vitriolic attacks on the Jewish people that I've ever seen," he said. "And yeah, it hurt me. I don't have the kind of respect for him except that he knows how to make money."

Death Certificate debuted at number two on the pop-album charts when it was released in October 1991 before going platinum. The album is regarded as a rap classic and, arguably, Cube's finest work. It was also met with controversy.

The Simon Wiesenthal Center, an LA-based Jewish human-rights organization, implored national record chains to stop selling copies of the *Death Certificate* album. "Recording artists these days like to use the excuse that their music reflects reality, but this record is dangerous," Rabbi

Abraham Cooper told the *Los Angeles Times*. "This is not a just theoretical issue here. Ice Cube is advocating violence against other ethnic minorities and given the climate of bigotry in the 1990s, we consider this kind of material a real threat."

A few critics were scathing, with a *Village Voice* review calling Cube "a straight-up racist, simple and plain, and of course a sex bigot, too" and *Billboard*, in a rather unprecedented move, penned an editorial condemning Cube for "the rankest sort of racism and hate-mongering."

He was confronted repeatedly about his lyrics, and claims that he was an anti-Semite—he was even asked how he'd feel if someone listened to his record and then went out and shot a Jewish person. "Taking rap music literally for everything that's said is like taking TV literally," Cube responded, bewildered by the question. "Of course the TV programs are most parts fiction and the news is real. And with my records, you have both. You have the news and you have the fictional things." Cube later admitted that he regretted using anti-Jewish language, but defended his position: "I didn't know what 'anti-Semitic' meant until motherfuckers explained why it was just not okay to lump Jerry with anybody . . . But I wasn't like, 'I wanna hurt the whole Jewish race'—I just don't like that motherfucker!"

For *Death Certificate*, Cube broke the album into two themes—the death side, a mirror image of where he believed we were at the time, and the life side, a vision of where we needed to go, the "we" being black America. "I was making a transformation, mentally, from knowing street knowledge to knowing world knowledge—history, seeing things from a different perspective," Cube said of his intention. "It was two different records, the life that I was coming out of into the life I was trying to envision and see myself going into. The death side is a lot of the craziness we do and go through. The life side was trying to make sense out of it and using it to better ourselves in a certain way."

Following *Kill At Will* shortly after *AmeriKKKa's Most Wanted*, Cube felt confident as he headed into *Death Certificate*. The recording never stopped once he started working on his debut, but seeing the response *Kill At Will* received was encouraging to Cube and Jinx, who did the project without the Bomb Squad. "We were just doing music. We had our own budget. We were confident," Cube said. "We felt like we were on a roll and we were just ready to keep going."

For the record, Cube eschewed the melange of textures that was the Bomb Squad's signature for a heavy assortment of seventies P-Funk and soul samples with production handled by himself, Sir Jinx, and the Boogie Men—the production team of Bobcat, Rashad, and DJ Pooh, who would become one of Cube's closest collaborators. "Having them in there, I felt like a running back with a Hall of Fame line. Ain't no way in the world I wasn't getting 100 yards, period. That's how I felt. I was in good hands," Cube said of his trusted producers. "For a rapper, there's nothing like knowing the production is going to be right. When all you can do is keep coming up with dope concepts and you got the right producers to help you create it, there's nothing like it."

Death Certificate showed Cube just scratching his prime. "Every song was better than the last one," he said, recalling the recording sessions.

Everyone was subjected to Cube's venom on the record: Whites, police officers, gays, President Bush, Jesse Jackson, and blacks. "Do I have to sell me a whole lot of crack, for decent shelter and clothes on my back? Or should I just wait for help from Bush," he asks on "A Bird in the Hand," a record that tackles the limited options for many men in the inner city who might have committed a small crime or not finished school. He rails against white supremacy on "I Wanna Kill Sam," sneers at black "sellouts" on "True to the Game," tackles gang warfare on "Color Blind," and stresses safe sex on "Look Who's Burnin'"—empowering and socially conscious messaging commingled with misogynistic, homophobic, and bigoted posturing. It made Cube a confluence of contradictions, something journalists worked overtime to challenge during interviews.

"No Vaseline" was but one controversial lightening rod on the album. "Black Korea" drew just as much ire from critics. On the short track, he blasts Korean shop owners for perceived prejudices toward the blacks who frequent their shops:

Look, you little Chinese motherfucker,
I ain't tryin' to steal none of yo' shit, leave me alone!

The relationship between the Korean immigrants who maintained liquor and convenience stores throughout South Central and their black customers became fraught with tension during the 1970s and '80s when, after a few clashes, the media became fascinated by the "Korean-black conflict." Stories of how Korean immigrants were "taking over" black communities in South Central were common.

"In their pursuit of the American dream, the new immigrants seemed oblivious to the African Americans' long history of struggle for their unfulfilled dreams," journalist Helen Zia explained. "In Los Angeles as well as New York and other cities, black people bristled over incidents of disrespectful treatment and false accusations of shoplifting."

In Brooklyn, an eight-month boycott of Family Red Apple market was initiated in 1990 after the store's Korean owner accused a black customer of shoplifting and the two got into a physical altercation. In Philadelphia, there were protests when a Korean-American merchant shot a black man to death inside a hoagie shop.

The strain between blacks and Koreans in South Los Angeles reached new heights on March 16, 1991, when Latasha Harlins walked into Empire Liquor Market and Deli in South LA. Soon Ja Du, a middle-aged Korean immigrant, was working the store that day instead of her son—who stayed home after he was threatened by some Crips he planned to testify against for an attempted robbery. Harlins, a fifteen-year-old high school student, grabbed a $1.79 bottle of orange juice, put it in her backpack, and pulled out two dollars to pay for it. Du accused her of shoplifting.

"You bitch, you're trying to steal my orange juice," Du shouted at the girl, before grabbing her by the sweater. Harlins punched Du in the face, breaking free of her grasp. Harlins tossed the orange juice on the counter and turned to leave the store, but Du took out a .38-caliber handgun and fired a round into the back of Harlins's head, killing the girl instantly. She died with two $1 bills clutched in her fist.

Police concluded there was no attempt at shoplifting and a jury found Du guilty of voluntary manslaughter, which carried a maximum sentence of sixteen years in prison. The judge, however, decided to give the woman probation, four hundred hours of community service, and a $500 fine after determining that the fifty-one-year-old's reaction, while inappropriate, was understandable, considering the string of robberies she and her family had experienced at their shop. Harlins's shooting inflamed blacks across LA, who were still reeling from the beating of black motorist Rodney King by LAPD officers following a high-speed car chase, the footage of which was captured by a witness and aired on the nightly news. For many blacks in LA, the Du verdict was confirmation that black lives meant nothing—feelings that were validated a week later when a Korean immigrant received thirty days in jail for abusing his dog.

"Look at the message," Cube told a reporter pressing him about "Black Korea.""A dog in this case is worth more than this black little girl's life. We're getting fed up. To say that we ain't is a lie. And to not express our frustrations and our anger when we had a chance to is wrong for the black community, because then when it gets to a boiling point . . . people from the Korean community can't say, 'We didn't know, nobody told us.'" He turned out to be correct: A handful of Korean-owned stores in South Central were firebombed one night in August 1991, including the store where Harlins was slain.

In response to "Black Korea," a boycott of Cube was called by the national Korean-American Grocers Association. Thousands of stores represented by the Southern California chapter pressured the owners of St. Ides malt liquor to drop Cube as their spokesman. Widely available across South Central liquor stores, St. Ides was popular for its low price and potency—at 8 percent alcohol, it's one of the strongest malt liquors on the

market. McKenzie River, St. Ides's San Francisco–based brewer, revamped
the brand by dropping soul crooners Four Tops as its endorsers and recruiting Gangsta rappers in an attempt to attract younger customers. The company hired DJ Pooh to produce its new commercials and he brought Cube
on board. In one commercial Cube crudely raps that the malt liquor "gets
your girl in the mood quicker [and] gets your jimmy thicker."

Cube was just one of many rap stars in the early nineties who lent
their likeness to the brew: Dr. Dre, Snoop Dogg, Tupac Shakur, and Notorious B.I.G. were among the brand's endorsers. McKenzie River declined
to remove Cube so stores decided to pull it off shelves. The brand was
a market leader at the time between its omnipresence in Gangsta rap
subculture and its spokesman's prevalent consumption of the product in
the successful film *Boyz n the Hood* (after the film's release, liquor store
owners couldn't keep product on shelves), and its owners couldn't afford
the controversy. McKenzie River caved to the pressures of the grocers
association and pulled Cube's advertisements from rotation. The dispute
was solved with an apology from Cube and a public commitment by
McKenzie, which announced a donation of up to $90,000 to Korean
American groups. The album's multiple controversies still surprises Cube.

"Nobody is safe when you listen to *Death Certificate*. Any of us that
has any kind of flaws in our character, *Death Certificate* was probably
going to find it. So, it didn't matter what color you are," he said. "I said
more about black people on that record than anybody else. It was much
ado about nothing. It's that saying, you throw a rock into a pack of dogs
and the only one that hollers is the one that got hit. The ones that were
hollering, to me, were the ones getting hit by the truth—as I seen it—in
a rap song. At the end of the day it's still music."

✳

Death Certificate and *Boyz n the Hood* thrust Cube deeper into the mainstream, though his rising profile came with its fair share of scrutiny, no

less for his affiliation with the Nation of Islam. Like many young black men, Cube was exposed to the Nation of Islam through Public Enemy. The rap group's pro–Nation of Islam lyrics were the source of much hand-wringing due to the inflammatory teachings of NOI leader Minister Louis Farrakhan, which have been labeled as anti-Semitic, antiwhite, misogynist, and homophobic. Farrakhan's notion of black advancement has often been seen as racial separatism. In 1989, Public Enemy found themselves at the center of a firestorm when its "Minister of Information" Professor Griff made anti-Jewish comments during an interview. It was PE affiliate the Drew who introduced Cube to Farrakhan's teachings by giving him tapes of the Minister speaking. For Saviours' Day one year—a NOI holiday that commemorates the birth of founder Wallace Fard—Cube flew to Chicago to see Farrakhan speak. The minister invited Cube back to his opulent Hyde Park mansion known as "the Palace" for a meal, which Cube accepted. "We kicked it and had a good time," he said.

"Cube is a sponge. He's a chameleon. The Nation were the brothers that held us down. It was just another kind of college that we needed to learn. With them being around, it taught us how to be a little bit more like gentlemen," Sir Jinx said. "We never got into trouble. No rape charges, nobody getting shot or killed, nothing. They ran it like a military. You wasn't playing around with Ice Cube. When the Nation came it was a breath of fresh air of men that I idolized. I didn't have a father, so I didn't know certain things. We were twenty-something-year-olds. The Nation provided guidance."

Although he never officially joined, Cube was attracted to the political and religious movement's philosophies on black advancement—philosophies he believed could rid blacks of societal ills such as drugs and violence. "[The] teaching is self-love, and everything we got from America is self-hate. Once you start loving yourself, you can respect anybody that looks like you," he once explained to a reporter.

Cube shaved off his Jheri curl, with help from Kam, a political rapper from Watts signed to the Street Knowledge Records production imprint

Cube founded in 1990 after leaving N.W.A. At a Nation of Islam func-
tion, he testified about how its teachings had changed his life. "I'm sick of
begging for the white man to put out my records . . . for him to treat me
equally. My father always taught me to always want to be equal. But once I
learned who the devil was, I would never want to be equal to him," Cube
said in his speech. In fact, in what's become yet another piece of infamous
rap lore, a furious Cube—vexed over his royalties from Priority—decided
to teach label head Bryan Turner a lesson by smashing up his office with
a baseball bat. "I swear to God . . . I remember him looking around the
room trying to look for something to break that wasn't too expensive,"
Turner said, "so he broke the TV, which we laughed about after."

Nation of Islam doctrine widely inspired *Death Certificate*. "No longer dead, deaf, dumb, and blind out of our mind . . . Look that goddamn
white man in his cold . . . blue eyes," controversial NOI spokesman Kha-
lid Abdul Muhammad implores at the conclusion of the death side of
the album. Muhammad's comments mirrored what Cube believed about
black people at the time. "The best place for a young black male or female
is the Nation of Islam," Cube inscribed on an image inside the album
picturing him reading NOI publication *The Final Call*. The image is a
crucial one to understanding Cube's mind frame at the time. To the left
of him is the Lench Mob, the backing crew of rappers and faceless hype-
men he originally formed as a concept for *AmeriKKKa's Most Wanted*—
its name a nod to the horrifying act of lynching of black men by mobs
of racist whites (Da Lench Mob spun off into a real group, releasing its
debut in 1992)—and on the right is the Nation of Islam, standing tall and
immaculately dressed in suits and bow ties. "We decided Cube needed a
backup group. Some no face niggas that nobody knows—faceless men
so that everywhere we went we had a gang. We were trying to re-create
Straight Outta Compton," said Sir Jinx. "At first the Lench Mob was the
Mad Circle. It was supposed to be Ice Cube and the Mad Circle. But
since we were working with WC [Dub-C], Cube remembered that he
wrote 'N.W.A is the lynch mob' [in 'Express Yourself'] and he changed it

to that." It was a literal representation of the duality of the album and the beliefs of the Nation. Cube put it this way: Black men and women were in a state of emergency, mentally dead because a limited knowledge of self has led to a "nigga mentality" and the Nation was the vision to bring them back to life.

Cube's Nation of Islam–influenced views made *Death Certificate* even more inflammatory and politically driven than its searing predecessor. He rapped how interracial dating and moving to the suburbs was stalling black men from reaching their potential, although to be fair, he believed selling drugs and gangbanging were just as ill. The racially charged lyrics of the album and the blowback from "No Vaseline" and "Black Korea" left Cube unfazed, though, which only further incensed his critics.

"The truth is, I don't care what the white community thinks about the record," Cube said. "I'm talking directly to my black brothers and sisters. I speak in a language we talk in the streets. Other people can listen too—they might learn something—but I'm talking to the black kids who need somebody to talk sense, honest sense, to them."

The media took particular interest in provoking Cube, between his increasingly confrontational and militant lyrics and his affiliation with the Nation of Islam. "Why are you so angry on your records?" he was asked in one interview. He regularly sparred with reporters over *Death Certificate*'s content. The media attention of his religious belief frustrated him. "That's why people have issues with the media now because they have an agenda. It's human nature to have an agenda. But when they are so forcefully trying to push on whoever they are trying to interview, some people take the bait and others wrestle with them," Cube said. "People aren't going to make me say something that I don't want to say, or that I don't mean or try to interpret my words or thinking without me correcting them. Ultimately, though, religion is private when it's all said and done. It's nobody's business what you believe."

And there was particular fixation on Cube's facial expression, a seemingly permanent snarl that particularly came in handy as he broke out in

Hollywood as an actor. References to Cube's menacing "scowl" became so frequent he eventually began playing it up.

"It's interesting, the people who are so intrigued by that," Cube said. "They think just the look on your face can define who you are and how you're feeling. It's cool, I'm fine with that. A lot of us are angry and mad and people need to feel us. I don't mind being the total opposite of what they try to project me to be or want me to be. We [as black men] have to show strength because showing weakness don't get us nowhere."

Cube and Public Enemy remain the most cited emcees who aligned themselves with the Nation of Islam, but the teachings of the Nation and the Five-Percenters, which teaches the ideology that black men are god personified and derived from the Nation, can be traced through decades of rap. Poor Righteous Teachers, Big Daddy Kane, Rakim, Wu-Tang Clan, Digable Planets, Jay-Z, LL Cool J, Common, Nas, and Jay Electronica, all to some degree, have embraced the teachings of both over the years.

N.W.A's MC Ren actually joined the Nation in 1993, converting to Islam after friend DJ Train gave him tapes about the history of Egypt and exposed him to Elijah Muhammad's *Message to the Blackman in America*. "I took that book everywhere I went . . . I couldn't put it down, read through it like twenty-three times. That book changed it for me," he said. Ren's conversion greatly informed his solo debut, 1993's *Shock of the Hour* (its title changed from *Life Sentence* to one referencing a speech from Minister Farrakhan), with the album playing like two separate sides—its first half rife with the gun-and-dick-slinging braggadocio he typically spit and the second half containing recordings he cut after joining the Nation of Islam.

TONIGHT'S THE NIGHT

Dr. Dre was becoming eager to start work away from the Ruthless fold. Before the release of N.W.A's swan song *Efil4zaggin*, Dre talked to Ren and Yella about exiting and joining Death Row, the new label he was starting with D.O.C and Suge Knight. Yella never answered him and Ren passed on the opportunity after Dre took him to Dick Griffey's SOLAR Records building in Hollywood where the label was seated. "Fuck this. This is a worse situation," Ren thought. Dre had also been in communication with Ice Cube to discuss the possibility of working on *Death Certificate* after Ruthless barred him from contributing to *AmeriKKKa's Most Wanted*, further proof of how Dre was looking to distance himself from Ruthless—though he changed his mind after learning about "No Vaseline."

CPO Boss Hogg, Ren's friend who was signed to Capitol Records through his MC Ren Productions was one Ruthless affiliate who would join Dre. CPO Boss Hogg, with his partners DJ Train and Young D, the other members of Capital Punishment Organization (CPO), released *To Hell And Black* in 1990. He was frustrated with the way Capitol handled the record at the time. Eazy had talked to him about doing an album under the Ruthless banner, but CPO declined because of his relationship with Ren. CPO was excited by the type of music Dre was creating and he wanted to be a part of it. "[The] beats were just too funky. He had this whole new thing," he said. "When you're working with Dre, it's the shit. I would sit on the back wall and just watch him. He'd be there, standing and bobbing his head and just mixing. Everybody talks about Dre's production, to me his talent isn't production—his mastery is mixing. He could probably make the worst sounding track ever put together sound like it was the shit, because of his mixing."

Dre's first non-Ruthless project was producing on the soundtrack to *Deep Cover*, a neonoir crime thriller starring Laurence Fishburne and Jeff Goldblum, that SOLAR was releasing with Sony's Epic Records. In late 1991, Dre's stepbrother Warren introduced him to a key collaborator that helped elevate Dre's work on *Deep Cover*. It was during a bachelor party Dre had thrown his friend and Ruthless keyboardist Andre "LA Dre" Bolton, when the music had run out. The DJ for the night had breezed through all the cassettes he had and asked Warren if he had any music. Warren had a demo of his trio 213 in the car and asked a friend to run and grab it. He had been shopping demos of the group he formed with his two lifelong friends, church singer Nathaniel "Nate Dogg" Hale and rapper Cordozar Calvin Broadus, who went by the name "Snoop," to no luck. Warren, Nate, and Snoop were thick as thieves growing up on the East Side of Long Beach, where they played Pop Warner football together. "We just stuck together as a crew all our lives . . . from elementary," Warren said.

Warren was nervous. He had played the music for his famous stepbrother a few times, and each time he passed, telling Warren they needed to get their shit together if they wanted a real shot. Their demo enjoyed some minor underground buzz, but they still couldn't get anyone to sign them. Warren put the tape in and played "Gangster's Life." "What is this shit? It's *banging*," Dre asked, stumbling in from a nearby room.

"Dre, this is me, Snoop, and Nate," his stepbrother told him. "This is what I've been trying to tell you about!"

Dre was impressed—especially with Snoop, who had a cadence similar to Slick Rick's smooth melodic flow, but incredibly laid-back and warm. He invited them to come to the studio and when an excited Warren called Snoop to tell him, Snoop refused to believe him.

"I said, 'Nigga, stop lying.' And someone said, 'Hello?' And I said, 'Who's this?' And he said, 'It's Dre. Man, that shit was dope. I want to get with you. Come to the studio Monday.'" Snoop recalled.

Like Dre, Snoop grew up loving old R & B, funk, and soul and was the class clown during high school. Snoop gleaned his nickname from his affinity with *Peanuts* comics as a child. While he was Snoopy at home, he started running the streets and eventually floated into petty drug sales with friends in the Rolling 20 Crips. The streets weren't kind to his friends from his football days: out of twenty-eight of them, twelve were killed, seven were behind bars, and three were strung out on crack.

Dre and Snoop clicked immediately, and he continued to invite them back to SOLAR and even let Snoop crash at his Calabasas home. Dre had barely any furniture in his place—"Jerry and Eazy were trying to starve me out, and they weren't paying me my royalties or anything like that," he admitted. Dre at least had a makeshift studio in his bedroom. One night, fooling around in the studio, Dre put on Sly Stone's "Sing a Simple Song," and longtime collaborator Colin Wolfe came up with a bass line with a jazzy feel similar to the A Tribe Called Quest record he was listening to heavily. Dre constructed a beat around Wolfe's melody and samples from the Sly & the Family Stone record, adding in a note from Undisputed Truth's 1975 cover of "(I Know) I'm Losing You" and some piercing piano keys he and Wolfe played.

Dre came up with a loose concept for the verses, giving Snoop instruction before taking a break for the gym. Build on the words, "Tonight's the night I get in some shit, Deep cover on the incognito tip," he said. When he returned Snoop had mapped out lyrics using his own arrest for slinging drugs as inspiration.

Dre turned the recording into a duet, building on the film's theme of killing an undercover cop. Before they knew it they had a refrain that was equally chilling and catchy, with its reference to the California penal code for murder that became wildly popular among thugs, both authentic and pretend. "*Yeah, and you don't stop, Cause it's 1-8-7 on a undercover cop.*"

"Deep Cover" was the first time listeners heard Dr. Dre on his own, no N.W.A behind him. The record also introduced the first of a handful of emcees that would go on to shape and define hip-hop under Dre's tutelage as he eased into a new role: Label mogul.

WHO GOT
THE CAMERA?

Rodney King's white Hyundai Excel came to a stop in front of an apartment complex on a busy street in Lake View Terrace. It was 12:30 a.m. on March 2, 1991, and the unemployed construction worker had just been given chase by the California Highway Patrol, a squad of Los Angeles police, and a helicopter after he was clocked speeding at about 115 miles per hour on the Foothill Freeway. The twenty-five-year-old was recently paroled after serving a year in jail for robbing a convenience store of $200 and assaulting the clerk. Fearing a speeding ticket could send him back to jail—not to mention the forty-ounce bottles of 8 Ball (Olde English 800) malt liquor and weed he'd indulged earlier that night while watching basketball with his homies—he kept driving. Now he had several patrol cars behind him and a police helicopter loudly circling overhead, attracting tenants to their windows and balconies.

For a second, no one moved, and then a shout from an officer forced King out of his vehicle. Officers claimed King acted erratically when he exited the vehicle, laughing at the helicopter lights and grabbing himself when instructed to put his hands up. Police swarmed him. Officers assumed, incorrectly, that he was high on PCP, a drug officers believed gave users near-superhuman strength. One officer shot him with a Taser, sending a searing electrical surge through his body, but King rose to his feet unfazed. The commotion awakened George Holliday, who thought to grab his Sony camcorder—it was still brand-new in its box—and went to his terrace. Holliday hit record on the chaos unfolding ninety feet away. The footage comes into focus as King, on his knees and surrounded by about a dozen cops, receives ten ferocious blows from one officer's baton.

Feeling the blows, the liquor, and the weed, a dazed King tries to stop the beating before falling to the ground. Two officers target his legs, slapping them with the batons to subdue him. *Crack! Crack! Crack! Crack! Crack! Crack! Crack! Crack! Crack! Crack! Crack!* A dizzying amount of blows were delivered to King, who laid connected to the Taser and never fought back. As he writhes around in pain, officers continue their assault. King is hit across his back, struck in the head, and has his neck stomped on as passing cars slow down to see what's happening, and nearby residents watch in horror from their balconies.

"Please stop. Please stop," King pleaded from the ground before he was hog-tied and dragged, facedown, to the side of the road, where he was left alone—the officers milling about as shocked and disgusted citizens spoke to each other from their apartments.

"That is sick!"

"It looked like they were trying to break his ankles."

"It's enough cops over there to fight an army."

King was transported to Pacifica Hospital of the Valley where doctors were unsettled by his injuries: Eleven broken bones at the base of his skull, a shattered eye socket and cheekbone, a broken leg, a concussion, numerous lacerations to his face, injuries to both knees, and nerve damage that left his face partly paralyzed. None of the officers reported they saw anything go wrong, unaware there was a video recording of the incident. "I haven't beaten anyone this bad in a long time," Officer Laurence Powell typed into the computer in his squad car. Later it was revealed Powell sent a dispatch earlier in the night describing a domestic disturbance involving blacks as "right out of *Gorillas in the Mist*," referencing the Sigourney

Weaver drama about naturalist Dian Fossey's work in Rwanda studying mountain gorillas.

The day after King's beating, Holliday took his tape to local news station KTLA and sold it for $500 after he was dismissed by his local precinct and ignored by CNN. Holliday's footage, and King's injuries, contradicted what officers had written in their reports. The tape became a sensation, with networks airing the footage "like wallpaper" as a CNN executive vice president was quoted as saying. It confirmed fears from blacks across Los Angeles that an encounter with the LAPD, which had a reputation for being prejudiced (the four officers were white), had the potential to end in violence, humiliation, or, worse, death.

"Did you see that shit on the news?" Cube remembered being asked one night in the studio. He had been busy recording and hadn't yet seen the tape. Cube took a break from the booth and ran to the television and the middle of the beating was playing on the screen. "I just kept thinking, 'These dirty motherfuckers.'"

Outrage ripped across LA, as well as the rest of the country. Hundreds rallied outside Parker Center, LAPD's headquarters, demanding the dismissal of the officers involved and calling for LAPD chief Daryl F. Gates to resign. Gates had proven particularly unpopular among black citizens for how he had militarized the police force during Reagan's War on Drugs. "Stop police brutality," one protestor's sign read. "LAPD = KKK," another stated. Powell and three other officers were charged with assault with a deadly weapon and use of excessive force after four days of grand jury testimony (charges against King for driving while intoxicated and evading arrest were never pursued).

Mayor Tom Bradley also called for Gates "to remove himself," which he refused to do. Mayor Bradley then ordered a comprehensive probe into the practices and procedures of the LAPD. Among the findings in the 228-page report? From 1986 to 1990, the city paid out more than $20 million in judgments, settlements, and jury verdicts for excessive-force lawsuits and in the same period more than 10 percent of the 1,800 officers against whom an allegation of excessive force or improper tactics was made were gross offenders. Racial bias was rampant in the department, with an LAPD survey agreeing that prejudice on the part of officers toward citizens contributed to a negative interaction between police and the community, and that bias often led to use of excessive force. The report also showed how often incidents involving racial slurs from white officers against minority colleagues were frequently ignored.

The culture of racism was so prevalent, officers were comfortable enough typing disparaging messages on computer transmissions between squad cars:

> *"If you encounter these Negroes, shoot first and ask questions later."*
> *"Sounds like monkey-slapping time."*
> *"I'm back over here in the projects, pissing off the natives."*
> *"Everybody you kill in the line of duty becomes a slave in the afterlife."*

A year after the beating, opening statements were made in the trial of the four officers charged with beating King. It was the first time the two sides formally presented their versions of the incident after months of debate and pretrial hearings.

The trial had the makings of a spectacle. The initial judge was removed for showing bias and it was decided to change the venue to Simi Valley, a sleepy town in neighboring Ventura County that was notably more white and conservative than LA, so the jury wouldn't be influenced by the extensive coverage of the case.

During the trial Eazy-E found himself in the center of controversy. A few weeks after the footage of King's beating had ignited the nation, Eazy suggested King record a remix to N.W.A's hard-core anthem, "Fuck tha Police." "We were criticized a lot when we first released that song, but I guess now after what happened to Rodney King, people might look differently on the situation," he said. "Not all cops are bad, but this kind of harassment has been going on for years in the ghetto. I think we'll probably call our new version 'F— tha Police, the King Remix.'" But he also publicly disparaged King, who had more run-ins with the law after the beating, including being arrested for solicitation: "[He's] all fucked up, man! Rodney King so fucked up he wouldn't know his own goddamn name!" Eazy also evoked King's beating by LAPD and made light of Dr. Dre's vicious assault on *Pump It Up* host Dee Barnes, joking how Barnes "was fucked up worse than Rodney King!" Eazy then drew the ire of blacks and hip-hop fans when he lent his support to Theodore Briseno, one of the officers being tried.

Eazy met Briseno through his lawyer. The unlikely pair made the front of the *Los Angeles Times*, with the paper identifying the rapper as a "supporter" in an image. Indeed, he was quite sympathetic to Briseno, attending the trial almost daily and frequently standing next to the embattled officer, and even helping to support Briseno's family. The general consensus was that this was an open-and-shut case; the video was quite damning for the officers. Eazy, however, disagreed. "Sure, I've seen that little stomp Briseno does on the video, and I'm not saying it's justified," he said. "But we don't know what it was about, do we? It could have been him just trying to tell Rodney, 'Stay down, man, stay down.' Who's to know?" The hip-hop community, still perplexed by Eazy's decision the year prior to attend a Republican luncheon with President Bush, was irate over his support for the cop. "Eazy-E is a sellout," Geto Boys' member Willie D said. "He got everybody all riled up about police injustice with 'Fuck tha Police,' but evidently he wasn't sincere. I guess maybe he should have called that song 'Fuck Bein' Broke,' because that's all Eazy-E seems to care about. He ain't about nothin but money."

After two weeks of testimony, the jury—which included no blacks— was dismissed to begin deliberations. Seven days later, a verdict was reached. All four men were acquitted on all charges except one count of excessive force against Officer Powell. The judge declared a mistrial, since the jury couldn't reach a consensus. A year later a federal jury found Officers Stacey Koon and Powell guilty of violating King's civil rights and sentenced them to two and a half years in prison. Again, the officers were acquitted.

WE HAD TO TEAR THIS MUTHAFUCKA UP

"This is for Rodney King!" a young black man shouted after cracking a bottle of 8 Ball over the head of David Lee, whose father owned Pay-less Liquor and Deli. The young man and his friends had gone to the Korean-owned convenience store known as "Mr. Lee's" around South Central to grab some bottles of Olde English 800 an hour after the verdict was announced. When they got there the men decided to steal the malt liquor, scooping up as many forty-ounce bottles as their arms could carry. Lee was struck in the head when he attempted to stop them from leaving the store without paying. The men tossed some of the bottles through the store's windows before fleeing.

Mayor Bradley condemned the verdict in an emotional public address. "No, our eyes did not deceive us. We saw what we saw. What we saw was a crime," Bradley said. "We will not tolerate the savage beating of our citizens by a few renegade cops." He urged the city to stay clam and refrain from violence but his comments were perceived by many as a tactful call to action for black citizens who were enraged not just about the case, but years of racial tension and police brutality that the footage had exposed. It was a breaking point for black Angelenos and less than two hours after the jury handed down its verdict, the city was on fire.

"It's a hellish night in the City of Angels," one newscaster said.

LA turned into a war zone, with scenes that looked like an apocalyptic thriller. Cops were unprepared as Gates was at a house in ritzy Brentwood campaigning against police reform when the unrest began. The intersection of Florence and Normandie, three blocks from the incident at Mr. Lee's, was the flash point of violence. A group of guys took baseball bats to a white man's car. An Asian man driving home from work was beaten and robbed after assailants got his car to stop, leaving his business attire soaked in blood. Fidel Lopez, a self-employed construction worker, was dragged from his truck and savagely beaten by a group of black men—a car stereo was smashed over his skull, his ear nearly severed, his pants pulled down to his knees so his assailants could spray paint his genitals black and douse him with gasoline. Lopez was saved from certain death when black reverend Bennie Newton intervened, hoisting his Bible in the air and warning rioters, "Kill him, and you have to kill me too." But there was no one to help Reginald Denny when he was pulled from his eighteen-wheeler and pummeled in a gruesome attack by members of the 8-Trey Gangster Crips. The assault on Denny was broadcast live by a news helicopter and became a jarring symbol of the mayhem. Denny was kicked and beaten with a claw hammer before Damian "Football" Williams took a cinderblock and crushed it on his head at close range, knocking him unconscious and fracturing his skull in ninety-one places—Williams even did a little victory dance afterward. The 8-Treys were linked to a police ambush where three officers were shot and injured, and authorities believed the gang looted clean a gun shop near Western and Florence Avenues. Although gangs did a great deal of looting during the riots, members of rival Crips and Bloods sets in nearby Watts had actually declared a truce to end violence the day before the riots (it didn't last long).

A lack of police presence made way for the increasingly brutal violence and mayhem to occur, although two blocks away from the madness unfolding at Florence and Normandie, there was a platoon metro division that refused to dispatch officers out of concern that the optics would exacerbate the sentiment behind the riots. When cops finally did show up, they were pelted with rocks and bottles, taunted by mobs of angry, disenfranchised blacks furious that, despite a video recording and national outcry, police officers still managed to get away with the types of brutality they had been complaining about for years. Knowing they were just as much a target of violence, and lacking shields or bulletproof vests, responding officers withdrew from the area. Retribution for Latasha Harlins was undoubtedly at the forefront of some who went into Koreatown to pillage shops and target Korean shop owners, who fired guns at thieves and exchanged gunfire with looters, as cops largely abandoned the area to instead protect Beverly Hills and West Hollywood. "Burn baby burn," a man screamed as buildings were set ablaze.

Sir Jinx was working with Kool G Rap at a studio in Atwater Village, a cute neighborhood nestled between Griffith Park and Glendale, when the verdict came down. It was supposed to be an off day, but G Rap was writing and Jinx was going through beats. In the room adjacent to his, Tupac Shakur was at work on his *Strictly 4 My N.I.G.G.A.Z . . .* album. The TV was off so they had no idea what was unfolding across LA until a few of his homeboys burst through the studio carrying hats, stacked one on top of another, and armfuls of liquor. "I know they ain't got no money," Jinx said. "So I'm like where did y'all get this stuff from?"

"LA is on fire," they told him. "Turn on the TV."

Jinx, G Rap, and Tupac decided to go see it for themselves. They piled into Jinx's Honda Accord and drove down Los Feliz Boulevard and south into South Central. Pac was strapped with a nine-millimeter, which he shot up into the sky as the car raced down the street passing burning cars. They got to Crenshaw and stopped in the middle of the street because traffic had come to a standstill. Cars were left in the middle of the road. "People were out everywhere, mad. The first place we stop was Tempo Records. We just went inside the motherfucker and it was on fire," Jinx said. "People was running in and stealing movies so we went in. People found Tupac and he's signing records that they stole."

The day the riots broke out, Ice Cube was moving from Baldwin Hills to a new home in the Valley with his wife, Kimberly Woodruff (they had just tied the knot a few days earlier after years of dating). With the movers doing their thing, Cube headed to Harrison-Ross Mortuary in Compton to pay respects to a homie that had gotten killed. "Some of the homies were like, 'Cube what you doing out here? It's getting crazy. You need to go back.'" As the violence fired up in South Central he went around checking on people, starting with his parents.

"Just crawling through it, it was crazy looking at everything that was happening and trying to get through," Cube recalled. "From there

I watched it from afar until the peace treaties and I wanted to be involved."

The images of strips of LA glowing amber as smoke billowed from dozens of fires were shocking. Men and women ran through the streets, their arms crammed with their stolen bounty—shoes, clothing, groceries, whatever. Classes were cancelled. The National Guard was called. A dusk-to-dawn curfew was implemented. And suddenly "Fuck tha Police," the record blasting from cars, became an unofficial motto during the unrest. Rioters chanted "Fuck the police," screaming it into news cameras and spray-painting the phrase on walls around South Central. The world watched in horror, and confusion. "Finally it took a motherfucker to videotape a nigga gettin' the shit beat out of him for everybody else to say 'fuck tha police,'" Eazy later said.

"Whether Rodney King happened or not, we would have still been saying that shit was real," Cube said of "Fuck tha Police" and how many saw the record foreshadowing the riots. "Nobody could tell us anything different because we had saw stuff like this with our own eyes. People probably needed validation for themselves, but we didn't need it because we weren't looking for none—we were spitting it how we saw it and how shit was around us. I had the feeling of 'we finally got y'all asses on tape.' That was the feeling: 'We finally got you, and this is why people are saying 'Fuck tha Police.'"

The D.O.C. and Warren G went out together and looted. "It seemed like the thing to do," D.O.C. said. What struck D.O.C. the most was how radically different the city felt in that moment. Before he was typically cognizant of where he was in the city as some areas were unsafe to travel in. But on that day, it didn't matter. "It didn't feel like LA at all. As long as you were black you were good. If you weren't black, you may have a problem," he laughed. "I didn't worry about Bloods or Crips that day, it was very much if you're black we're in this bitch together—let's go." Added Sir Jinx: "It was like a big-ass picnic."

"The events in the USA are evidence—again—of the sense of exclusion by which minorities feel themselves victimized in the country that was conceived to be a paradise of opportunities for all of its citizens, and even for the millions it has welcomed as immigrants," a Brazilian paper wrote, while a publication in Rome proclaimed "Los Angeles is paying today what other cities and nations tempted by the same illusions could be called upon to pay tomorrow: the price of indifference and of judicial disgrace which protects the (white) police attackers and condemns the (black) victims; which acquits a Kennedy and condemns a Tyson for the same crime of rape."

When the rioting finally ended five days later, more than sixty people (mostly black and Latino) had lost their lives in shootings or incidents tied to the unrest, more than two thousand people were injured, eleven thousand arrested, and $1 billion in damage had been done, in what was the most devastating civil disturbance since the 1863 Draft Riots in New York City.

"It was more than just the verdict. More than just the white cops. It was a lot of shit building up—issues with the Koreans and blacks, the Mexicans and the blacks. It was boiling over and it just needed one thing," Jinx said. "People didn't really give a fuck about Rodney King like that, but we thought it was fucked up what they did to him and it was on tape. It wasn't like they beat this nigga up and there was no proof. There was a video."

"Born, wicked, Laurence, Powell, foul / Cut his fuckin throat and I smile," Ice Cube rapped on "We Had to Tear This Muthafucka Up" from his album *The Predator*.

Released months after the LA riots, *The Predator* touches on the events from earlier that year and became his first number one album. "Who Got the Camera?" is inspired by the Rodney King beating, imaging a scenario in which a black motorist is brutally beaten by cops and hoping its filmed. He seethes at the Simi Valley jury that acquitted the four officers charged with beating King on "Now I Gotta Wet 'Cha" and "We Had to Tear This Muthafucka Up." And on the album's closer, "Say Hi to the Bad Guy," Cube envisions revenge on a cop by enticing him with donuts and blasting him in the head. *The Predator*, however, is mostly remembered for "It Was a Good Day," a mellow, celebratory jam created around an Isley Brothers' sample describing the perfect day where there was no gang violence, police confrontation, or drama, that's become his most famous recording—so famous in fact, a blogger calculated the exact day that Cube describes in the song as January 20, 1992, two months before the killing of Harlins and King's beating. Goodyear decided to fly its blimp over South Central like the song said to pay tribute.

✳

By the time the riots had inflamed LA and captivated a nation, Gangsta rap had already embedded itself into the pop zeitgeist of the 1990s, going from scandalous musings of urban miscreants to a lucrative industry.

The year prior, N.W.A notched the first number-one Gangsta-rap album with its final release, *Efil4zaggin*, and three of its former members—Ice Cube, MC Ren, and Dr. Dre—put out hit projects that year. Tupac Shakur emerged with his debut, *2Pacalypse Now*, offering raw mediations on racism, police brutality, poverty, black-on-black crime, and teenage pregnancy from the lens of a twenty-year-old black man. DJ Quik, an inventive rhymer and producer from Compton, became the first rapper from the Bloods to break big. Ice-T dropped *O.G. Original Gangster*, which still remains a seminal entry in the genre. And Hollywood, seeing the growing commercial success of Gangsta rap, embraced films that told the same grim and violent stories emcees were rapping about. With Cube's *Boyz n the Hood* launching a subgenre of hood films, rap continued to deepen its influence. In fact one of the biggest singles of 1992 came from a young teenage rap duo named Kris Kross that rapped about missing the school bus on one song while sampling Eazy-E on another. But in 1992, rap was such a hot button in politics it led to the *Los Angeles Times* to label the months of controversy and debate over race and class as "The Uncivil War."

After the riots, political rapper and community activist Sister Souljah gave an interview where she levied the unrest as "revenge" against years of white oppression.

"I mean, if black people kill black people every day, why not have a week and kill white people? . . . In other words, white people, this government and that mayor were well aware of the fact that black people were dying every day in Los Angeles under gang violence. So if you're a gang member and you would normally be killing somebody, why not kill a white person? Do you think that somebody thinks that white people are better, or above dying, when they would kill their own kind?" she asked.

Souljah, born Lisa Williamson, appeared on several tracks with Public Enemy before briefly becoming a member, replacing the exiled Professor Griff as the group's "Minister of Information." In 1992 she tried her hand at a rap career, releasing her only album, *360 Degrees of Power*, which featured her explosive oratories. "Souljah was not born to make white people feel comfortable. I am African first. I am black first. I want what's good for me and my people first. And if my survival means your total destruction, then so be it," she yells on "The Hate That Hate Produced," one of her two singles banned by MTV because of their language and imagery.

An edited version of Souljah's words reached Arkansas governor and presidential candidate Bill Clinton. Needing to appeal beyond the Democratic vote, Clinton saw an opportunity to try to get the support of Republican voters disillusioned by President Bush and those considering Ross Perot when he was invited to speak at the Reverend Jesse Jackson's Rainbow Coalition Leadership Summit. To the surprise of the organization hosting him, Clinton used his speech to denounce Souljah and criticize them for allowing her to speak at a youth forum. "She told the *Washington Post* . . . 'If black people kill black people every day, why not take a week and kill white people?' . . . If you took the words 'white' and 'black' and reversed them, you might think David Duke was giving that speech," Clinton said, comparing her to the former grand wizard of the Ku Klux Klan who ran for governor of Louisiana the year prior. His denouncement, based on a quote taken out of context, angered Jackson and other black leaders who accused Clinton for exploiting Souljah "purely to appeal to conservative whites." It was an embarrassing hiccup for Clinton who later won over black voters when he pulled off a smooth saxophone solo on the *Arsenio Hall Show* and won the election—he was even labeled America's "first black president."

Clinton's takedown of Souljah wasn't the only political shaming of hip-hop. The Combined Law Enforcement Associations of Texas and the Dallas Police Association united to call for a boycott of "Cop Killer," a song from Ice-T and his thrash metal band Body Count. Ice, the first rapper signed to Sire Records, was no stranger to his music attracting political attention. After founding the Parents Music Resource Center, a committee established to keep explicit music away from kids, Tipper Gore, wife of Clinton's running mate Senator Al Gore, and Susan Baker, wife of longtime Bush confidant and secretary of state James Baker, used their political influence to initiate the 1985 Senate hearings on explicit lyrics, which led to the Recording Industry Association of America being pressured into introducing a labeling system that identified potentially offensive albums. Ice-T's debut, *Rhyme Pays*, was the first album to be labeled with a warning sticker under those guidelines. Released a few weeks before the LA riots and months before law enforcement got their hands on its lyrics, "Cop Killer" was a rock song that was a dark fantasy about snuffing a member of the law. The song was dedicated to "every cop that has ever taken advantage of somebody, beat 'em down or hurt 'em, because they got long hair, listen to the wrong kinda music, wrong color, whatever they thought was the reason to do it."

"Cop killer, I know your family's grievin' . . . FUCK 'EM! / Cop killer, but tonight we get even," Ice sings over brash guitars and drums.

"Cop Killer" unleashed a furor not even seen by "Fuck tha Police" (the phrase is actually shouted repeatedly in the song's final refrain). Law enforcement associations held a press conference calling for a boycott of Sire's parent company, Time Warner, if it wasn't removed from future pressings. Vice President Dan Quayle joined the outcry, denouncing the company for marketing "obscene" entertainment that, he said, ran counter to the traditional values of mainstream culture. "The problem is that records like 'Cop Killer' do have an impact on the streets—the wrong impact," he decried, while President Bush offered an attack on the entertainment industry at large, saying it was "sick" to produce anything that glorified cop killing. The outcry was especially strange considering the previous year's highest grossing film featured Arnold Schwarzenegger playing a cop-slaying cyborg and there was no one up in arms.

Sixty members of Congress signed a letter to Warner Brothers, slamming "Cop Killer" as "vile" and "despicable," and there was a call for divestiture of stock from Time Warner. California attorney general Daniel E. Lungren sent letters to chief executives of eighteen record-store chains in the state urging them to stop selling the record, printing the missive on government stationery for extra potency. Oliver North, the former National Security Council aide who was entangled in the Iran-Contra scandal, called on the governors of all fifty states to persecute Time Warner for marketing "Cop Killer" in violation of sedition and antianarchy statutes. The National Rifle Association took out full-page ads in newspapers pledging legal assistance "to the interests of any police officer shot or killed if it's shown that the violence was incited by Ice-T's 'Cop Killer,'" and future NRA president Charlton Heston read the lyrics aloud at a Time Warner stockholders meeting in Beverly Hills while hundreds of members from local and national police organizations, including the Los Angeles Police Protective League, protested outside.

As demonstrated with N.W.A's "Fuck tha Police," national fury is damn good for business. The protests led to the *Body Count* album selling 100,000 copies in a month, sending it racing up the *Billboard* chart despite it being pulled by about 1,500 stores. Citing his First Amendment right to free speech, Ice-T defended his band's record saying, "If you believe that I'm a cop killer, you believe David Bowie is an astronaut." The National Black Police Association denounced the boycott and Time

Warner co-CEO Gerald M. Levin wrote an editorial for the *Wall Street Journal* suggesting that instead of "finding ways to silence the messenger" critics and listeners should be "heeding the anguished cry contained in his message." Tired of the public condemnation as a violent thug and constant death threats, Ice-T agreed to pull the song from future pressings of the album and gave it out for free. Later that year, he split amicably with Sire/Warner Brothers after the label sought to censor lyrics on his solo project, *Home Invasion*, instead taking the album to Priority Records, a label familiar in dealing with public outcry over Gangsta-rap lyrics. Ice-T continued releasing albums, both solo and with Body Count, but he's still most famous for his role on *Law & Order: SVU*—a drama in which he portrays, in one of the greatest ironies of all time, a detective.

NUTHIN'
BUT A 'G' THANG

Michael Harris, better known as Harry-O, made a fortune moving cocaine across the country—money he then funneled through legitimate business dealings, investing in real estate, a limousine service, hair salons, and a construction company. But the South Central drug kingpin was itching to get into show business. Harry-O got a shot in 1988 by coproducing a Broadway production called *Checkmates*, which starred Ruby Dee and Paul Winfield and served as the stage debut of Denzel Washington. Most impressively he managed to do this while behind bars, sentenced months before the show opened to twenty-eight years for crack dealing, kidnapping, and attempted murder.

In the autumn of 1991, Harry-O introduced his lawyer David Kenner to Suge Knight and asked Kenner to bring him in for a jailhouse visit so the two could confab about cutting a demo of his wife, Lydia Harris, an aspiring singer who served as his proxy on the outside. They discussed partnering for the label, with the incarcerated dealer particularly interested in Dr. Dre's involvement. Within months he put up $1.5 million in capital for a 50-percent stake in a multimedia company called GF Entertainment, which commissioned Death Row Records as its record division (pay-per-view concerts and a movie division were also part of the plan).

Suge and Harry-O frequently discussed business over the phone—despite
it being illegal for an inmate to run a business while in state prison—
and Suge would make the two-hour trek to the California Correctional
Institution in Tehachapi to sit with his business partner, going nearly two
dozen times in the next eighteen months after they met. Lydia and Kenner filed incorporation papers in May 1992 to establish GFE Inc., which
stood for Godfather Entertainment Inc.

The "springing of Death Row Records" was celebrated with a flashy
party thrown by GF Entertainment at Chasen's restaurant in Beverly Hills.
Video footage of the party shows Suge and Kenner toasting Harry-O,
a seemingly intoxicated D.O.C. declaring the label's greatness, and Dre
hamming it up with Michel'le. But the celebrations were short-lived
for some of the label's key players. Harry-O and Suge fell out after he
learned Suge and Dre inked a deal with Jimmy Iovine's burgeoning Interscope Records. The deal with Interscope also pushed out D.O.C. and
Dick Griffey, with them later suing Suge for secretly incorporating the
label and fraudulently transferring all its assets. "By the time it made it to
Jimmy, I didn't own anything. It was tough. Everybody knew it. And I
knew everybody knew it, but there was nothing I could do about it. Dre
was supposed to be my guy, and so if he's not gonna stand back to back
with me that means I'm out here by myself. For me, it was let's just ride
this thing out and see how I could get mine off of it and move on," said
D.O.C., who found out about the deal the night before shooting a video
for *The Chronic*.

"Suge used to always say to me, 'We don't fatten no frogs for no
snakes,' meaning he didn't want undeserving individuals in the corporate world to benefit from our hard work," Harry-O said. "As it turned
out, Suge ended up being both the frog and the snake." Harry-O threatened to sue in 1996 and received a $300,000 settlement—in 2002 Lydia
sued Suge and a judge awarded her $107 million, though only $1 million
was paid after Suge was forced into bankruptcy—and a year later Griffey
and D.O.C. sued Suge, who was incarcerated at the time, for $150 mil-

lion and won a small six-figure settlement. D.O.C. likens the speed with which Suge changed on him to the old story of Dr. Jekyll and Mr. Hyde. "It happened that fast," he said. "The words don't exist to explain how demoralizing it felt."

It was during these early days for Death Row when Dre was recruiting and auditioning artists to join the fold, acts that would soon help him craft his debut, *The Chronic*. D.O.C., despite getting shafted by Suge, stuck around. "Even when me and Dre were beefing and fighting and I thought this motherfucker was doing me wrong, I still took my ass to work every day to make that record as good as I could because it represented me just as much as anybody else," he said. "One of the things that made the music so great is we all loved and cared for each other. We were a family. [But] none of those monies ever came to me, none of those accolades ever came to me."

Snoop Dogg was pegged as a banner act along with Dre. Snoop's fellow 213 members, Nate Dogg and Warren G, were heavy in the mix when it came to the new music being created at Death Row, even though Dre never signed his stepbrother Warren to a deal. "My brother told me, 'You need to go on and be your own man,'" Warren said. "So that's what I did!" Also brought on board was Jewell, who sang alongside Eazy on N.W.A's raunchy "I'd Rather Fuck You." Snoop met Kurupt, a rail-thin rapper who moved to South Central from Philadelphia as a teenager, at the famed Roxy on the Sunset Strip where emcees would battle-rap. Impressed with his skills, Snoop took him to meet Dre and Suge, who signed him on the spot. Snoop also brought his cousins, Delmar Arnaud known as Dat Nigga Daz, or Daz for short, and Eric Collins, who rapped for fun as RBX (or "Reality Born Unknown") and actually played football with Suge at the University of Nevada. Dre discovered a fiery female rapper from Virginia named the Lady of Rage, after LA Posse, a local production team, let him listen to their album *They Come in All Colors*, which featured Rage. He flew her out to LA not long afterward.

Around Dre was a stable of hungry, raw talent. And it pushed him further. In the course of a day maybe fifty people would drop by, mostly hangers-on. The sessions at the studio became parties. People only stopped drinking and smoking long enough to get in the booth. The goal was "all hits and no bullshit" as D.O.C. recalled. Dre would throw whoever was closest into the booth to record a vocal. D.O.C. coached the newcomers, who were tested to some degree, but eventually Snoop broke out as the most valuable player, popping up on song after song. "It was fun, no different from when it was me, Dre, Ren, and Cube," D.O.C. said of the first days of Death Row. "It was a change in style, the music, but it was still just us having fun."

But the party atmosphere was often ruined by Suge's unpredictable, violent behavior. D.O.C. and others have said things were always tense at the studio, but nights would get especially crazy if Suge didn't like someone who was there—or if he just felt like flexing his power, which was routine. One night he saw George and Lynwood Stanley, two brothers he'd known for years, among the crowd in the studio at Dre's invitation. Dre gave them permission to make a call on a phone in the studio, which angered Suge. "I don't give a fuck what Dre says, Dre ain't payin' no bills," Suge huffed. An argument erupted and Suge beat the shit out of the men. He grabbed a gun and fired a bullet through the wall to scare them. Suge didn't stop there. He then humiliated the men, forcing them to strip to their underwear—just one instance of the sadistic things he did to intimidate people, behavior that became commonplace in the studio. "It was great working with Dre, but the elements that surrounded him? Interesting," CPO Boss Hogg said of the environment around Suge. "There was always something in the air. Always this underflowing tension. There was this Blood and Crip element that was going on, which we didn't have at Ruthless. Ruthless was much more of a family, whereas Death Row felt like a set. It was an eggshell situation, you knew it was going to crack at some point. I never wanted to do anything huge there because I didn't want to be, literally, standing on Death Row."

It was all too much for D.O.C. He could only show up to the studio if he was drunk or high on weed or dope. "I was in hell at that moment. Just going to SOLAR [where Death Row was based], most of the time was like going to the yard in the penitentiary," he said. "For a nigga that's not of that world, that shit was murder. But when I was high or loaded as fuck I was just one of the niggas and when they wanted to do crazy shit like whoop some nigga's ass or slap a muthafucka or spit or piss or whatever the fuck they was doing, I was with it."

Trouble also followed Dre while he worked on *The Chronic* in 1992. In mid-July he joined some friends at a party in South Central when he got into a spat with a guy, who shot him four times in the leg. Dre rebuffed the claim he was shot, downplaying the event the way he did after allegedly assaulting music producer Damon Thomas, striking a police officer in New Orleans, or his house catching fire during a wild pool party.

"Shot at," Dre said incredulously during one interview. "I got shot at a whole bunch of times. They never reported it before, though." Dre's account was that he and his friends were outside a hotel, calling one guy's girl ugly. "So we came downstairs to talk about her, right? Shots rang out. We ran back into the hotel. I don't even know where they came from."

Reporters from *Spin*, *Rolling Stone*, and the *Los Angeles Times* inquired about the incident. He wasn't budging from his story. "I ain't got nothing to tell y'all," he said. But he was honest with one reporter, flat out telling him that "1992 was not my year." There was a hotel lobby brawl, an incident where he allegedly hired thugs to threaten a former associate, and as his debut album was arriving in stores, Dre had to face a judge for assaulting Thomas with a single jawbreaking punch. Eazy was vocal about Dre's troubles, pushing the blame on his association with Suge. "He had the Dee Barnes thing, breaking that kid's jaw, driving his car off the cliff, getting shot, New Orleans. None of that ever happened when he was down with us," he offered.

*

Interscope Records couldn't have been a better home for Death Row, given the pedigree of its head, Jimmy Iovine. Introduced to music production as a teenager while growing up in Brooklyn, Iovine started his career as a recording engineer. He worked with John Lennon on his experimental *Mind Games*, Bruce Springsteen's *Born to Run*, Meat Loaf's *Bat Out of Hell*, Patti Smith's *Easter*, U2's *Rattle and Hum*, and Stevie Nicks's stellar solo debut, *Bella Donna*. After a term at A&M Records, he teamed with businessman Tim Field in 1991 to launch the $30 million start-up Interscope records. Iovine was given Dre's *Chronic* album and publicity materials—including Death Row's grim logo of a man being executed by electric chair. Iovine was initially hesitant to play the music. He didn't know hip-hop, but as an accomplished producer himself, Iovine felt much of the rap he heard sounded cheaply produced. But he was astounded by Dre's project, which sounded more polished than a great deal of rock records. "I knew nothin' about hip-hop. The only thing I was familiar with was my speakers. I had heard every producer who came in during the first year of Interscope, and the hip-hop sounded terrible. I couldn't take it. I was such a sound fanatic," Iovine said. "When Dre came in with that fuckin' thing, I said, 'Who produced this?'"

Dre and Iovine hit it off immediately. Iovine was impressed by Dre's prowess behind the boards. Dre, in turn, was wowed at Iovine's cred and his passion for music. As Death Row and Interscope mapped out its partnership, Eazy filed his federal lawsuit, claiming Dre sent goons to intimidate him into releasing him, the D.O.C., and Michel'le from their contracts.

In response, Dre wrote a statement claiming he and Eazy started Ruthless in 1985 as a joint venture and had a verbal agreement to split all profits. "I could have gone after half of Ruthless 'cause me and Eazy was equal partners from the jump street," Dre told a reporter. Ruthless denied the claim.

In a controversial interview with the *Source* for its November 1992 cover, Dre denied almost every single incident embroiling him—hitting Damon Thomas, beating Dee Barnes, getting shot four times, totaling his car, burning down his home accidentally, and Eazy's claim that Dre was the reason he got shook down to sign over contracts. Dre even posed with a .44 Smith & Wesson pointed at his own temple. "That's how I felt at the time," he said.

Iovine had a solution. With Eazy refusing to release Dre from his contract, asserting that Dre still owed the label four albums, Iovine decided to offer payment to Eazy, and also Death Row, for the right to release *The Chronic*. The deal, which was solidified in early December, a few weeks before the album's release, recognized Dre's contracts with Ruthless by giving Ruthless a percentage of royalties from whatever Dre produced. In exchange, Ruthless gave Interscope the rights to Dre as an exclusive producer and artist. Eazy was said to make 25–50 cents off every copy of *The Chronic* and bragged that he was earning more from Dre's albums than Dre did, and that Dre would have been better off staying at Ruthless.

In light of his mounting troubles, *The Chronic* unfolded as a semi-autobiographical look into the genius producer. From a production point of view, the album is a slam dunk, as Dre relied deeply on his beloved Parliament-Funkadelic samples to create the album's hallmark sound, incorporating those high-pitched "funky worm" Moog synths to get the warm, lush throwback groove that became known as Gangsta funk, or G-funk for short.

Revenge is the dominant theme in the intro, and "Fuck wit Dre Day (And Everybody's Celebratin')" takes some potent shots at Eazy. The violent streets of South Central inspired "Let Me Ride," a record in which he makes it quite clear that the album will stray far away from the pro-black messaging Cube was bringing into Gangsta rap: "No medallions, dreadlocks, or black fists," he rapped. "The Day the Niggaz Took Over" is a mediation on the destructive, deadly LA riots from earlier in the year. "Nuthin' but a 'G' Thang" is a funky anthem for gangster posturing that was originally recorded over a Boz Scaggs track while Snoop was in jail on a drug charge. "He called in, and I taped the receiver of the phone to the mic. You can hear jail sounds in the back and everything," Dre said. The final version of the record is built over a sample of Leon Haywood's "I Want'a Do Something Freaky to You," a record he found in his mom's collection—he knew it was special after he played it at a house party and people kept asking him to rewind it. Black-on-black crime is dissected in "Lil' Ghetto Boy" in a tale of a drug dealing gangster shot after trying to rob a younger gangbanger. And the album's concluding track, "Bitches Ain't Shit," contained Dre's most scathing lines toward Eazy. "I used to know a bitch named Eric Wright . . . now she's suing cause the shit she be doing ain't shit," he raps.

While work on *The Chronic* was under way, Death Row moved its headquarters from the SOLAR building into a suite near Interscope at a Westwood office tower. Suge hired new staff, including his wife, Sharitha, to manage acts. The office was also rife with thuggish guys like Buntry, Jake the Violator, Heron, and Hen Dogg (he was responsible for designing the label's grim logo)—all men who would be killed by gunfire in separate incidents. Suge moved away from the boots and jeans he typically favored and began incorporating red into his wardrobe to play up his affiliation with the Mob Piru Bloods. The omnipresence of thugs made the air thick the second you arrived. Interscope employees, terrified, started evading the elevator since it dumped you directly into Death Row's lair.

For all its hard-core ways, Death Row still wasn't immune to the corporate censorship of Gangsta rap happening across the industry in the wake of protests and lyric controversies. Interscope wanted "Mr. Officer" off *The Chronic*—a song in which Dre had a chorus chant of "Mister Officer, Mister Officer, I wanna see you lying in a coffin, sir." It was as rancid and brash as N.W.A work, but Interscope's parent company, Time Warner, wanted no part. It had already spent a chunk of the year catching heat over Ice-T's inflammatory "Cop Killer," released with his metal side act Body Count. Dre wasn't interested in a battle. Thinking as a business-man, he yanked the offending record from the album and kept it moving.

To further show how much control he had over his project, Dre stepped into the director's chair for "Fuck Wit Dre Day (And Everybody's Celebratin')." In the video he wore a heavy Carhartt jacket, black jeans, and a black baseball cap—drinking had him a bit heavier than normal—and filmed himself driving around in a lowrider, standing near Snoop, waving a gun, and rapping in front of a dancing crowd. The video is most remembered for its cruel, comedic assault on Eazy. Dre casted actor A. J. Johnson to play a Jheri-curled parody of Eazy named Sleazy-E. In a skit opening the video, Sleazy gets a new contract from a white, money-grubbing record producer of "Useless Records" (an obvious dig toward Jerry Heller and Ruthless), played by executive producer from Interscope Records, Steve Berman. It's an exchange that presents Sleazy as an Uncle Tom of sorts, happily serving his fat-cat master.

"You know, the problem with this business, people just don't trust each other. I'm glad you and I trust each other. You trust me, don't you?" Berman asks, doing his greatest Jerry Heller impression.

"Yeah, boss," Sleazy assures him.

"Oh, no, no, I work for you. I work for Sleazy-E—I wouldn't have it any other way," the Heller character stresses before giving him orders to find some rappers to sign. "Go, boy! Go, boy!"

Dre lays on the humiliation thick in the clip, as we see Sleazy shuck and jive with rappers he's trying to recruit, get chased by armed men, and finally, standing on the Pasadena Freeway with a sign: "Will Rap for Food." Eazy was then savvy enough to place the same character in the video for his single, "Real Muthaphuckkin G's," from his *It's On (Dr. Dre) 187um Killa* EP—released the following year in response to *The Chronic*—in which he brags about playing Dre and profiting off his records, and makes digs at his pre-N.W.A stint with electro group the World Class Wreckin' Cru. "But Dre Day only meant Eazy's payday . . . so nigga please, nigga please, don't step to deez," he gloated.

To promote *The Chronic*, Interscope purchased minute-long ads featuring music from the album that aired on dozens of stations. Label executives worked the phones to convince MTV to air Dre's videos, since they couldn't get radio to touch the record. "They think it's a bunch of black guys cursing who want to kill everybody," Iovine said his radio guys were told. "I said, 'Okay, make a commercial—nothing in front or back of it, just a minute of the song. Don't say who it is, and buy it on fifty stations, drive time. I want the program directors to hear it in their cars.' What I didn't know would happen was kids heard it and started calling for it. That's how that got on the radio."

Released in December 1992, *The Chronic* hit number three on the *Billboard* 200 and would sell three million copies in a year. MTV aired "Dre Day" on repeat, but for some reason blurred out Dre's directing credit, with "Nuthin' But a 'G' Thang" and "Let Me Ride"—the video of which Cube appeared in after they reconciled—also dominating airplay. Reviews for the album were exceptional. *Rolling Stone* called it "A hip-hop masterwork," as the *Source*, *Entertainment Weekly*, and other publications lobbied it with praise. *The Chronic* became a pop phenomenon that yielded Dre radio hits and catapulted him and Snoop to superstardom. Dre helped establish Gangsta rap with N.W.A and *Straight Outta Compton*, but it was *The Chronic* that revolutionized the genre, as it would define hip-hop and inspire generations to come. "*The Chronic* is the only album that rivals *Niggaz4Life* . . . and I don't think of them as rivals, I see them as some of the best works of hip-hop that has ever come out," CPO Boss Hogg said. "The attention to detail. The mixing. The mastering. Everything."

IT'S ON

Ruthless looked to move beyond Dre and Cube. Eazy and Jerry Heller juggled a staggering twenty-nine simultaneous projects, one of which was Eazy's EP *5150: Home 4 tha Sick* released just days before Dre's *The Chronic*. The EP was his first solo material since *Eazy-Duz-It*, which dropped four years earlier. Eazy needed to show that he still had it, but how could he do that when much of his formula relied on Dre's studio wizardry and Cube, Ren, and the D.O.C.'s pens?

Gleaning its name from the California code allowing involuntary confinement of someone suspected of being a danger to themselves or others, *5150* is a mostly forgettable collection of serviceable tunes— though it did include a collaboration with Naughty by Nature and the debut of will.i.am, then a young rapper signed to Ruthless as Will 1X. He was signed to the label with his group Atban Klann or A Tribe Beyond a Nation, a jazzy conscious outfit that fit nicely with the trend of emcees embracing their blackness and snubbing Gangsta rap's hard-core imagery in exchange for enlightened rhymes. Will 1X was one of a handful of acts drafted to ghostwrite for Eazy and other acts on the label. The Atban Klann's debut album, *Grass Roots*, would end up shelved and they were eventually dropped from Ruthless before rebranding as the Black Eyed Peas and going on to massive pop stardom. Jewish rap group Blood of Abraham was also apart of the new crop of Ruthless recruits, as were trio of dirty rapping vixens dubbed H.W.A or "Hoez with Attitude." Above the Law's sophomore album, *Black Mafia Life*, was the first record Ruthless issued in 1993, despite being recorded two years prior as N.W.A worked on *Efil4zaggin*. Dre and Above the Law's Cold 187um often fed off each other in the studio, and there are great similarities between the way both albums married the psychedelic rock and soul of Parliament-Funkadelic and classic 1970s soul with hard-core lyrics. *Black Mafia Life* didn't take off the way *The Chronic* had, but it's impossible to think the latter could have existed if it wasn't for what Cold 187um did on *Black Mafia Life*—just listen to "Never Missin' a Beat" and "Nuthin' But a 'G' Thang" back-to-back, for starters. While many have accused Dre of jacking the G-funk sound, Cold 187um doesn't see it that way. "Coming up under Dre's tutelage, I wanted to be different then what we were doing at Ruthless.

In order for my crew to get an identity I wanted us to have a sound. I didn't want us to sound like spin-offs of N.W.A. I wanted to actually try a lot of different fusions of music: Funk, soul, blues, jazz, and hard-core hip-hop—a gumbo of sounds," he said. "A combination of all that funky soulful seventies stuff, with the boom and the bap of the eighties and the slap of the nineties. Melodies and chords and all these different things on top of hard drums and synthesizers, and filling it with breakbeats. Those were things people weren't doing. It's crazy because the template and the blueprint of the theory became the same one that *The Chronic* has. A lot of people get it wrong and say Dre bit it, but no he was just influenced by me being a young producer with a fusion of music that he tried it on *The Chronic*. It was great to see the idea that I thought of really work, but it was disheartening because I never got any credit for it."

Eazy's pockets were well greased from the success of *The Chronic*, but to anyone on the outside looking in, the optics were humiliating. Both Cube and Dre walked away from what they had built with Eazy and found even success without him. Eazy, of course, had listened to *The Chronic*, flipping through it in the studio one day, surrounded by groupies. "This shit is wack," he sneered to Ren, with his hangers-on joining the chorus.

"Nigga, this shit is hard," Ren countered.

Eazy knew a real game-changer would be an N.W.A reunion album; it would be massive, given all the guys had gone through and what they meant to rap. Earlier in the year at a premiere for Chris Rock's N.W.A parody/mockumentary *CB4*, he announced to *Yo! MTV Raps* host Fab Five Freddy that the group was getting back together without Dre because they were "staying sucka free." Ren looked uncomfortable during the exchange and when asked if he was down, he tactfully said if they all couldn't sit and talk about it like men then he wouldn't be involved. He balked at the idea altogether when Eazy told him the album would be produced by Yella, Cold 187um, and new producers he'd recruit. "I wasn't about to rap over any nigga's beat back then . . . I mean, how you gonna go from the top muthafucka to that?" Ren said.

Granted, Eazy's deal he brokered with Death Row and Jimmy Iovine to collect royalties from a massively successful album he had absolutely nothing to do with was a major power move, but rap fans were unaware of the behind-the-scenes dealings. What he really needed was to show that he could stand without Dre, the same way *Efil4zaggin* and *100 Miles and Runnin'* sought to prove N.W.A didn't need Cube. Eazy replaced Dre with a new in-house producer, Rhythm D. The South Central producer was on the come-up after crafting Oakland rapper Paperboy's debut album, *The Nine Yards*, including the funky, Zapp-sampling "Ditty," which went platinum and became a top ten hit on the pop charts in 1993—it was even nominated for a Grammy for Best Rap Solo Performance, but lost to Dre's "Let Me Ride." Before he joined Ruthless, Rhythm D was briefly affiliated with Death Row when he was introduced to Suge by Lady of Rage. He wrote and produced a record on the *Deep Cover* soundtrack for Paradise, a female rapper Suge had signed to the label. While doing some beats for Tracy Jernagin, Eazy's girlfriend and the mother of their daughter Ebie, Jernagin told Rhythm D that Eazy could use beats from someone like him. She offered to link them and Eazy invited him to his Norwalk home; Rhythm came prepared, bringing a tackle box filled with discs of his beats. "It just seemed like everything was kind of dead musically over there. Nobody was in there making beats," he said. "Niggas was laying all around on the couch and stuff. Seeing all that equipment, I was excited." Rhythm played him a beat that was a pastiche of Sir Jinx and the Bomb Squad. "Eazy went nuts. He went crazy off this beat . . . He pulled a few stacks out of his sock and was like 'Rhythm, you rollin' with Ruthless.'" And so Rhythm, who said he wasn't getting paid from Suge, stopped coming around Death Row.

Eazy almost entirely devoted his next release, *It's On (Dr. Dre) 187um Killa*, to dissing his former friend and collaborator. He assembled a new team of collaborators to make up for the absence of Dre, D.O.C., Cube, and MC Ren, who had converted to Islam and was working on his solo debut, *Shock of the Hour*. Yella was still around to handle production, but there was also Rhythm, Dr. Jam, Madness 4 Real, and Cold 187um—who more or less took Dre's place—to help. "[Eazy] was cocky. He was very confident in his position and him having a voice without Dre," Cold 187um said. "He was like a football coach—he just replaced the player and kept it moving. That was his attitude on that record."

It's On (Dr. Dre) 187um Killa opened with Eazy thanking his "bitch" Dre for making him money with *The Chronic* and the EP's centerpiece was the scathing diss track, "Real Muthaphukkin' G's" ("Real Compton City G's" for the radio).

> *Damn it's a trip how a nigga could switch so quick*
> *From wearin' lipstick to smoking on chronic at picnics*

"If Dre just left and didn't say anything or said, 'I just wanted to do my own thing,' I don't think Eric would have even tripped," Cold 187um said. "But when it's out there like, 'Oh he fucked me over' and this and that, it wasn't right. If you're brothers, family deals with business like family."

Eazy and his collaborators, Dresta and B. G. Knocc Out—brothers from the Nutty Blocc Crips—blasted Snoop and Dre as "studio gangstas," and the assaults continued throughout the eight-track EP. "Eazy would tell us stories about Dre, Death Row, and all these things and that's how [we] came up with the lyrics," B. G. Knocc Out said. The album art even included a publicity still from the World Class Wreckin' Cru showing Dre, with his handsome baby face and thin athletic frame, dressed in a tailored white-sequined body suit fashioned out of a medical supply store smock, stethoscope around his neck, and his face touched with powder and eyeliner. It was included in a mock obituary or as *The Eazy Times* called it, an "Obitchuary," announcing the EP as the death of Dre, a point he drove home by having his name crossed out in the graffiti-styled title on the cover the way gang members did when sending a threatening message—he's even pouring out a bit of his forty, a hood tradition marking someone's passing. And to further poke at his rift with Death Row, Eazy thanked Rhythm D for going AWOL. Released in October 1993, *It's On (Dr. Dre) 187um Killa* was the first issue under Ruthless's new distribution deal with Relativity Records. It's his most successful solo record, peaking at number five on the *Billboard* 200 and going on to sell over two million copies.

The beef between Eazy and Dre, unlike that of N.W.A and Cube, felt like it could explode beyond wax at any second. Although Cube and Ruthless signees Above the Law came to physical blows, the dissension between the group and Cube was contained to lyrical jabs and potshots in the press. Eazy, by many accounts, seriously contemplated killing Suge. The heavy presence of gangs at Death Row meant there were plenty of thugs ready to blast if things heated up. Extra muscle was employed at Ruthless and Death Row. A number of run-ins between the rivals happened, including a brief yet intense standoff at the 1994 Billboard Music Awards (legendary Crip Michael Concepcion intervened) and a melee between affiliates of Ruthless and Death Row on the set of a Montell Jordan video. Rap beefs would only escalate in later years as regions and rap empires fought on record, in the media, and in public. "It actually was some unnecessary bullshit," said Nate Dogg, who can be seen on video hitting Dresta over the head with a gold club as pandemonium sweeps the set of Jordan's "Somethin' 4 da Honeyz" music video.

Death Row quickly emerged victorious in the battle for supremacy between Dre's former home and his current one. At its height, Death Row was generating $100 million a year in profits. After the sensational release of *The Chronic*, an album that remained on *Billboard*'s Top 10 for months, work began on Snoop's highly anticipated debut, *Doggystyle*. Dre had been through a gamut of legal troubles the year prior and was under house arrest, allowed to leave his Valley estate only for work. Like *The Chronic*, *Doggystyle* was another all-hands-on-deck approach to record making. *Doggystyle* elevated the G-funk sound Dre trademarked on *The Chronic*. Layered with P-Funk samples, that indelible and eerie "funky worm," crisp drums, organs, and numbing basslines, the album was another slam dunk in Dre's canon as a producer—there are some who would argue *Doggystyle* is superior to *The Chronic*. D.O.C. served as a mentor of sorts to Snoop, helping him craft his rhymes. During production, Dre's beats and Snoop's flow had sessions feeling like an all out party. "We were having a bunch of fun," Dre once said, recalling a time the crew got kicked out of the studio because of the rambunctious atmosphere. *Doggystyle* was rife with the dark mores of gangster life, but the songs were injected with so much funk and catchy melodies, the actual content was easy to overlook. The album's first single, "Who Am I? (What's My Name?)" heavily samples George Clinton's funky earworm "Atomic Dog"—a record that's been worked into hundreds of songs since its 1982 release—and is one of a handful of classic tracks on the album that still moves the masses today. "Gin and Juice" is probably one of the greatest party anthems ever created, with a laid-back groove that literally sounds like the first day of summer captured on record. "Lodi Dodi" flipped the Doug E. Fresh and Slick Rick classic (though its preceding interlude took an uncomfortable dig at Eazy), and "Ain't No Fun (If the Homies Can't Have None)" is a swinging ode to group sex that's as ribald as it is infectious. Seriously, if the reaction these records continue to get when performed is any indication, Snoop will be rapping them for the rest of his life.

But Snoop Dogg's Death Row debut was also marred by real-life death. Shortly after the album was released in November 1993, Snoop was in a West Los Angeles courtroom to face a murder charge in connection with a shooting three months earlier. The rapper and his bodyguard McKinley Lee were accused of gunning down Philip Woldemariam after he tried to flee from a confrontation with them at Woodbine Park in Palms, where Snoop lived. Woldemariam was said to be a member of a local gang called the By Yerself Hustlers, who were at odds with Snoop and his crew. There was a fracas between the crews, and Woldemariam allegedly brandished a .380 automatic handgun; Lee fired as the rapper drove off. Snoop and his bodyguard evaded the cops for a week, with

LAPD detectives trailing him to the 1993 MTV Video Music Awards at Universal Amphitheater where he presented the first-ever award for R & B video alongside Dre and George Clinton. After handing the VMA to En Vogue, Snoop snuck away and later turned himself in. Snoop and his bodyguard were charged with murder, with Death Row posting the million-dollar bail. The 1996 trial was a media circus. Prosecutors said the self-defense case was contrived and that Woldemariam was followed, taunted, and gunned down as revenge. Snoop's defense team said the man was a hotheaded gangster looking to protect his turf and felt threatened when Snoop moved into the neighborhood. The defense said he was the one who brandished arms first after the heated argument, not anyone in Snoop's entourage. Woldemariam's family, a tight-knit clan of Ethiopian immigrants, said the man was an innocent victim whose biggest troubles were his health, and not gang beef. They condemned Snoop of not just killing in cold blood, but also using the murder to promote his own career. The LAPD was accused of inadvertently destroying the victim's clothing and evidence, including shell casings. After six days of deliberation a jury reached a verdict, acquitting Snoop and his bodyguard of murder. The judge declared a mistrial as the jury was deadlocked on a lesser count of voluntary manslaughter and a charge of conspiracy after the fact.

Though he'd been in and out of jail over drug charges, which he was quite open about, Snoop became the latest representation of the confluence of Gangsta rap's hard-core lyrics and real life. And he wasn't the only emcee getting into serious trouble that added to the seemingly unrelenting backlash against the music. Public Enemy's kooky Flavor Flav was charged with attempted murder and Tupac Shakur had released his hit sophomore album *Strictly 4 My N.I.G.G.A.Z.* . . . (N.I.G.G.A.Z. being an acronym for Never Ign'ant Getting Goals Accomplished) and was enjoying a blossoming film career—his ravishing debut in 1992's *Juice* earned him rave reviews—when he was charged of shooting two off-duty policemen in Atlanta and sexually abusing and sodomizing a woman in a New York hotel. Both charges were within a month of each other. Like Snoop, extra attention was placed on his venomous lyrics. With hard-core albums from Cypress Hill, Wu-Tang Clan, Scarface, Too $hort, former N.W.A members Eazy-E, Ice Cube, and MC Ren, and Snoop doing big business, it was enough to keep conservatives and the media wringing its hands. Jesse Jackson denounced record labels for issuing rap music and making money from "pain and degradation," calling for a boycott. Reverend Calvin Butts of Abyssinian Baptist Church in Harlem denounced the music at a rally. Surrounded by a few hundred supporters chanting "Negative rap is not all right!" he planned to take a steamroller over boxes of explicit albums but opted not to at the last minute, instead saying he would confab with rappers. And *Newsweek* in a November 1993 cover story asked "When is Rap 2 Violent?" alongside an image of a scowling Snoop.

"The media is quick to point their finger when trouble strikes, but nobody ever asks a successful rapper like me how he feels about what's going on in the 'hood," Snoop said at the time. "I guess they think I'm macho and I don't care or something."

Despite all this, *Doggystyle* was a smash. Dre wanted to produce the perfect rap record, one that would redefine the genre. *Doggystyle* achieved just that. Before its release, the hype was palpable. *Doggystyle* was declared the most anticipated rap album in history by the same publications covering the denouncement of the genre. "They had trucks lined up, and they were waiting to ship it," Chris "the Glove" Taylor said. During the final moments of editing the record, Taylor said Suge and Jimmy Iovine were literally breathing down his neck since production problems had already delayed its release six weeks. Record stores stayed open through the night, and fans waited in lengthy lines to purchase it. *Doggystyle* delivered on expectations, selling more than 800,000 copies in its first week—then a sales record for a debut—and becoming the first Gangsta rap album to open at number one. And yes, critics heaped on the praise. Snoop was called "the gangsta Marvin Gaye of Dr. Dre's Motown," *Rolling Stone* gave the collection four stars, and one review labeled it the smoothest gangsta album to date, but noted "it's easy to be impressed one moment and appalled the next." The album went quadruple platinum, eclipsing *The Chronic* and both N.W.A records—offering further, more definitive proof that Gangsta rap wasn't slowing down any time soon.

NATURAL BORN KILLAZ

Dr. Dre wanted to follow up Snoop's album with Lady of Rage, whom he long kept on the back burner, despite constant promises that she was up next to bat. She'd gladly guested on *The Chronic* and *Doggystyle* but like Nate Dogg, Tha Dogg Pound, and Warren G, she had yet to get any work done on her own project. The wait for Dre's attention would continue as Suge inked a deal to executive produce the soundtrack to the Tupac Shakur–starring urban drama *Above the Rim*, which would be released through Death Row and Interscope in the spring of 1994. Although the film was about a cocky high school basketball player in New York City, the soundtrack was aggressively West Coast, with Death Row artists filling most of the slots. Dre took on the role of supervising producer, crafting Lady of Rage's fiery breakout single "Afro Puffs" and pulling in CPO Boss Hogg to contribute to the project. Warren G was finally able to break out of his famous stepbrother's shadow with "Regulate," a G-funk staple featuring Nate Dogg. Warren's work on *The Chronic* and the *Poetic Justice* soundtrack—he produced "Indo Smoke" for Mista Grimm and Tupac's "Definition of a Thug Nigga"—got the attention of Chris Lighty at Violator, who signed him to a deal through Def Jam. "Regulate" was built around Michael McDonald's mushy 1982 hit "I Keep Forgettin' (Every Time You're Near)" and was a crossover smash, peaking at number two on the *Billboard* Hot 100. The success of "Regulate" set the stage for Warren's debut album, *Regulate . . . G Funk Era*, which went triple platinum (without any help from Dre).

The *Above the Rim* soundtrack was another hit for Death Row. The soundtrack peaked at number two on the pop charts and remained atop the R & B charts for ten nonconsecutive weeks, before going double platinum. It was a rare feat for a hip-hop soundtrack to have that type of commercial success (critics praised it, too), and the record showed Death Row as an industry leader and that hip-hop's pop appeal was continuing to widen. In the summer of 1994, the Bad Boy Entertainment label was the next big push of bringing hip-hop to mainstream audiences with the release of its first singles, a hypnotic groove called "Flava in Ya Ear" by Craig Mack, and "Juicy," a celebratory anthem from a burly former crack dealer with a poetic flow who called himself the Notorious B.I.G. Both records were instant rap classics that launched Sean "Puffy" Combs's New York upstart. Bad Boy instantly became Death Row's fiercest rival, and the war between labels anchored on opposing coasts would end in bloodshed.

By many accounts, Dre and Suge were rapidly growing apart. The label that was positioned as a fifty-fifty venture between the two men— that is, once Harry-O, D.O.C., and Dick Griffey were iced out—was being usurped by Suge and his callous ways. Dre was getting more and more fed up. Despite the mounting riff between Suge and Dre, he agreed to Suge's next project, *Murder Was the Case*, an extended-length video for Snoop. Dre was to direct the short film, in which Snoop would play a gangster killed in a drive-by, who then sells his soul to the devil, and returns to Earth to make it as a rap star, before the devil hatches a plan to send him to prison for murder.

Dre saw the project, which also included an accompanying soundtrack he would produce on, as an opportunity to link up with Ice Cube. Both men had found much success in their years apart. Dre was the creative genius behind one of the hottest rap labels in the country, while Cube had sold six million records, was a married father and a Hollywood player, and had just issued his forth album, *Lethal Injection*, a few months earlier.

One day, in the middle of production for *Murder Was the Case*, Dre heard some in-progress productions from collaborator Sam Sneed. One in particular struck his ear.

"Yo, what you gon' do wit' that, Sam?" Dre asked about the records.

"Whatever you wanna do."

"Man, we need to put that on the soundtrack," Dre told him.

The record turned into a duet, "Natural Born Killaz," and Dre had the idea of putting Cube on the chorus.

Interscope, however, was excited about the on-wax reunion between the former N.W.A members (Cube previously appeared in the music video for "Let Me Ride") so Dre was asked to remove Sam and have additional verses from Cube. "They gave me the boot. I was a little salty about that," Sneed confessed. "But I understood; it was a political move."

"Natural Born Killaz" was acidic. Dre rapped that his verse was a journey through the mind of a maniac and that he was "doomed to be a killer since I came out the nut sack." Cube referenced Charles Manson, O. J. Simpson, Jeffrey Dahmer, and the vicious assault on trucker Reginald O. Denny during the LA riots. The duo filmed a cinematic music video playing up the record's grim lyrics and timed the release to Halloween to further exploit its eerie theme. In it they satirize the stabbings of Nicole Brown Simpson and Ronald Lyle Goldman, and the Menendez brothers' murder of their parents, all the while surrounded by corpses. The idea was to deliver a tongue-in-cheek commentary on the nation's obsession with high-profile murder mysteries—O. J. Simpson's murder case was one of the most sensationalized events in American history—and create shock value, as Dre told the *Los Angeles Times*. "Of course we're exploiting violence, but there's nothing unusual about that in America," Cube said. "This country's national anthem is full of rockets' red glare and bombs bursting in air. That's just the way America is, so why shouldn't Dre and Cube be able to exploit a little violence every now and then? If people don't like it, let 'em ban it. Who cares?"

Dre and Cube's reunion was to extend to more than one record, as they soon plotted to do a joint album called *Helter Skelter*. They announced the project alongside "Natural Born Killaz." Death Row and Priority were going to handle its release. "We weren't trying to bullshit each other," Cube said of his rekindled friendship with Dre. "He was the same motherfucker I had met, and I was the same motherfucker he had met. We just clicked, started laughing about old shit."

The album's theme was the end of the world and Dre put his trusted collaborator D.O.C. to work. He started drafting lyrics, even though he was apprehensive about the likelihood of the project coming to fruition.

"Dre is feeding me these books about the Illuminati and stuff like that and I wrote a couple records," D.O.C. said. "Of course I knew the shit wasn't going to work because I know those men."

Disillusioned with his career progress, resentment consumed D.O.C. He reached out to Dre about how he could get back in the studio and rap, but Dre didn't want to hear it. Besides, he had already told D.O.C. that with his voice the way it is, writing was the best option. D.O.C. was furious. He believed Dre owed a great debt to him. He stuck around Death Row, the label he helped build and got pushed out of, and helped shape *The Chronic* and *Doggystyle* into the rap classics they became. "Nobody is really putting any energy into what D.O.C. is gonna do next," he said. "We made the Dre album and it's great, Snoop's album has been released and it's on, now what are we gonna do to make sure D.O.C. has something? Nobody was talking about that or gave a fuck about that."

D.O.C. decided he was done with Death Row—and with Dre. He packed up and went to Atlanta, but not before snatching a track he had written for the album. "I went into his vault and took two beats. The nigga had a zillion beats, I took two and left. That was my glorious departure." To further spite Dre, he lifted both the title and the concept of the record, which he released in 1996 to middling reviews. The *Los Angeles Times* wrote that listening to the album, his first since his near-fatal car accident in 1989, was "like seeing Superman trying to fly with Kryptonite shackles on his legs. It's painful to witness."

"I suppose that probably wasn't my most shining moment, stealing that guys music," D.O.C. admitted, his raspy voice quieting to a pause. "But I was in a really tough spot and I didn't know how to get out of it."

✳

Over at Ruthless, Eazy continued his mission to rebuild. He signed a breadth of acts like female rap duo Menajahtwa (pronounced "ménage à trois"); Blood of Abraham, a consciously Jewish duo whose most famous song is called "Niggaz and Jewz (Some Say Kikes)"; raunchy girl group Hoez With Attitudes; and Mexican rapper Kid Frost. It was Eazy's discovery of Bone Thugs-N-Harmony in 1993 that turned things around at Ruthless.

Originally named the Band Aid Boys when the group formed in junior high school, they changed their name to B.O.N.E. Enterpri$e and recorded an album filled with horrorcore called *Faces of Death*. Their style was incredibly unique to rap, with its members layering their vocals as stacked harmonies, switching between singing and rapid-fire rhyming, a skill they perfected by learning each other's verses front to back—hence the "harmony" in their name, which Eazy came up with. The group left their native Cleveland to come out to LA, scrimping together the money for Greyhound tickets, in search of Eazy. When they finally reached Eazy, by phone, he told them he was performing in Cleveland so they returned home and auditioned for Eazy in his dressing room. Bone Thugs-N-Harmony's Ruthless debut EP *Creepin On Ah Come Up* dropped in June 1994 and went four times platinum thanks to hits "Thuggish Ruggish Bone" and "Foe tha Love of $"

Eazy also looked to extend his reach outside of music. He started a film company, Broken Chair Flickz, and had plans to star in *Smilin' Facez*, a bloody revenge tale set in South Central he helped develop, with screenwriter Preston Whitmore II promising it would make Cube's *Boyz n the Hood* look like an afterschool special (a sentiment Eazy once used as a jab toward Cube). "The characters are really N.W.A," Whitmore said. "So that should give it a lot more edge." He was also spending lots of time with KDAY programmer Greg Mack. The two had been tight since the N.W.A days and had made plans to purchase radio stations, the first seated in Phoenix. Mack had preached to Eazy that the real growth of hip-hop meant having some control on radio. It was the medium that was the slowest to embrace the genre, and even though Def Jam, Ruthless, Death Row, and Bad Boy were powerhouses with artists enjoying cross-over radio success, the radio landscape was still devoid of a rap presence when it came to ownership. "You've got rock and rollers, country western singers, even R & B artists, but never has there been one rapper—even today—not one rapper owns a radio station and I attribute that to the fact that some of them think they can't because of where their money came from or federal [laws they have broken]," Mack said. Before they could get going they were waiting for a big check (Mack doesn't remember for what), and in the interim Mack suggested Eazy start a radio show. He went down to 92.3 the Beat and pitched the idea of the show. It would cost the station nothing, so long as Eazy was able to play his Ruthless records, and in the summer of 1994 he began hosting the *Ruthless Radio Show*, a weekly, party-style show where he and his friends Julio G., Tony G., and Jesse Collins interviewed artists, took requests, and talked lots of shit.

On the *Ruthless Radio Show*, Eazy had no problem playing Death Row records—particularly *The Chronic*, since he was making money on it—even if it angered Suge (which it absolutely did). One infamous episode featured Eazy attempting to talk with Death Row artists Tha Dogg Pound and the D.O.C., but the conversation exploded into a curse-filled screaming match between Eazy and Daz, who got on the phone and began insulting Eazy. At one point Michel'le jumps in, Kurupt chides them for acting "silly," and an unidentified woman interrupts to yell at Eazy for how he treated his baby's mother Tracy Jernagin (the two had a tumultuous history; once Eazy shot at Tracy's car and another time she wrecked it while arguing with Eazy). "When you can sell a million records you come talk to me," Daz screamed, sending Eazy over the edge, with him shouting that he bets Daz never got paid for his work at Death Row. "Y'all jumped into something that had nothing to do with y'all.

This between me, Dre, Snoop, and whomever [Suge undoubtedly the 'whomever' here]."

"Eric was funny as hell. He had a warped personality," Mack said. One time they heard screaming and stepped outside to see a guy beating his wife and Mack wanted to intervene. "Nah, fuck that," said Eric, who began egging the guy on. "Beat that bitch's ass, beat her fucking ass," he shouted.

"The very next day he's taking ten busloads of kids out of South Central to Magic Mountain," Mack added. "He never wanted anyone to know about that, all the good things he did. He didn't want people to know that. He wanted to keep that gangster image."

Everyone remembers Eazy as incredibly generous. He gave to Make-A-Wish and the City of Hope regularly, visited juvenile correctional facilities to talk to kids there, and was extensively involved with mentoring organization Athletes & Entertainers for Kids. He let friends stay in his houses, and if anyone got in trouble they knew he was a call away.

Beyond caring for his friends, Eazy was an exceptionally devoted father. In all he had eleven kids, but he only knew of seven. His daughter, Erica Wright, said he would take the kids to Disneyland often, and holidays were lavish affairs. "No matter what he did in his entertainment life, he was family oriented. Always had time for us period," Erica said.

"My most memorable time with him was for my birthday, he took me to an amusement park, Bullwinkle's in Orange County," younger daughter Ebie remembered. "We rode all the rides."

But for all Eazy had going on in his life, he remained quite ardent on getting the old crew back together.

There had previously been talks of partial N.W.A reunions, though Eazy's assertion that the group would reassemble without Dre led to a two-year estrangement between him and Ren, after the latter turned the idea down. Later Ren, along with Cube and Dre, was said to be plotting a project titled *N.W.E—Niggaz Without Eazy*.

During a trip to New York in early 1995 to help Bone Thugs-N-

Harmony promote its *Creepin On Ah Come Up* album, Eazy ran into Cube. Bone and Eazy had gone out to a nightclub called the Tunnel. When they got to the back of the club they spotted Cube, whom Eazy hadn't seen or spoken to. "As soon as they saw each other it was all smiles and love," Krayzie Bone said, remembering the group also met LL Cool J and Notorious B.I.G. that night—the introduction to B.I.G. led to their collaboration, "Notorious Thugs," from *Life After Death*, B.I.G.'s landmark second album released a few weeks after his 1997 murder.

Amid the reminiscing between the two men, the conversation steered toward a reunion album. "I told Eazy I was down; I thought it was a good idea," Cube said. "He was in his feud with Dre at the time. I told him if he could work that out, call me, and I'd be ready to go." Dre and Eazy eventually started discussing the prospects of a reunion. Dre had gone on record saying the only way he'd entertain it was if it was put out on Death Row, which of course would never happen. The tension between the former friends had softened considerably, and Dre too was on board with a reunion, so long as Jerry Heller wasn't involved. "I would have gladly done so—well, maybe not gladly. But I would have gotten out of the way," Jerry wrote in his memoir. Reuniting N.W.A was going to be Eazy's goal when he returned to Los Angeles.

"We gonna get the whole family back together and we gonna start riding again on this shit," Eazy excitedly told Cold 187um.

Two weeks later, however, Eazy was in the hospital.

ETERNAL E

It started with a cough. The weather was frigid when Eazy was in New York City with Bone Thugs-N-Harmony and the Southern California boy was poorly dressed for winter on the East Coast. "Before we went out, Eazy had gone and bought us all leather jackets," Krayzie Bone remembered. "Eazy had one but when he came out the hotel room and went out to the club he ain't have nothing on but a sweatshirt. Plus his Jheri curl was wet. We were like, 'Man you're going to catch pneumonia.' We're from Cleveland. We know about having Jheri curls in the wintertime. You got to cover your shit up."

After a run-in with Cube sparked talks of a real N.W.A reunion album, Eazy intended to make the project his top priority when he returned to Los Angeles, alongside a double album called *Temporary Insanity* he was already working on. Eazy wanted to get Dre on his solo record, as well as Guns N' Roses. He also reconciled with Ren and the two recorded together for the project. After the club closed, Eazy walked back to his hotel, unable to catch a cab. There was no way he didn't shiver the entire way back.

For weeks after his return, Eazy had cold symptoms and difficulty breathing. He wasn't pressed to get to a doctor, which those close to him didn't find out of the ordinary considering the bouts of bronchitis he'd had since childhood. "It was never anything serious. He'd go in the hospital every now and then," said Greg Mack. "Honestly, we thought it was because of all the weed he smoked."

Many believed Eazy's affinity for marijuana, a habit he developed in the years after N.W.A split, and which Mack estimated cost tens of thousands of dollars per month, combined with chronic bronchitis was the source of his ailment. Though as Eazy's coughing fits began to last longer, his friends grew more concerned. "In the studio, I knew something was wrong with him," MC Ren said. "[H]e would be coughing a lot, for five or ten minutes straight, like he had bronchitis or something. Then he'd stop for a while and start back again with this hard cough. I was just thinking, 'Man, you need to quit smoking that weed.'"

More sick than anyone could have known, including himself, Eazy's cough grew more violent, and breathing became more and more difficult. In mid-February of 1995, a crushing pain in his chest and a rage of coughs took over. It was decided to take him to Norwalk Community Hospital's emergency room. "He sounded worse than I'd ever heard him," said Eazy's longtime friend Mark "Big Man" Rucker, "but he wouldn't have gone if it were up to him. We practically had to force him to go." He was admitted, and a test confirmed it was bronchitis.

The wheezing and coughing continued after Eazy was released from the hospital. Following a short stay at his Topanga Canyon home, he was taken to Cedars-Sinai Medical Center in Beverly Grove on February 24. He was admitted under an alias, Eric Lollis, and treated for an infection in his lungs with antibiotics. Doctors working to discover his ailment ordered a full panel of tests. The result was startling: he was HIV positive.

Eazy phoned his girlfriend, Tomica Woods, who unbeknownst to anyone but them was pregnant with their second child. "I got a call from him, but he was on the phone crying and couldn't talk and then the doctor got on the [line], asked me was I sitting down, and then he told me," Woods said. "I just remember sitting and crying, and I got myself together and went to the hospital." Woods and their unborn daughter tested negative, though there was still fear, as the virus could take months to show up in tests.

In just a matter of days of his initial diagnosis, doctors informed Eazy that he was in the final stages of full-blown AIDS.

At the time, the American public was still wildly uneducated about human immunodeficiency virus (HIV), or the AIDS (acquired immune deficiency syndrome) disease it could lead to. Since it was first discovered in the early 1980s, the epidemic was largely stigmatized as a gay men's disease after a 1984 study traced many early HIV infections to Gaëtan Dugas, a Canadian flight attendant.

Dugas, known as patient "O" (for "outside California"), was a gay man with a voracious sexual appetite. By his own estimation, he averaged hundreds of sexual partners per year, and believed he had had more than 2,500 partners across North America since becoming sexually active. Dugas was thought to have contracted the virus in Haiti or Africa and spread it to hundreds of men before his death in 1984, and has long been blamed for starting the AIDS epidemic in America. More than thirty years later, in 2016, researchers determined through newly available genetic evidence that Dugas couldn't have possibly been the first person in the US to have the virus, instead concluding he was one of thousands infected by the late 1970s, years before it was officially recognized in 1981.

Because there was little public education about the disease and the belief it only infected gay men, the nation reacted in disbelief when basketball player Earvin "Magic" Johnson announced at a November 1991 press conference that he had contracted the virus and would not return to the Lakers because he was positive. Before him the last major public face of the disease was closeted Hollywood heartthrob Rock Hudson, who died from an AIDS-related illness in 1984. But Johnson, a heterosexual black man, looked nothing like what the public had seen or believed they knew of the disease. He didn't know who he contracted the disease from because of the volume of women he had slept with during his days as a bachelor star athlete. "I was never at a loss for female companionship. . . .

I did my best to accommodate as many women as I could—most of them through unprotected sex," he wrote in a piece for *Sports Illustrated*.

Johnson's public disclosure was heralded by public-health officials and activists, and although his career as a basketball player was over (he played a few more times, including on the Dream Team at the 1992 Olympics), his work in HIV/AIDS prevention has helped dispel the stereotypes of the disease. He became tangible proof that the disease wasn't a death sentence. But AIDS was ravishing Eazy, and quickly. His mother would bring him home-cooked meals and fresh fruit as he spent most of his time in a cramped hospital room watching television surrounded by a few friends. Woods stayed at his bedside around the clock. He tried keeping his spirits up. To walk was difficult due to shortage of breath. Eventually Eazy required an oxygen mask.

"I was too young to understand that my dad was sick," said Ebie Wright. She was three at the time and kept busy by playing in the lobby of the hospital.

The mood at Cedars was somber—and tense as Eazy's health declined, leaving the future of his Ruthless Records empire in jeopardy. "It got chaotic. Everyone was lost," Tracy Jernagin said. She and the other mothers of Eazy's children had descended upon the hospital, and, according to Jernagin, things were contentious between the women and Woods. "He had ties to many people, not just one girl. And she didn't respect that. The fact that you know someone is dying and you do have those last moments they should be utilized very wisely and I think they should have been utilized [differently]," Jernagin said.

Uncertain if he would survive a procedure to drain excess fluid from his lungs, Eazy and Woods decided to get married in the hospital. They exchanged vows late in the evening on March 14, surrounded by his parents, sister, and brother. The groom was unable to stand.

"He went through the whole list of who to trust, who not to trust, who to look out for, who not to look out for . . . and that was basically it," Woods-Wright said. Right after the short ceremony, a will was drafted naming Woods-Wright and his attorney Ron Sweeney coexecutors of his estate.

Eazy's surgery never happened. Instead, he was transferred to the intensive-care unit at Cedars and attached to a ventilator. He was in critical condition.

"By the time I seen my dad, he was already in a coma," Erica Wright said. "He wasn't talking, laughing, or joking—nothing. He was on life support, lying there, eyes closed."

On March 16, 1995, a news conference was held by Sweeney to announce to the world that Eazy had AIDS. As Sweeney read the press statement drafted on Eazy's behalf, Woods-Wright and DJ Yella sobbed nearby as they were embraced by relatives and friends.

I may not seem like a guy you would pick to preach a sermon, but I feel it is now time to "testify," because I do have folks who care about me hearing all kinds of stuff about what's up.

Yeah, I was a brother on the streets of Compton doing a lot of things most people look down on—but it did pay off. Then we started rapping about real stuff that shook up the LAPD and the FBI, but we got our message across big time and everyone in America started paying attention to the boys in the "hood." Soon, our anger and hopes got everyone riled up.

There were great rewards for me personally, like fancy cars, gorgeous women, and good livin'. Like real nonstop excitement. I'm not religious, but wrong or right, that's me. I'm not saying this because I'm looking for a soft cushion wherever I'm heading—I just feel that I've got thousands and thousands of young fans who have to learn about what's real when it comes to AIDS. I would like to turn my own problem into something good that will reach out to all my homeboys and their kin, because I want to save their asses before it's too late. I'm not looking to blame anyone except myself. I've learned in the last week that this thing is real and it doesn't discriminate. It affects everyone.

My girl, Tomica, and I have been together for four years, and we recently got married. She's good, she's kind, and [she's] a wonderful mother. We have a little boy who's a year old. Before Tomica, I had other women. I have seven children by six different mothers. Maybe success was too good to me. I love all my kids and always took care of them.

Now I'm in the biggest fight of my life, and it ain't easy. But I want to say much love to those who have been down with me, especially my brothers from N.W.A, and thank you all for your support. Just remember: It's your real time and your real life.

Fans and hip-hop reporters wept in the street. Hours later Snoop Dogg called into LA radio station 92.3 the Beat to say he was praying for Eazy. The hospital's switchboard was inundated with calls from Eazy's fans. About 2,500 calls per day were coming in—more than any other celebrity patient had attracted, including Lucille Ball—though some of the calls came from women claiming to be former lovers who phoned in death threats, believing they, too, were infected. To this day, no woman has ever stepped forward to say she contracted the disease from Eazy.

MC Hammer and Above the Law were among hospital visitors, and the former members of N.W.A visited Eazy at different times, according to legendary Hollywood publicist Norman Winter, who was representing Eazy at the time. "I can remember the way everybody looked; it was like everybody knew that he was gone," Dre remembered. "I felt . . . stupid, because the couple of years we spent mad at each other was nothing compared to the time we spent together and had happy times."

Heavily sedated, Eazy fell unconscious as a form of pneumonia commonly seen in people with weakened immune systems ravaged his body. His lung collapsed, causing heart problems. Two hours later he was dead. It was March 26, 1995—a little more than three weeks after he was told of his diagnosis. Eazy was just thirty years old.

Despite the work Magic Johnson had done to quell the perception about the disease, Eazy's prognosis was the subject of gossip. There were rumors that he was closeted like Rock Hudson and speculation that he was a drug user. How Eazy contracted HIV, and the speed his health deteriorated, has been up for debate ever since his death.

"I've never seen anybody die that quick, and I've seen people die from AIDS," said Cold 187um. "It was crazy to me. He always had bronchitis and stuff like that. I've never seen him looking sickly, [and] I would be with Eazy from sunup to sundown."

Family members and close friends have long refuted Eazy died from AIDS. Cold 187um and Greg Mack both admit his proclivity for women was undeniable. Mack recalls a time when they were traveling and he went into Eazy's hotel room, where there were ten naked women in a circle on the floor. "Eazy's right in the middle and he's like, 'Greg, come on grab you one.' He was just wild," Mack said. "He was enjoying the fruits of his labor, although it was a little reckless." Tracy Jernagin, however, maintains the image that Eazy ran through women at his leisure is overrated. "I don't think he was any more promiscuous than any other male that's in their prime," she said. His lyrics said differently, though, as did former band members who mentioned his penchant for going bareback when he slept with women. "It would be hard to imagine a pussyhound more rabid than Eazy," Jerry Heller once said.

Conspiracy theories around Eazy's death have only grown more wild as time passes. One popular theory is that he was injected with the virus, a theory Suge Knight spread on national television during an appearance on *Jimmy Kimmel Live* in 2003, his first appearance since his release from jail. "See, technology is so high. If you shoot somebody, you go to jail forever. You don't want to go to jail forever. They have a new thing out. They have this stuff . . . they get blood from somebody with AIDS and they shoot you with it," Suge said, almost braggingly. "That's a slow death. The Eazy-E thing. You know what I mean?"

Another theory is he was given HIV through acupuncture needles infused with the virus, something that is scientifically impossible despite former Ruthless artist Kid Frost's assertion.

"Do I think something fishy happened to Eazy? Absolutely," Jerry

Heller said in a radio interview. "I don't believe for a second that someone with as much money as we [had] and could afford whatever like Magic Johnson could, who doesn't even test positive anymore. I don't believe that he could have possibly died that quickly from full-blown AIDS."

Like many others, the fact that no one has stepped forward claiming Eazy gave them the virus or that none of his children were infected is a point that comes up often. "None of us have anything. The girls he was dealing with didn't have anything. There was no autopsy. Why?" wondered Erica Wright, admitting the severity of her father's illness was hidden from her until he was in a coma. Ebie Wright is blunt when asked about her father's death: "I believe he was murdered," a sentiment son Marquise Wright has also shared among other relatives.

HIV is a difficult virus to catch sexually and it's possible to contract it without showing any symptoms or change in health for quite some time. It's even more likely that Eazy had been living with the virus for years before knowing it. In fact, one in eight people living with HIV have no idea they have it. Regular testing is still promoted far more aggressively among gay and bisexual men, and according to data from the Centers for Disease Control and Prevention, blacks continue to experience the greatest burden of HIV compared to other races and ethnicities.

The idea that Eazy had possibly lived with the virus for years isn't far-fetched. Greg Mack said on multiple occasions over the year before Eazy passed that he had what appeared to be an outbreak of shingles on his face. Mack said Eazy would get a painful, nasty looking rash on his face, which is common among people living with HIV, particularly young people infected with the virus.

"We'd be like, 'Man, get that shit away from us, what the fuck.' We'd laugh with each other, but we never really thought . . . we looked at it like no big deal," Mack said. "There's all the conspiracy theories about someone injecting him, or there were reasons for him to be dead. Do I believe any of them? No. I think he just had a very promiscuous lifestyle, and it caught up."

Even before Eazy's death, those around him were jockeying for control over Ruthless. The label was valued at $30 million, though it had racked up over $1 million worth of debt. Mike Klein, who was appointed as Ruthless's director of business affairs by Eazy without any terms put on paper, filed a $5 million suit against the estate, claiming to have a 50 percent stake of the label. Ruthless's Woodland Hills office was locked after a Superior Court judge barred the rapper's trustees and business associates from entering the premises. Child support to his children ceased and payments to Ruthless artists stopped. Klein alleged Eazy was "forced to sign" his trust and marriage certificate, and there was speculation in the industry that the deathbed marriage was orchestrated by Woods-Wright and Sweeney in a bid to help Motown Records gain control of Ruthless—they both previously worked with Motown chairman Clarence Avant—but none of it was substantiated, with a probate judge finding the marriage and will legally binding.

Woods-Wright has been the target of much vitriol and criticism. At twenty-six she was thrust into a position of executing an estate worth millions and running an infamous label whose best days were thought to be behind it—and that was even before its founder and flagship artist died. "That is a strong lady," Greg Mack said. "Because with everything that was going on, she was dealing with all the bill collectors, baby mamas, lawyers, and she just hung in there like a champion."

Jerry Heller has accused Eazy's widow of never operating in her husband's best interests, his kids have labeled her as greedy and conniving, Ruthless artists have questioned her business acumen, and others have said far worse.

"Opinions are like assholes—everybody's got one," she told *Vibe* in 1998. "I was not the cause of his death. I did not kill him. I was the one by his side, and I am the one trying to keep his dream alive. As far as anybody else who might be saying stuff, I could give a damn."

Woods-Wright settled with Klein out of court and when Jerry Heller claimed more than a million dollars in unpaid fees she countersued him for fraud and misuse of company funds—the two settled in 1999 for an undisclosed sum with the terms including a nondisparagement clause. There was a seemingly endless list of claims that kept Woods-Wright in court for years. The other mothers of his children sought to contest Eazy's will and marriage. As part of that settlement, trusts valued at $75,000 were established for each child. "We got the short end of the stick; we lost our father and we lost everything that was his," Ebie said, noting that any prof- its from merchandise or record sales aren't seen by any of his kids. "Every day you'll go somewhere and someone will say 'I've seen this and that in the store, do you guys see any of that?' Every day, constantly, it's a slap in the face. You see stuff, but we can't even get a box shipped to us."

More than three thousand fans descended upon the First African Methodist Episcopal Church for Eazy's homegoing on April 7, 1995. Harvard Boulevard was crammed with onlookers, including many teen- agers who skipped school, as friends, family, industry associates, and even gangbangers wearing their colors filed into the church to pay their final respects. Eazy was dressed in a Compton hat, Pendleton shirt, khakis, and boots. Compton Mayor Omar Bradley, who had previously berated Eazy for perpetuating negative stereotypes of the city in his lyrics, declared "Eazy-E Day" in the city and proclaimed the fallen Gangsta-rap pioneer "Compton's favorite son." Of N.W.A's five former members, only DJ Yella showed up to send off Eazy's golden casket. "I never turned my back on him. I was there in the beginning, and I was there putting dirt on him when nobody else was around in the end," Yella said.

Four months after Eazy's death, Ruthless issued *E. 1999 Eternal* from protégés Bone Thugs-N-Harmony. It was another landmark for Gangsta rap, selling four million records largely in part to the emotional, Grammy- winning ballad "Tha Crossroads," which was dedicated to their late men- tor. Eazy's final record, *Str8 off tha Streetz of Muthaphukkin Compton* was completed with Yella's assistance. It was cobbled together using leftover records and scraps of songs he had yet to complete for his *Temporary Insan- ity* project. There were hundreds of tracks to sort through, the majority of which didn't have any vocals on them. Yella took snippets from an old interview and inserted them between songs. *Str8 off tha Streetz of Mutha-phukkin Compton* was completed as a single disc and released in January 1996—nine months after Eazy's death.

The last song Eazy ever recorded, "Tha Muthaphukkin Real," is included, and serves as the centerpiece of the record. Unsurprisingly, it's a partial N.W.A reunion with Yella and MC Ren. Recorded three months before his untimely death, a few lines felt prophetic, and still do now.

> *When I die, niggas bury me.*
> *Make sure my shit reads Eazy-muthaphukkin'-E.*
> *And it's a fact, to be exact, my tombstone should read,*
> *"He put Compton on that map."*

EPILOGUE

At a lavish estate in Beverly Hills, the scene looked like a more sophisticated take on N.W.A's infamous Wet 'N Wild parties from the early nineties. The place was exquisite, with Romanesque statues, lush greenery, and a sparkling infinity pool taking second place only to the breathtaking views of Los Angeles. It was the quintessential Saturday afternoon in LA—the sun hot enough to warm your skin but tempered by a crisp breeze. There were beautiful women everywhere. The liquor was flowing, and quite bountifully. And the ground slightly shook as the vibrations of classic G-funk records from Dr. Dre and Snoop Dogg blasted from speakers placed throughout the property. Plumes of marijuana smoke wafted from a few of the cabanas in the backyard, as guests danced and sipped on gin and juice, albeit a far more artisan dressing-up of the elixir.

If this were Wet 'N Wild, things might have gotten freaky as intoxicated guests lost their inhibitions as the afternoon went on, but this August 2015 gathering wasn't about toasting unbridled hedonism. It was a celebration of Dre's new radio show, *The Pharmacy*, which he recently debuted on Apple Music. The private bash served as a live watch party for an episode that helped drum up even more anticipation for *Straight Outta Compton*, the highly anticipated biopic of N.W.A. Dre was also using the occasion to make a stunning announcement to fans: he was releasing his first album in sixteen years, and the record, inspired by the film, would be his last.

It was a few weeks before the premiere of *Straight Outta Compton*, and Dre and Ice Cube were ruminating on N.W.A's legacy and the group's controversial rise in the late eighties, which managed to jolt America, put law enforcement on high alert, and define a new era for rap simultaneously. Nearly three decades have passed since N.W.A made its incendiary debut, which the film is named after. They became Gangsta rap antiheroes on the strength of one brazen album, before crumbling amid beef with leader Eazy-E over money and management. The debut of the biopic, like that of the group, couldn't have arrived at a more opportune moment.

Depending on whom you ask, N.W.A's music was either grossly obscene or prophetic tales of the rage brewing among blacks struggling to survive in South Central. Long before the police beating of Rodney King stunned the nation, N.W.A screamed about police brutality in their hood. When LA exploded in violent unrest after the cops were acquitted of wrongdoing, many pointed to N.W.A's collection of polemics as the warning, with the group's brazen "Fuck tha Police" becoming a mantra during the fiery 1992 riots. Though much has changed since then—especially for the group's surviving members—the arrival of *Straight Outta Compton* struck a nerve as the deaths of unarmed blacks in Ferguson, Missouri; Baltimore; Cleveland; Staten Island; North Charleston, South Carolina; Cincinnati; and Waller County, Texas; became footnotes in the ongoing debate over the treatment of minorities by law enforcement and flash points of civil unrest all over the country.

"'Fuck tha Police' did change the world," Cube said, when asked to look back on the record's impact. "If you think about how the police were getting away with murder before 'Fuck tha Police' and then you see how much scrutiny they get after you say, 'Okay this song changed [something].' Before that song and after, now police have to tell the truth."

The men of N.W.A might be decades removed from the brash gangster personas that saw them hyped as the World's Most Dangerous Group, but their message was still just as potent, as the film became a summer blockbuster—making history as the highest-grossing music biopic of all time—and sparked renewed interest in the group. That their story was made for the big screen wasn't entirely a shock, especially considering the stratospheric ascent of Dre and Cube—N.W.A's most famous members— in the years since they departed the group to pursue solo interests.

Dre built his own rap empire in Death Row, the most controversial rap label since Eazy launched Ruthless at the tail end of the eighties. He dropped *The Chronic*, arguably one of the most groundbreaking rap albums of all time, and launched Snoop Dogg to rap stardom before splitting with Death Row's infamous co-owner Suge Knight and starting Aftermath. Dre's Midas touch continued, with his imprint serving as the launching pad for Eminem, 50 Cent, the Game, and Kendrick Lamar. And as if the unanimous distinction as one of the world's most successful producers wasn't enough, Dre has become a rap magnate, with his electronics company Beats, which he founded with longtime friend and business partner Jimmy Iovine, being acquired by Apple for $3 billion in August 2014 (*The Pharmacy* is one of many live, personality-driven shows broadcast across the globe on Apple's innovative twenty-four-seven Beats 1 online radio station). Dre has also endowed an arts academy at the University of Southern California and pledged $10 million to fund the construction of a performing arts complex at Compton High School. As a solo artist, Cube's earliest recordings were pivotal in defining West Coast hip-hop in the nineties, with his angry narratives of disenfranchised life in the ghetto among some of the genre's finest work, and he's continued to be one of rap's most respected emcees. Although he's long enjoyed being an independent artist, in the spring of 2017 he inked a deal with Interscope Records, which controls the catalog of music he did with Priority, to launch a series of anniversary reissues for some of his most seminal releases, starting with *Death Certificate*. And he's planning on releasing twenty-fifth-anniversary editions of *The Predator* and *Lethal Injection*. But even more impressively is the way he's parlayed rap success into a career in Hollywood, becoming a major industry player whose bona fides and broad reach have been proved multiple times over. His film and television production company, Cube Vision, has produced multiple hit franchises including *Friday*, which he wrote; *Barbershop*; the family-friendly *Are We There Yet?*; and *Ride Along*. Altogether his movies have grossed nearly $2 billion at the box office, and in the spring of 2017 Cube became only the sixth rapper to earn a star on the iconic Hollywood Walk of Fame—a stunning turn of events from the days when he'd been labeled an anti-Semite and a racist.

\#

Before Eazy-E died of complications from AIDS on March 26, 1995, the Ruthless Records mastermind wanted nothing more than to reunite his old group. In spite of the petty beef that came after Cube and Dre exited, he knew how big a reunion could be. In the months after his tragic death, attention turned to getting an Eazy project to fans. His final album, *Str8 off tha Streetz of Muthaphukkin Compton*, was released, and while it was certified gold, the company he built struggled to remain relevant in his absence. Eazy's widow Tomica Woods-Wright was calling the shots and doing her best to keep her late husband's dream going. She fought off a seemingly endless list of opportunists looking to cash in on Eazy's throne, even amid accusations that she manipulated her husband on his deathbed so that she could control the company.

"When he died, to me, Ruthless died. All Ruthless Records is now is just a name," said DJ Yella, who helped piece together Eazy's swan song after he passed away. Yella was the last of N.W.A to issue a solo album, which he aptly titled *One Mo Nigga ta Go* and dedicated it to Eazy (he poses next to his grave on the cover), but it wasn't issued on Ruthless. The album, released exactly a year after Eazy's death, was the only solo material from Yella, who went on to a career in adult films, directing titles such as *H.W.A.: Ho's With Attitude*, *West Side Stories*, and *DJ Yella's Str8 Outta Compton* before again focusing on his DJ career and touring the world.

MC Ren, the group's core lyricist next to Cube, stuck around Ruthless for a few years before taking a hiatus. He's never really gotten the proper due for his contributions to the group, the unfortunate pitfall of being in a group with a producing savant, an acerbic poet, and a charismatic frontman who sold himself as a maniacal thug.

N.W.A is mostly remembered for its polarizing controversies and the members it launched to rap stardom. Sadly, Eazy doesn't get exalted the way other rappers have whose lives were cut tragically short. He's rarely placed in the conversation alongside seminal emcees like Tupac Shakur, the Notorious B.I.G., J Dilla, Big L, Ol' Dirty Bastard, or Big Pun. Some of it probably has to do with the fact that he didn't always write his own rhymes and some of it has to do with him dying of AIDS—and not as a martyr of street violence. Even the coverage of his diagnosis and his death paled in comparison to the frequent media attention he got when he was in the midst of controversy, a real shame considering the teachable moment this was for a community largely uneducated about AIDS. Eazy had done the unthinkable with Ruthless Records. During its height, Ruthless was the biggest black-owned independent label since Berry Gordy's Motown empire. He created the blueprint for the street rap mogul that remains foundational decades after his death. Dre took Eazy's cues when he launched Death Row and, later, Aftermath. An enterprising business major at Howard named Sean "Puffy" Combs was able to take his Bad Boy Entertainment to the top of the pop charts after Ruthless kicked the door down. It's hard to imagine a No Limit or Cash Money had it not been for Eazy-E.

"He's not just some rapper who died from AIDS. Without Eazy-E the world of hip-hop would be very different now," said Cold 187um, whose group Above the Law was signed to Ruthless. "He never got behind anything he didn't believe in. From [Above the Law] to Bones to J. J. Fad. Everything he believed in, he believed in it for real."

In November of 1999, Dre and Cube were in the studio mulling the idea of an N.W.A reunion. It wasn't long before Ren was back in the fold. He hadn't worked with Dre since the group split, but Cube had appeared on "Comin' After You," the second single from Ren's third studio album, *Ruthless for Life*—the first time they worked together since Cube left in 1989. There were even talks that the reunion would include Snoop. A superstar on his own, Snoop directly traced his success to the door opened by N.W.A and his mentor, Dre. Cube, who was deep at work on *War & Peace, Vol. 2 (The Peace Disc)*, the second of a two-album project, was about to release the long awaited sequel to his 1995 stoner comedy *Friday*, appropriately titled *Next Friday*. For the film's soundtrack, the guys got together and recorded "Chin Check." "Nobody was talking about old beefs," Ren remembered of the recording sessions. And why would they be? It was over ten years since the men had been together in the studio, and it felt like old times. Dre and Cube were like "two field generals" in the studio. Cube eased into his old role as lead writer with Dre taking the reins behind the board. "The chemistry is just incredible," producer Mel-Man said of the three day recording sessions.

"Chin Check" was the first N.W.A single since 1991. *Vibe* gave it a negative review, stating that Dre's G-funk beat was "bland" and that MC Ren and Ice Cube sounded "geriatric" and "lukewarm," respectively. There was some praise for Snoop, who fans were largely rejecting as a replacement for Eazy.

It was a test run for a proposed reunion album, *Not These Niggaz Again*, which was announced in the summer of 2000 as Dre, Cube, and Snoop coheadlined the Up in Smoke Tour. The tour was a celebration of West Coast hip-hop with Dre, Snoop, Cube, and Eminem headlining. A stable of acts connected to the four rap titans also joined the bill including Kurupt, D12, Westside Connection, Warren G, Xzibit, the D.O.C., and MC Ren. Dre set up a mobile recording studio in one of the tour buses to record while they were on the road—but their respective solo careers were a constant impediment. No music ever came from the sessions.

*

On a film set in Leimert Park in the fall of 2014, Dre and Cube watched as a parking lot behind an old dilapidated theater was transformed into Compton circa the late eighties. Lowrider Impalas bounced around, and extras rocking glistening Jheri curls milled about. Near their trailer were racks of neatly arranged wardrobe with vintage LA Raiders gear and LAPD uniforms peeking out. Dre found himself immersed in a rerun of *The New Detectives: Case Studies in Forensic Science*, a true crime series on the Investigation Discovery channel. He wasn't someone who liked to look in the past, and watching it literally unfold in front of his eyes wasn't the easiest thing to do. "It's fucking weird. This whole process. Watching somebody re-create scenes . . . when I met my wife or realizing my brother died. Having to pull those emotions out again. Its been really difficult. It's weird [watching someone] portray you. You're being immortalized," Dre said, admitting he was 100 percent against a film based on N.W.A because he thought it would blemish the group's legacy.

As challenging as it was for Dre to relive his past during production of *Straight Outta Compton* in 2014, it was even more difficult bringing the film to the big screen. Coproduced by Dre, Cube, and Tomica Woods-Wright, the biopic tracing the group's humble beginnings in the eighties to its controversial success, infighting, and the death of Eazy had been in the works for more than a dozen years. An early draft of the screenplay focused the story on the group's leader and Ruthless Records founder before Cube came aboard and spearheaded rewrites. Those placed Eazy, Dre, and Cube as the story's coleads—with Ren and Yella as peripheral characters (they served as consultants on the film)—before it landed at Universal Pictures with a $29 million budget. Directed by F. Gary Gray, the film's cast was made up of mostly unknowns, aside from Paul Giamatti as Jerry Heller. Heller had been publicly talking about his plans for an N.W.A film for years, and Cube's own son played him in one of the most spot-on castings for a biopic.

It wouldn't be an N.W.A affair without scandal, and *Straight Outta Compton* certainly had its share. On the afternoon of January 29, 2015, a few months after production had wrapped, filming was under way for a promotional video for the movie when Suge Knight arrived on set unannounced. While many of the artists affiliated with N.W.A and Death Row have abandoned the Gangsta rap image over the years, Suge never seemed to grow out of it. Instead he continued to amass a mountain of legal and personal troubles that have tarnished the Death Row legacy.

After Dre gave up his stake of Death Row in 1996, the label descended into chaos with the drive-by shooting of its marquee act Tupac Shakur—with fingers pointing at everyone from Suge, who was driving with Shakur and injured in the gunfire, to Puffy and the FBI. Not to mention Suge's nearly five-year imprisonment following the brutal beating of a rival of Shakur's that was caught on camera hours before the shooting. "Ultimately Suge was gonna destroy it, one way or another," the D.O.C. said of Death Row. Suge and Dre's relationship since then has been mostly contemptuous.

Suge wanted to be paid for his likeness when he discovered that he was being portrayed in the film (the actor cast for the role, stuntman-turned-actor R. Marcos Taylor, bared an uncanny resemblance to Suge). So he did what Suge does when he feels he's owed money: he shows up to collect. Suge drove his red Ford pickup truck to set past security. As soon as he arrived he spotted Cube's head of security, Kebo, and the men had a cordial conversation about Suge's desire to set up a meeting with Cube. But before he could leave Suge got into an argument with Cle "Bone" Sloan, an affiliate of the Bloods working as a technical adviser to the movie, who Suge had longstanding beef with. The spat was diffused and Suge left without incident before he got a call from Terry Carter, a revered South Central businessman. Carter told Suge to return so he could help ease the tension further. They agreed to meet at Tam's Burgers, a Compton fast-food institution located close to set.

Accounts vary, but Sloan told police Suge was talking shit as he arrived, so he unleashed a barrage of punches at Suge through his car window. However, surveillance video shows what appears to be Sloan immediately attacking Suge upon his arrival. Suge, these days, was a shell of his once formidable self, having not yet recovered from being shot six times a few months prior at a party thrown by R & B star Chris Brown during the weekend of the 2014 MTV Video Music Awards. Suge threw his car into reverse, knocking Sloan down before putting it in drive and crushing his ankles. And he kept going, taking down Carter, crushing his skull and killing him before he fled. Suge has now been in jail for more than two years, shuffling through several lawyers as his family worries about his declining health while he sits in solitary confinement. His murder trial begins in January 2018, and if his defense team can't persuade a jury that he acted in self-defense, the rap mogul will likely spend the rest of his days behind bars. "It makes no sense," said Nina Bhadreshwar, who worked as Suge's assistant. "He has chosen that route. He has lost a lot of friends. He lost his business. A lot of stuff has happened to him. It's a tragedy."

Straight Outta Compton was a smash upon its August 2015 release. It opened to critical acclaim, topped the box office, and made more than $200 million. But not everyone was pleased with the film. MC Ren felt his contributions to the group were greatly diminished, and after doing a deluge of press for the film he got to the point where he was done being asked about N.W.A. Founding member Arabian Prince questioned why he was omitted—a question J. J. Fad, Michel'le, and a host of other Ruthless acts asked after the film's release. "They were our family. They were like brothers," J. J. Fad's Dania "Baby D" Birks said. "We go to sleep with them, wake up with them . . . work with them. It was everything. It just seemed like, you don't forget about people that easily. I mean, I didn't."

Eazy's kids weren't too pleased either.

"It was like seventy-five percent accurate," said Eazy's daughter Ebie Wright. "Everybody else wanted to make themselves look good, and he was not here to make himself look the way [he] really was. If he were alive, [it] would have been a whole different movie, completely."

Cube was unbothered by the gripes, suggesting instead that anyone pissed off should tell their own version of the story. "There's been several movies made about Elvis; go make your own N.W.A movie if you don't like the way the one the four surviving members, and everybody else we could find that was around, put together. If you can do one better than that, knock yourself out."

"This movie was just a blip on the radar. You can't sum up a group's life in a hundred or so scenes," Cube continued. "There's no way to sum up ten years. It's just an eye blink of what happened."

Jerry Heller was actually trying to do just what Cube intimated, but he never got his project further than teasing it to the press. After *Straight Outta Compton*'s release he filed a $110 million libel lawsuit against Dre, Cube, Woods-Wright, Eazy's estate, Universal, and a host of others involved with the production of the film. He claimed it was "littered" with inaccuracies that made him into the "bad guy" and depicted him as a sleazy manager.

Jerry also claimed he had never consented to the use of his name and likeness, and that the film's writers had lifted scenes from his memoir, *Ruthless*. Everyone interviewed for this book had differing views of Jerry and his role at Ruthless, but they all agree that Eazy remained loyal to him until the very end, despite popular belief that he fired him. *Straight Outta Compton*'s success struck a nerve with Jerry. He was incredibly hurt by the film and wanted to be publicly exonerated for what he felt was unjustified blame for the group's demise. "I want to concentrate on other important areas right now," Jerry said when asked to participate in this book. Jerry was open to showing off the collection of N.W.A memorabilia he kept in his Calabasas home (Eazy used to live two doors down, a marking of their closeness) but like Ren, he had grown tired of discussing N.W.A—particularly its famous former members, Cube and Dre. It was a meeting that never took place, though, as Jerry died from a heart attack in September 2016 at the age of seventy-five. His lawyer blamed the stress of the film lawsuit as a contributing factor.

What the film chose to omit has been among its biggest criticisms. Long before it hit theaters, N.W.A fans wondered how the biopic would handle some the more difficult moments in the group's history such as Eazy's death from AIDS, its often misogynist and homophobic lyrics, and allegations of physical abuse from Dre by women associated with the group. In the end, none of the incidents were explored or they were intentionally left out, including his well-documented attack on female hip-hop journalist Denise "Dee" Barnes fueled by the group's rivalry with Cube. Yet Barnes's run-in with Dre was actually included in an earlier version of the film's screenplay.

In the scene, the fictional Dre, "eyes glazed, drunk, with an edge of nastiness, contempt" (per notes from the script), spots Barnes at the party and approaches her. "Saw that bullshit you did with Cube. Really had you under his spell, huh? Ate up everything he said. Let him diss us. Sell us out." "I just let him tell his story," Barnes's character retorts. "That's what I do. It's my job." The confrontation escalates, and Barnes throws her drink in Dre's face before he attacks her, "flinging her around like a rag doll, while she screams, cries, begs for him to stop."

"I don't think [my abuse] should have been in the movie, but I don't think it should have been left out," Michel'le said. "Maybe he didn't want to show me in a bad light or whatever, and I appreciate that, but the truth is the truth. I get it, you want to tell your story and you want to make yourself look good. Why would you waste your time showing the bad part?"

A gripping essay from Barnes and the revelation that the scene was omitted helped reignite conversations about Dre's treatment of women, something he has never seriously addressed as he remade himself into a corporate mogul. With the chorus of outrage growing louder, and likely because of his relationship with Apple, Dre issued a blanket statement apologizing to all the women he hurt without addressing any specific incident. "Twenty-five years ago I was a young man drinking too much and in over my head with no real structure in my life. However, none of this is an excuse for what I did. I've been married for nineteen years and every day I'm working to be a better man for my family, seeking guidance along the way. I'm doing everything I can so I never resemble that man again. I apologize to the women I've hurt. I deeply regret what I did and know that it has forever impacted all our lives."

✳

In early 2016 the prospect of an onstage N.W.A reunion seemed like a real possibility. The making of *Straight Outta Compton* had led to discussion of a European tour, with Eminem sitting in as an honorary member, but like previous talks nothing came of it. There was a partial reunion before the film's release, with Ice Cube performing a short medley alongside Ren and Yella during his headlining slot at the BET Experience where the group juxtaposed images of the 1992 LA riots and Rodney King beating with footage of recent civil unrest in the wake of police brutality cases across America. But still, fans were eager to see Cube, Ren, Yella, *and* Dre together on the same stage again. The announcement that N.W.A would be inducted into the Rock and Roll Hall of Fame that spring (after they were passed over three times before) felt like the perfect opportunity. They didn't perform at the ceremony, opting instead to relish the night with heartfelt speeches. "To the man . . . The late, great, often-imitated but never duplicated Eazy-motherfucking-E. This is his vision. He wanted us to be honest, he wanted us to be truthful, say what we feel," Cube said. "He didn't care if we got any record play. He didn't even care if we got signed to a major label. All he cared about was for our story to be recognized and heard." It was a breathtaking sight, a group once accused of destroying the moral fiber of America inducted into the Rock and Roll Hall of Fame, the highest validation the group could receive that its music made an impact—though the proof was there long before they were recognized by the voting committee.

A few weeks after the Rock and Roll Hall of Fame induction ceremony the impossible finally happened during Cube's closing set at the Coachella Valley Music and Arts Festival in Indio, California. Ahead of the festival all hope was lost that the group would actually ever unite, considering the number of opportunities that had come and gone since *Straight Outta Compton* reignited interest in N.W.A. "When we all come back together, we want it to be enormous," Cube said a few weeks before the festival. And what was bigger than the preeminent music festival on the West Coast with nearly one hundred thousand fans in attendance? Cube was the lead up for Guns N' Roses, a fitting double bill of rebellious bad boys grown out of LA during the late 1980s. And to the shock of thousands, he had a surprise planned: all the surviving members of N.W.A would perform together. It was the first time the four surviving members performed together since 1989. The occasion came with a slight caveat, though, as the quartet didn't actually perform any N.W.A numbers, opting instead to tackle some of Dre's classics that have defined rap and remained a bit more durable as crowd movers than any of N.W.A's music.

"It was amazing, like magic," Cube said of the reunion. "It felt special. Every time we used to hit the stage it felt special so getting back up there, it always feels good to get on stage with those dudes . . . it's always fun."

Much has changed since the last time these men performed together—a black man has been president of the United States, same-sex marriage has become law, marijuana is legalized in some states, hip-hop is one of the most commercial genres of music—but the themes N.W.A yelled about are still prevalent today, as evidenced by the discourse around the group's biopic. (Even the irony of N.W.A, of all rap acts, receiving the blockbuster treatment didn't fall upon deaf ears.) *Straight Outta Compton* the album was a sonic Molotov cocktail that ignited a firestorm with acidic lyrics that shocked the world. It's a record that now sits in the Library of Congress's National Recording Registry and is perhaps the best example of the short-lived group's brilliance. One wonders what would have happened had N.W.A stayed together just a little longer or if Eazy never got sick. We'll never know, but what we do know is their legacy is undeniable. It was a marvel to see tens of thousands of music fans from every facet of life unified by a group that had to fight for the right to speak their mind. As N.W.A rocked the stage, one guy moved through the crowd exchanging high fives, posing for selfies, and grabbing girls to dance with as he took swigs of liquor from a flask. He couldn't have been more than twenty but he was dressed in black Dickies, with a Compton hat and wraparound shades—even though it was nightfall—and his curly hair shiny with product. It's doubtful anyone in the audience had ever seen an Eazy-E impersonator, let alone one that was of Hispanic descent. And he was fiercely dedicated to his bit, quoting lyrics like gospel, and doing his best impression of a squeaky voice. After watching him for a bit, one girl tapped him on the shoulder and asked him who he was supposed to be.

"Call me Eazy," he told her. The man fist-bumped a few more strangers before disappearing into the crowd.

ACKNOWLEDGMENTS

First, my deepest gratitude to William LoTurco. When you reached out about this project, I nervously stumbled through all of our conversations, as I had no idea what you even saw in me. Your encouragement and honesty guided me tremendously, and eased the avalanche of fear and anxiety that made me want to quit more than once. Incredibly lucky to have you as an agent.

Blessings to the entire team at Aevitas Creative Management for having a kid's back.

Todd Hunter, you are the greatest editor I have ever worked with. This project wouldn't have happened without you. From our first chat, I knew I was in good hands and that feeling never changed, regardless of how frustrated—or defeated—I felt at times. Thank you for the trust and guidance. Thank you for being a tremendous copilot. And thank you for challenging me and never letting me off the hook. Still can't believe we reached the finish line. Now can we please do it again?

A million thanks to the team at Atria and Simon & Schuster. You only get to write your first book once and I'm still pinching myself that my first is with this imprint.

To my parents, Jessica and Robert, what a journey this has been. Mom, my earliest memory in life is walking to preschool, your hand tightly clutching mine, and we haven't let go of each other since. I couldn't have gotten through this with you—period. You were my ear, my shoulder, and the fire under my feet that got me to the end. Your feedback (and real talk) has sustained me just as much as your love and support has.

Dad, you are the greatest man I know. It takes one hell of a man to step into the gap the way you did. I spend my days trying to make you proud and upholding the values you instilled in me. Dedicating this book to you, my grandfather, and my brother—the three men who have molded me into the man I am—brought me a sense of pride I didn't know existed. I will never be able to thank you enough for the sacrifices made to get me where I am today.

There are countless journalists and authors whose reporting and interviews helped shape this book. Wishing I could name them all, but please know I am humbled by your genius.

After reading and watching more than 1,500 texts and videos (films, documentaries, etc.) on N.W.A, I must give praise to Ronin Ro, Terry McDermott, Jeff Chang, Brian Coleman, Chuck Philips, Frank Owen, Dennis Hunt, Brian Cross, Kevin Powell, Peter Spirer, Davey D, Nelson George, and Jonathan Gold, whose work I especially leaned on.

Ben Westhoff, *Original Gangsters* is a beast—hope you dig my take on the guys as much as I loved yours. Thank you for the kindness and help.

Special thanks to Lorraine Ali and Randall Roberts, two former editors I have the pleasure of calling friends. I owe a great deal of debt to the two of you. Lorraine, thank you so very much for the outtakes with Cube and Dre. Randall, thank you for connecting me with Jerry and J. J. Fad.

Chad Kiser, you are a lifesaver and the true definition of an "O.G." Thank you for having my back the way you did and really looking out for me as I navigated this project.

CJ Shaw, you are *THE* man. Thank you for all your help.

Jermaine and Adrienne, our brainstorming sessions kept me focused and inspired.

Much appreciation to S. Leigh Savidge and Jeff Scheftel, Keith Murphy, Alonzo Williams, Dave Marsh, Phyllis Pollack, MC Ren, DJ Yella, and Verna Griffin.

The biggest thanks to my interview subjects. There were LOTS of closed doors in the pursuit of this book and I'm appreciative to those who took the time to speak to me (on and off the record)—most importantly Ice Cube and the D.O.C., whose generosity was invaluable to this project.

Kudos to Sir Jinx, Jerry Heller (RIP), Cold 187um, Craig Schweisinger, Susan Yano, Greg Mack, CPO Boss Hogg, Tracy Jernagin, Michel'le Toussaint, Erica Wright, and Ebie Wright. Blessings to Lil Eazy-E and Tomica Woods-Wright.

Todd Schweisinger and Erica Varela, thanks for digging in the archives for me.

A very special thanks to Andres Tardio, one of the most talented photographers in the game. Your passion for hip-hop inspires me, and I didn't want to do this without your art gracing these pages.

I am blessed to have an incredible family that has kept me encouraged and grounded beyond their love and support. My stepmother Melani influenced me to believe in the man I am and to never stop dreaming. My brother Jermaine is the first hero and role model I had (and that will never change). My sisters Adrienne, Charlisa, and Whitney taught me confidence and self-love and my special little homies Khari and Jalil remind me to lead by example in all that I do. Demetrius, I don't think I need to tell you what you mean to me.

To my friends who held me up through these past three years, thank you. Endless love to Brittany Michels, Yvonne Villarreal, Kevin Nelson, Brianne Pins, Wesley Lowery, Aishah White, Erica Davis, Jessica Herndon-Newton, Shawn Higgins, Amina Khan-Ghazi, Eric Burse, Dexter Mullins, Shaeden Madi, Ari Bloomekatz, Danny Rust, Christina Williams, Kalyd Odeh, Latifah Muhammed, Devin and Cameron Lazerine, Nate Jackson, Siobhan Gabrielle, Mervyn Marcano, Chelsea Fuller, Marlene Meraz, Chris Basler, Zach Schemenaur, John Ketchum, Lauren Jacobs, Mesfin

Fekadu, Cara Donatta, Nekesa Mumbi Moody, Roderick Scott, Mike Navarra, Lilah Kojoori, Cara Vanderhook, Caroline Yim, Tre'vell Anderson, and Anthony Williams. If I have forgotten anyone, please blame my mind and not my heart.

I wouldn't be half the journalist I am without Sarah Hoye, Steve Wartenberg, Elise Woolley, Delano Massey, Sherri Williams, Nicole Kraft, Eileen Holliday, Janessa Castle, Michelle Johnson, Belinda Thurston, Tracie Powell, Randy Hagihara, and Kelley Carter.

Jamie, you are my partner in life. You shared the brunt of this project with me and there are no words to explain how much your love, support, and beautiful spirit has meant to me. You believed when I didn't and you stayed positive when I couldn't. WE DID IT! I love you, always.

My dear sweet Feeney, I will spend the rest of my days trying to be as generous and loving as you were. Everything I write is for you.

Charles Kennedy, you led me to a dream when I was six—one I've never stopped chasing. You knew the true strength of street knowledge. I hope I've made you proud.

—GK

NOTES

PROLOGUE

2   *"You're not going to be looking at 1987 Eazy-E"*: Tomica Woods–Wright, author interview, September 6, 2013.

COMPTON'S N THE HOUSE

6   *"It was good music"*: Greg Mack, author interview, September 24, 2016.

8   *"We had lyrics"*: Ice Cube, unpublished interview by Lorraine Ali, fall 2014.

8   *the single most influential genre in American pop music*: Matthias Mulch et al., "The Evolution of Popular Music: USA 1960–2010," *Royal Society Open Science* 2 (May 2015).

10   *"If you sat on this porch at night and just listened real hard"*: Ice Cube, quoted in Mark Cooper, "NWA: 'Our Raps Are Documentary. We Don't Take Sides,'" *Guardian*, October 1989.

10   *"I grew up in the hood, I'm going to die in the hood"*: Anonymous, *Crips and Bloods: Made in America*, directed by Stacy Peralta (2008).

10   *"It was a dangerous time"*: Vince "CPO Boss Hogg" Edwards, author interview, November 17, 2016.

10   *Integration of the city*: Kelly Simpson, "A Southern California Dream Deferred: Racial Covenants in Los Angeles," KCET.org, February 22, 2012, https://www

.kcet.org/history-society/a-southern-california-dream-deferred-racial-covenants -in-los-angeles.

11   *property owners received threats*: Josh Sides, "Straight Into Compton: American Dreams, Urban Nightmares, and the Metamorphosis of a Black Suburb," *American Quarterly* 56, no. 3 (September 2004).

14   *"We all got pissed and went out and burned up our neighborhood"*: Anonymous, *Wattstax*, directed by Mel Stuart (1973).

PANIC ZONE

16   *"workin' for somebody else"*: Eazy-E, interview in *Rap Pages*, February 1993.

16   *as addictive as it was cheap*: Eric Lichtblau and Gaylord Shaw, "Problem in 46 States: Crack: It's Not Just a 'City Drug,'" *Los Angeles Times*, April 5, 1988.

16   *typical one-gram package of powdered cocaine sold for $100*: Ibid.

16   *"That boy could fight"*: Mack interview.

17   *"That was his structure. Even early on, he was very business"*: Tracy Jernagin, author interview, September 26, 2016.

17   *"If you looked at [his] knuckles, they were gone"*: Mazik Saevitz, quoted in Jeff Chang, "The Last Days of Eazy-E," *Swindle Magazine*, no. 2.

18   *"I thought, 'I can cleanse the neighborhood'"*: Stanley Tookie Williams, quoted in Amy Goodman, "A Conversation with Death Row Prisoner Stanley Tookie Williams from his San Quentin Cell," *Democracy Now!*, November 30, 1995.

19   *"I had to learn the color scheme"*: Mack interview.

20   *"The whole idea of the gangbanging shit was a bit much"*: The D.O.C., author interview, December 8, 2016.

22   *"It just swept through the neighborhood"*: Ice-T, *N.W.A: The World's Most Dangerous Group*, directed by Mark Ford (2008).

DOPEMAN

23   *"I'd probably be dead right along with him"*: Eazy-E, *Rap Pages*.

24   *"whatever the Beatles did was acceptable, especially for young people"*: Al Aronowitz, *Rock & Roll: Shakespeares in the Alley*, WGBH Media Library & Archives.

24   *"a better, more honest, more tolerant member of society"*: Peter Brown and Steven

Gaines, *The Love You Make: An Insider's Story of the Beatles* (New York: Berkley, 2002).

24 *"America's public enemy number one . . . is drug abuse"*: Richard Nixon, "Remarks about an Intensified Program for Drug Abuse Prevention and Control" (speech, White House, Washington, DC, June 17, 1971).

25 *"a merciless destroyer"*: Richard Nixon, "Message to the Congress Transmitting Reorganization Plan 2 of 1973 Establishing the Drug Enforcement Administration," memo, March 28, 1973.

25 *"We knew we couldn't make it illegal to be either against the war or black"*: John Ehrlichman, quoted in Dan Baum, "Legalize It All: How to Win the War on Drugs," *Harper's Magazine*, April 2016.

27 *"taken out and shot"*: Ronald J. Ostrow, "Casual Drug Users Should Be Shot, Gates Says," *Los Angeles Times*, September 6, 1990.

28 *"We'd take them to jail for anything and everything we can"*: Anonymous LAPD officer, *N.W.A: The World's Most Dangerous Group*.

28 *"the rotten little cowards"*: Daryl F. Gates, quoted in Paul Feldman, "War on 'the Rotten Little Cowards': Irate Gates Pledges 1,000 Officers for Gang Sweeps," *Los Angeles Times*, April 3, 1988.

28 *"It had such a psychological impact on all of us"*: Ice Cube, interview by Ali.

29 *"These people in here are beyond the point of teaching and rehabilitating"*: Louis Sahagun and Carol McGraw, "Ex-First Lady Just Said Yes to Drug Raid: Nancy Reagan Regains Visibility as Crusader," *Los Angeles Times*, April 8, 1989.

30 *"He was family oriented, always been"*: Erica Wright, author interview, September 26, 2016.

30 *"I seen that it wasn't really worth it"*: Eazy-E, quoted in Davey D and Keith Moerer, "N.W.A—Art or Irresponsibility?" *BAM Magazine*, April 21, 1989.

SOMETHING 2 DANCE 2

32 *"In South Central, all you had to do was open your window"*: Mack interview.

34 *Eve's After Dark was the only teen club in the city*: Alonzo "Lonzo" Williams, *N.ot W.ithout A.lonzo* (The Lonzo Infotainment Company, 2015).

35 *"People came out in droves"*: Ibid.

35 *"there wasn't no money in it"*: Dr. Dre, quoted in Ronin Ro, "Moving Target," *The Source*, November 1992.

38 *"Andre was so excited when he unwrapped his mixer"*: Verna Griffin, *Long Road Outta Compton: Dr. Dre's Mom on Family, Fame, and Terrible Tragedy* (Cambridge, MA: Da Capo Press, 2008).

39 *"That's what your name should be"*: DJ Yella, interview by Maximus Clean, *PROP$ Magazine*, May 1996.

40 *As Brooklyn trio Whodini opened*: Jess Cagle, "All Hell Breaks Loose at a Run-D.M.C. 'Raising Hell' Rap Concert in California," *People*, September 1, 1986.

41 *"it's all right to beat people up"*: Tipper Gore, quoted in Ed Kiersh, "Run-D.M.C. Is Beating the Rap," *Rolling Stone*, December 4, 1986.

41 *"This is it?"*: DJ Yella, quoted in Terry McDermott, "Parental Advisory: Explicit Lyrics," *Los Angeles Times*, April 14, 2002.

41 *"I would have done this different"*: Dr. Dre, quoted in Andre Torres, "The Architect," *Scratch Magazine*, 2004.

41 *It took them forty-five minutes*: Williams, *N.ot W.ithout A.lonzo*.

42 *"We sold five thousand of them"*: Ibid.

43 *"We wanted to put on a show"*: Dr. Dre, *N.W.A: The World's Most Dangerous Group*.

44 *"We'd split up the money right there on the corner"*: Jerry Heller, *Ruthless: A Memoir* (New York: Gallery Books, 2006).

44 *"Larkin was like the black godfather of music"*: Alonzo Williams, quoted in McDermott, "Parental Advisory."

44 *"From that point on, we had nothing but dissension over money"*: Ibid.

LA IS THE PLACE

49 *"a self-made monster of the city streets"*: Ice-T, "6 'n the Mornin'," *Rhyme Pays*, 1986.

51 *"the consumer didn't define him as rock"*: Bob Pittman, quoted in R. Serge Denisoff, *Inside MTV* (New York: Routledge, 1988).

51   *"You cannot be all things to all people"*: Ibid.

51   *"Rock and roll is not a guitar, it's not long hair"*: Ice Cube, author interview, April 6, 2016.

52   *Yetnikoff threatened to go public*: Walter Yetnikoff and David Ritz, *Howling at the Moon: Confessions of a Music Mogul in an Age of Excess* (London: Abacus, 2004).

54   *"I had never heard the kind of music they were playing"*: Mack interview.

55   *"They weren't normal mixes"*: Ibid.

56   *"Anytime somebody got smoked I usually got a phone call"*: Ibid.

57   *"It's awful"*: Bob Pool, "Station's Neighbors Rap Its Wrap-Around Sound," *Los Angeles Times*, November 4, 1989.

60   *"Pretty soon Lonzo is coming to me"*: Steve Yano, quoted in McDermott, "Parental Advisory."

60   *"He'd tell Steve, 'This one is gonna be a hit'"*: Susan Yano, author interview, May 15, 2016.

61   *"Next thing I know"*: Steve Yano, quoted in McDermott, "Parental Advisory."

I AIN'T THA 1

63   *"I remember seeing Run-D.M.C. and Public Enemy"*: Ice Cube interview.

64   *"Yo, you ever write a rap before?"*: Ice Cube, quoted in Stephen Galloway, "Ice Cube Says Hollywood Isn't Cool Enough," *Hollywood Reporter*, February 25, 2016.

64   *"And then you had hip-hop, which was something new"*: Ibid.

65   *"a chance to see that the world was bigger than Compton"*: Ice Cube, "Not My Job: Ice Cube Answers Three Questions about Very Bad Days," NPR, January 9, 2016.

65   *"I was mad at everything"*: Ice Cube, quoted in McDermott, "Parental Advisory."

65   *"That cadence, I was drawn to it"*: Sir Jinx, author interview, November 17, 2016.

65 *"We'd be in there smelling dog shit"*: Ice Cube, interview, November 1993, http://www.oocities.org/sunsetstrip/lounge/5705/icecube.html.

66 *"Next thing I know I'm ditching school to go hang out with Dre"*: Ice Cube, *N.W.A: The World's Most Dangerous Group*.

66 *"The place was rowdy as a motherfucker"*: Dr. Dre, quoted in Ronin Ro, *Dr. Dre: The Biography* (Cambridge, MA: Da Capo Press, 2007).

66 *"We used to sneak and listen to that"*: Sir Jinx interview.

67 *"He robbed us"*: Ibid.

67 *"We didn't like the label situation with the Stereo Crew"*: Ice Cube, quoted in Brian Coleman, *Check the Technique: Volume 2: More Liner Notes for Hip-Hop Junkies* (Berkeley, CA: Wax Facts Press, 2015).

69 *"It is unlikely that any Negro-owned center of this kind"*: "Dooto Music Center: A Community Asset," *Los Angeles Sentinel*, March 21, 1963.

69 *"Majority of them said, 'Fuck no'"*: Craig Schweisinger, author interview, November 17, 2016.

71 *"They said, 'Look at all these fucking gangsters out here'"*: Ibid.

72 *"You know what? I'm gonna let your butt sit in jail for a while"*: Alonzo Williams, quoted in McDermott, "Parental Advisory."

73 *But when Dre played the record*: *N.W.A: The World's Most Dangerous Group*.

74 *"I was like, damn"*: Ibid.

75 *"I wasn't crazy about it, to be honest"*: Mack interview.

77 *"We were broke"*: Arabian Prince, lecture, Red Bull Music Academy, 2005.

NIGGAZ . . . WITH ATTITUDE

79 *"Using it instead of getting abused by it"*: Ice Cube, *Behind the Music: Ice Cube*, VH1, June 20, 2011.

80 *"I wanted to go all the way left"*: Dr. Dre, quoted in Brian Cross, *It's Not About a Salary . . .: Rap, Race and Resistance in Los Angeles* (New York: Verso Books, 1993).

80 *"I used to make people buy records"*: Eazy-E, *Welcome to Death Row*, directed by S. Leigh Savidge and Jeff Scheftel (2001).

83 *"You want to play me something?"*: Heller, *Ruthless*.

85 *"My uncle told us, Jerry loved your dad"*: Erica Wright interview.

85 *"They had a great dynamic"*: Jernagin interview.

85 *"People callin' me, askin' me"*: Eazy-E, *Rap Pages*.

87 *"Nigga, you the shit"*: The D.O.C., ThaFormula.com.

87 *"to get the fuck away"*: The D.O.C. interview.

87 *"They just didn't want me in the group, I guess"*: Ibid.

87 *"I've always known how to talk to white people"*: The D.O.C., quoted in Alex Pappademas, "The Man Behind Dre and N.W.A: Hip Hop's Ghost (Writer) in the Machine," *Playboy*, August 7, 2015.

88 *"[Lonzo] called me back the next day"*: Michel'le Toussaint, author interview, September 28, 2016.

88 *"didn't say anything other than hello"*: Ibid.

89 *"I wanted to get up outta that shit"*: Dr. Dre, quoted in Ro, "Moving Target."

90 *"The cool thing about Eazy"*: Gregory "Cold 187um" Hutchinson, author interview, November 4, 2016.

90 *"If they don't want us, we don't want them"*: Salt-N-Pepa, "Did Jay-Z Boycott the Grammys Again?" *MTV News*, February 14, 2011.

91 *"What you heard is one take"*: Mack interview.

91 *"He sounded and looked like a little kid"*: DJ Yella, interview by Clean.

92 *"I'd get calls from them"*: Ice Cube, quoted in Sean Daly, "The Warm and Fuzzy Side of Ice Cube," *Washington Post*, January 19, 2005.

92 *"That shit was like some wack shit"*: MC Ren, ThaFormula.com, 2004.

GANGSTA GANGSTA

93 *"Oh, fuck, here we go"*: Heller, *Ruthless*.

94 *"The world was changing"*: The D.O.C., quoted in Pappademas, "The Man Behind Dre and N.W.A."

95 *"What makes you think anyone is going to buy this garbage?"*: Heller, *Ruthless*.

96 *"He'd tell you, 'Try to make it like this'"*: MC Ren, quoted in McDermott, "Parental Advisory."

96 *"Everybody was trying to showcase their wares and do their best"*: The D.O.C. interview.

96 *"They were having a ball, being young dudes just having fun"*: Edwards interview.

100 *"Just as they were getting ready to go out"*: Schweisinger interview.

100 *"Eazy was a hard-core little Crip"*: Ibid.

100 *"We just knew the image—that pirate, the silver and black"*: Ice Cube, *Straight Outta L.A.*, directed by Ice Cube (2010).

101 *"N.W.A in purple and gold?"*: MC Ren, *Straight Outta L.A.*

102 *"N.W.A made the Raiders more official to LA"*: Chuck D, *Straight Outta L.A.*

102 *"It went right to the point"*: DJ Yella, DVD extras, *Straight Outta Compton*, directed by F. Gary Gray (2015).

103 *"One day Ren said they'd finished the album"*: Edwards interview.

103 *"It was like . . . we wasn't doing that type of shit"*: MC Ren, quoted in Ro, *Dr. Dre*.

104 *"I was a solo artist first"*: Arabian Prince, quoted in Wendy Brandes, "Kept Outta 'Compton': N.W.A's Arabian Prince Has No Regrets," *Huffington Post*, September 8, 2015.

105 *Eazy propped his Air Jordans up on a desk*: Jonathan Gold, "N.W.A: A Hard Act to Follow," *LA Weekly*, May 5, 1989.

PARENTAL DISCRETION IZ ADVISED

107 *"If you rose to the bait, you were a racist"*: Jonathan Gold, "Twenty-Seven Years Later, N.W.A Still Rubs a Raw Spot," *Los Angeles Times*, September 5, 2015.

107 *"illicit, forbidden fruit"*: McDermott, "Parental Advisory."

108 *"I realized this could actually cause a riot"*: Rupert Wainwright, quoted in Craig Marks and Rob Tannenbaum, *I Want My MTV: The Uncensored Story of the Music Video Revolution* (New York: Dutton Books, 2011).

109 *"On MTV they play heavy-metal music"*: MC Ren, *N.W.A: The World's Most Dangerous Group*.

110 *"We're not putting down women"*: Eazy-E, quoted in Dennis Hunt, "The Rap

Reality: Truth and Money: Compton's N.W.A Catches Fire with Stark Portraits of Ghetto Life," *Los Angeles Times*, April 2, 1989.

111 *"Words like bitch and nigger may be shocking"*: Ice Cube, quoted in Robert Hilburn, "Rap: Striking Tales of Black Frustration and Pride Shake the Pop Mainstream," *Los Angeles Times*, April 2, 1989.

112 *"Basically, I got arrested for humping a couch"*: LL Cool J, *Jimmy Kimmel Live*, October 9, 2014.

113 *Reverend Floyd E. Rose went public*: Dave Marsh and Phyllis Pollack, "The FBI Hates This Band," *LA Weekly*, October 10, 1989.

114 *"We just showed your City Council"*: Ice Cube, quoted in Marsh and Pollack, "The FBI Hates This Band."

114 *"These people aren't doing anything but capitalizing off of death and violence"*: Lieutenant Harry Taylor, *N.W.A: The World's Most Dangerous Group*.

114 *"We're not talking about all police"*: Ice Cube, interview by David Mills, 1989.

114 *Late on the night of June 25, 1989*: Griffin, *Long Road Outta Compton*.

115 *"Neck got broke and all kind'a shit"*: Dr. Dre, quoted in Ronin Ro, "Escape from Death Row," *Vibe*, October 1996.

115 *"So it kinda fucked with me"*: Ibid.

115 *The case originally went to trial*: "Woman, Rappers Settle Rape Claim Suit," Associated Press, December 16, 1993.

116 *"Eazy-E was kind of a smart-ass during the deposition"*: Gusty Yearout, quoted in Asawin Suebsaeng, "When N.W.A Was Sued for Rape," *Daily Beast*, September 2, 2015.

116 *"And dude was like, 'Nah, this is Eazy-E money'"*: Ice Cube, *Beef*, directed by Peter Spirer (2003).

116 *"It's either him or me"*: John Mendelsohn, "Poison the Hood: Niggaz with Attitude," unpublished, *Playboy*, 1991.

117 *"Jerry Heller lives in a half-million-dollar house in Westlake"*: Ice Cube, quoted in Frank Owen, "N.W.A: Hanging Tough," *Spin*, April 1990.

117 *"There was no money"*: Sir Jinx interview.

117 *"Jerry told me that lawyers were made to cause trouble"*: Ice Cube, quoted in Owen, "N.W.A."

118 *"It was kinda like, why didn't you sign the contract"*: DJ Yella, *N.W.A: The World's Most Dangerous Group.*

118 *"I couldn't really attach myself to the N.W.A thing"*: The D.O.C., interview, VladTV, November 23, 2015.

119 *"It was me and you bustin' a song called 'The Formula'"*: Dr. Dre, quoted in Jake Brown, *Dr. Dre in the Studio: From Compton, Death Row, Snoop Dogg, Eminem, 50 Cent, The Game & Mad Money: The Life, Times and Aftermath of the Notorious Record Producer . . . Dr. Dre* (Phoenix: Amber Communications Group Inc., 2007).

119 *"I was going from chick to chick's house high on ecstasy and liquor"*: The D.O.C. interview.

120 *"It was never even possible for it to ever heal"*: The D.O.C., interview, VladTV.

120 *"That was my first piece of loot, and even that was a fuck job"*: The D.O.C. interview.

121 *"I didn't know anything about the business"*: Ibid.

122 *"Laylaw got this pacifier and put it around my neck"*: Toussaint interview.

122 *"We can't only have all this rap shit on Ruthless"*: Heller, *Ruthless.*

122 *"I knew nothing about hip-hop"*: Toussaint interview.

123 *"I do remember when he first hit me"*: Michel'le Toussaint, interview, *The Breakfast Club*, 2015.

123 *"It just never stopped"*: Toussaint interview.

124 *"At the time it felt like if he didn't hit me . . . something was wrong"*: Ibid.

125 *"What are they gonna do?"*: Eazy-E, quoted in Owen, "N.W.A."

125 *"You kidding? It was the FBI"*: Bryan Turner, quoted in McDermott, "Parental Advisory."

125 *"Oh, I didn't know they were buying our records, too"*: Ice Cube, quoted in Marsh and Pollack, "The FBI Hates This Band."

127 *"That letter wasn't for N.W.A"*: The D.O.C. interview.

128 *"There were close to two hundred of us"*: Larry Courts, quoted in John Counts,

"Retired Detroit Sergeant Recalls Telling N.W.A They Couldn't Play 'F★★★ tha Police' at 1989 Concert," MLive.com, August 27, 2015.

128 *"Oh man, y'all shouldn'ta come if y'all wasn't gonna do that"*: Ice Cube, interview by Mills.

129 *"The cops are charging us!"*: Heller, *Ruthless*.

130 *"It was a trip"*: The D.O.C. interview.

AMERIKKKA'S MOST WANTED

131 *"It wasn't like Jerry was all the brains"*: Jernagin interview.

131 *"Man, I ain't got no money"*: MC Ren, quoted in Ro, *Dr. Dre*.

131 *"[The] other guys' positions as far as business was concerned?"*: The D.O.C. interview.

131 *"Nobody in N.W.A fucking coughed"*: Rupert Wainwright, quoted in Marks and Tannenbaum, *I Want My MTV*.

132 *"Stay with the group, man"*: Chuck D, interview by Nick Huff Barili, 2014.

132 *"Go out and be a flop like Arabian Prince"*: Ice Cube, interview, *Juan Epstein*, 2012.

133 *"I was like, 'Aw, shit'"*: Dr. Dre, quoted in Ro, "Moving Target."

133 *"Is your money right for sure?"*: Ice Cube, quoted in Ro, *Dr. Dre*.

133 *"From the inside looking out"*: Hutchinson interview.

133 *"He was with it"*: Ice Cube, interview, *Juan Epstein*.

134 *"You wanna jump on there"*: Ibid.

134 *"I don't like to do pieces of records"*: Hank Shocklee, quoted in Coleman, *Check the Technique: Volume 2*.

134 *"I realized this could be a really good project"*: Chuck D, quoted in Coleman, *Check the Technique: Volume 2*.

135 *"When I went out there I had my ears closed"*: Sir Jinx interview.

135 *"Jinx was the gatekeeper"*: Ice Cube interview.

135 *"With Dre, it was like, 'Here's the sound'"*: Ice Cube, quoted in Coleman, *Check the Technique: Volume 2*.

135 *"that kinda represents the America we were dealing with"*: Ice Cube, quoted in "The Making of Ice Cube's *AmeriKKKa's Most Wanted,*" *XXL*, June 7, 2010.

137 *"Eazy said he wanted to have two supergroups"*: Hutchinson interview.

138 *"We wanted Cube on it whether he was leaving or not"*: Ibid.

138 *"Ice Cube, how's he going to write about something he's never been through?"*: Go Mack, quoted in Jonathan Gold, "Above the Law Is Happy to Take the Rap for 'Murder,'" *Los Angeles Times*, April 7, 1990.

138 *"New jacks [poseurs] from Pomona should only talk about the 10 Freeway"*: Ice Cube, quoted in Gold, "Above the Law Is Happy to Take the Rap for 'Murder.'"

138 *"For me and my crew, that was really messed up"*: Hutchinson interview.

139 *"I was like, 'Yo, we can't do business together'"*: Ice Cube, quoted in Keith Murphy, "Eazy-E: The Ruthless Lie of an American Gangster," *Vibe*, August 19, 2015.

140 *"He hit me like Tyson, but I took it"*: Tairrie B, interview, *Record Mirror*, December 1, 1990.

141 *"It means we get more money"*: Eazy-E, quoted in Owen, "N.W.A."

141 *"Yeah, it got better"*: MC Ren, *N.W.A: The World's Most Dangerous Group.*

141 *"You could've grabbed anybody off the street"*: Dr. Dre, quoted in Ro, "Moving Target."

144 *"Then Dre picks me up by my hair"*: Dee Barnes, interview by Louis Flores, *The Source*, December 1992.

144 *"I was like, 'What?'"*: Dr. Dre, quoted in Ro, "Moving Target."

144 *Ren said Barnes "deserved it"*: MC Ren, quoted in Alan Light, "N.W.A: Beating Up the Charts," *Rolling Stone*, August 8, 1991.

144 *"He grabbed the bitch by the little hair that she had"*: Eazy-E, quoted in Mark Blackwell, "Niggaz4Dinner," *Spin*, September 1991.

APPETITE FOR DESTRUCTION

147 *"There was tension all through that album"*: Dr. Dre, *N.W.A: The World's Most Dangerous Group.*

148 *"As soon as I was old enough"*: Suge Knight, quoted in Burhan Wazir, "Mutha Knows Best," *Guardian*, August 5, 2001.

149 *"They wanted me to be the gangster"*: The D.O.C. interview.

149 *"He was the first one to tell me"*: Ibid.

150 *"By any means necessary"*: Dr. Dre, *N.W.A: The World's Most Dangerous Group*.

151 *"'Look, we'll give you a couple of dollars'"*: Suge Knight, interview by BET, 1996.

151 *"He had me look over the edge"*: Vanilla Ice, interview, *Primetime Live*, 1996.

152 *"You're talking about many, many years"*: Nina Bhadreshwar, author interview, January 30, 2015.

152 *"I got a hold of one on my own"*: Suge Knight, quoted in Chuck Philips, "The Big Mack," *Spin*, August 1994.

153 *"They had the worst contracts I had ever seen"*: Dick Griffey, *Welcome to Death Row*.

153 *"Look, man, I'm not dealing with Jerry Heller anymore"*: Dr. Dre, *N.W.A: The World's Most Dangerous Group*.

153 *"He played the divide-and-conquer game"*: Dr. Dre, quoted in Kevin Powell, "Live from Death Row," *Vibe*, February 1996.

154 *"Hey, yo, you know we got to work this shit out"*: Heller, *Ruthless*.

154 *"I heard you was trying to get me killed, Blood"*: Suge Knight, quoted in Jory Farr, *Moguls and Madmen: The Pursuit of Power in Popular Music* (New York: Simon & Schuster, 2001).

154 *"I figured he did know where my mother lived"*: Eazy-E, quoted in Farr, *Moguls and Madmen*.

155 *"It was like The Godfather"*: Michael Bourbeau, quoted in Farr, *Moguls and Madmen*.

155 *"[It's] a simple dispute"*: Wayne Smith, quoted in Farr, *Moguls and Madmen*.

156 *"[People] like Suge Knight are just takers"*: Jerry Heller, quoted in Philips, "The Big Mack."

156 *"That Mike Klein deal brought a lot of confusion to Ruthless"*: Mack interview.

156   *"Eric felt bad for Dre"*: Hutchinson interview.

158   *"When Cube left, you really didn't miss anything but his essence"*: Ibid.

160   *"the single most important event"*: Mulch et al., "The Evolution of Popular Music."

160   *"From doing 'Boyz-n-the-Hood,' the song"*: Ice Cube, interview by Ali.

162   *"He was real sharp about the business of show business"*: Hutchinson interview.

162   *"I paid $2,500 for a million dollars' worth of publicity"*: Eazy-E, quoted in Blackwell, "Niggaz4Dinner."

SA PRIZE

166   *"That first line, 'Goddamn, I'm glad y'all set it off'"*: Sir Jinx interview.

166   *"Once I found that track, I knew"*: Ice Cube interview.

167   *"I was ready to mash"*: MC Ren, ThaFormula.com.

167   *"When the song was done"*: Ice Cube interview.

167   *"I think it's one of the most vitriolic attacks"*: Jerry Heller, quoted in Amos Barshad, "Jerry Heller Expresses Himself," *Grantland*, August 11, 2015.

168   *"Taking rap music literally"*: Ice Cube, interview by Barbara Nevins, *Talk Live*, 1991.

168   *"I didn't know what 'anti-Semitic' meant"*: Ice Cube, quoted in Brian Hiatt, "N.W.A: American Gangstas," *Rolling Stone*, August 27, 2015.

168   *"I was making a transformation"*: Ice Cube interview.

169   *"We were just doing music"*: Ibid.

169   *"Having them in there, I felt like a running back"*: Ibid.

169   *"Every song was better than the last one"*: Ibid.

170   *"In their pursuit of the American dream"*: Helen Zia, *Asian American Dreams: The Emergence of an American People* (New York: Farrar, Straus and Giroux, 2000).

170   *"You bitch, you're trying to steal my orange juice"*: Soon Ja Du, quoted in Clarence Lusane, *African Americans at the Crossroads: The Restructuring of Black Leadership and the 1992 Elections* (New York: South End Press, 1994).

171 *"Look at the message"*: Ice Cube, quoted in Robert Gordon, "Ice Cube Lets Off Steam," *Creem*, 1991.

172 *"Nobody is safe when you listen to Death Certificate"*: Ice Cube interview.

173 *"We kicked it and had a good time"*: Ice Cube, interview by Michael Williams, *RapCity*, 1993.

173 *"Cube is a sponge"*: Sir Jinx interview.

173 *"[The] teaching is self-love"*: Ice Cube, interview by Williams.

174 *"I'm sick of begging for the white man to put out my records"*: Ice Cube, speech at a Nation of Islam event, https://www.youtube.com/watch?v=48x2SE 60a0Y.

174 *"I swear to God"*: Bryan Turner, quoted in Hiatt, "N.W.A."

174 *"We decided Cube needed a backup group"*: Sir Jinx interview.

175 *"The truth is, I don't care what the white community thinks"*: Ice Cube, quoted in Dennis Hunt, "Outrageous as He Wants to Be," *Los Angeles Times*, November 3, 1991.

175 *"That's why people have issues with the media now"*: Ice Cube interview.

176 *"It's interesting, the people who are so intrigued"*: Ibid.

176 *"I took that book everywhere I went"*: MC Ren, quoted in Michael Cooper, "N.W.A's MC Ren Is Ready to Be *Renincarnated*," BallerStatus.com, October 2, 2009.

177 *"Fuck this. This is a worse situation"*: MC Ren, ThaFormula.com.

177 *"[The] beats were just too funky"*: Edwards interview.

178 *"We just stuck together as a crew"*: Warren G, interview, DubCnn.com, 2003.

178 *"I said, 'Nigga, stop lying'"*: Snoop Dogg, quoted in S. Leigh Savidge, *Welcome to Death Row: The Uncensored History of the Rise & Fall of Death Row Records in the Words of Those Who Were There* (Hawthorne, CA: Xenon Press, 2015).

179 *"Jerry and Eazy were trying to starve me out"*: Dr. Dre, *The Pharmacy*, October 10, 2015.

WHO GOT THE CAMERA?

182 *"Please stop. Please stop"*: Hector Tobar and Richard Lee Colvin, "Witnesses Depict Relentless Beating," *Los Angeles Times*, March 7, 1991.

182 *"I haven't beaten anyone this bad in a long time"*: Tracy Wood and Sheryl Stolberg, "Patrol Car Log in Beating Released," *Los Angeles Times*, March 19, 1991.

183 *"Did you see that shit on the news?"*: Ice Cube interview.

184 *"Not all cops are bad"*: Eazy-E, quoted in Chuck Philips, "Rodney King Gets Rap Offer," *Los Angeles Times*, March 20, 1991.

185 *"was fucked up worse than Rodney King!"*: Eazy-E, quoted in Blackwell, "Niggaz4Dinner."

185 *"Sure, I've seen that little stomp"*: Eazy-E, quoted in Chuck Philips, "Rapper Takes Officer's Side," *Los Angeles Times*, April 6, 1993.

185 *"Eazy-E is a sellout"*: Willie D, quoted in Philips, "Rapper Takes Officer's Side."

188 *"I know they ain't got no money"*: Sir Jinx interview.

188 *"Some of the homies"*: Ice Cube interview.

189 *"Finally it took a motherfucker to videotape a nigga"*: Eazy-E, "Eternal E," *Str8 off tha Streetz of Muthaphukkin Compton*, 1996.

189 *"Whether Rodney King happened or not"*: Ice Cube interview.

189 *"It seemed like the thing to do"*: The D.O.C. interview.

189 *"It was like a big-ass picnic"*: Sir Jinx interview.

190 *"It was more than just the verdict"*: Ibid.

192 *"I mean, if black people kill black people every day"*: Sister Souljah, quoted in David Mills, "Sister Souljah's Call to Arms," *Washington Post*, May 13, 1992.

194 *"The problem is that records like 'Cop Killer' do have an impact"*: Dan Quayle, quoted in Chuck Philips, "The Uncivil War: The Battle between the Establishment and Supporters of Rap Music Reopens Old Wounds of Race and Class," *Los Angeles Times*, July 19, 1992.

194 *"If you believe that I'm a cop killer"*: Ice-T and Douglas Century, *Ice: A Memoir*

of *Gangster Life and Redemption—From South Central to Hollywood* (New York: One World Books, 2011).

NUTHIN' BUT A 'G' THANG

198 *"By the time it made it to Jimmy, I didn't own anything"*: The D.O.C. interview.

198 *"As it turned out, Suge ended up"*: Harry-O, quoted in Chuck Philips, "Probe of Rap Label Looks at Entrepreneur Behind Bars," *Los Angeles Times*, September 1, 1997.

199 *"It happened that fast"*: The D.O.C. interview.

199 *"Even when me and Dre were beefing"*: Ibid.

199 *"My brother told me"*: Warren G, interview, DubCnn.com.

200 *"all hits and no bullshit"*: The D.O.C., interview by Charlie Braxton.

200 *"It was fun"*: The D.O.C. interview.

200 *"I don't give a fuck what Dre says"*: Dick Griffey, *Welcome to Death Row*.

200 *"It was great working with Dre"*: Edwards interview.

201 *"I was in hell at that moment"*: The D.O.C. interview.

201 *"I got shot at a whole bunch of times"*: Dr. Dre, quoted in Ro, "Moving Target."

201 *"1992 was not my year"*: Dr. Dre, quoted in Chuck Philips, "The Violent Art, Violent Reality of Dr. Dre," *Los Angeles Times*, December 15, 1992.

201 *"He had the Dee Barnes thing"*: Eazy-E, quoted in Ro, *Dr. Dre*.

202 *"I knew nothin' about hip-hop"*: Jimmy Iovine, quoted in David Fricke, "Jimmy Iovine: The Man with the Magic Ears," *Rolling Stone*, April 12, 2012.

203 *"That's how I felt at the time"*: Dr. Dre, quoted in Ro, *Dr. Dre*.

204 *"He called in, and I taped the receiver of the phone to the mic"*: Dr. Dre, interview, *Big Boy's Neighborhood*, March 26, 2015.

206 *"I said, 'Okay, make a commercial'"*: Jimmy Iovine, quoted in Fricke, "Jimmy Iovine."

206 *"The Chronic is the only album that rivals Niggaz4Life"*: Edwards interview.

207 *"Coming up under Dre's tutelage"*: Hutchinson interview.

208   *"This shit is wack"*: MC Ren, ThaFormula.com.

208   *"I wasn't about to rap over any nigga's beat back then"*: Ibid.

209   *"It just seemed like everything was kind of dead musically"*: Rhythm D, interview, *Murder Master Music Show*, May 8, 2015.

210   *"[Eazy] was cocky"*: Hutchinson interview.

210   *"If Dre just left and didn't say anything"*: Ibid.

210   *"Eazy would tell us stories about Dre"*: B. G. Knocc Out, interview, VladTV, September 22, 2015.

211   *"It actually was some unnecessary bullshit"*: Nate Dogg, *Straight Outta Compton* [film], https://www.youtube.com/watch?v=J4vqQFKoyrM.

212   *"We were having a bunch of fun"*: Dr. Dre, *Behind the Music: Snoop Dogg*, VH1, 2000.

214   *"The media is quick to point their finger"*: Snoop Dogg, quoted in Chuck Philips, "The Saga of Snoop Doggy Dogg," *Los Angeles Times*, November 7, 1993.

214   *"They had trucks lined up"*: Chris "the Glove" Taylor, quoted in Tim Sanchez, "Chris 'the Glove' Taylor Talks Death Row, Aftermath, and Dr. Dre," AllHipHop.com, January 28, 2012.

217   *"Yo, what you gon' do wit' that, Sam?"*: Sam Sneed, quoted in Paul Arnold, "Sam Sneed Talks Dr. Dre's Abandonment and 'That Crazy Meeting' with Tupac," HipHopDX.com, December 28, 2010.

217   *"Of course we're exploiting violence"*: Ice Cube, quoted in Chuck Philips, "Is America Ready for 'Natural Born Killaz'?" *Los Angeles Times*, October 20, 1994.

217   *"We weren't trying to bullshit each other"*: Ice Cube, quoted in Ro, *Dr. Dre*.

218   *"Dre is feeding me these books about the Illuminati"*: The D.O.C. interview.

218   *"Nobody is really putting any energy"*: Ibid.

218   *"I went into his vault and took two beats"*: Ibid.

218   *"I suppose that probably wasn't my most shining moment"*: Ibid.

219   *"The characters are really N.W.A"*: Preston Whitmore II, quoted in Steve Hochman, "N.W.A's Founder Follows Ice Cube to the Flickz," *Los Angeles Times*, February 9, 1992.

220   *"You've got rock and rollers"*: Mack interview.

221   *"Eric was funny as hell"*: Ibid.

221   *"No matter what he did in his entertainment life"*: Erica Wright interview.

221   *"My most memorable time with him"*: Ebie Wright, author interview, September 26, 2016.

222   *"As soon as they saw each other it was all smiles and love"*: Krayzie Bone, quoted in Paul Meara, "Firsthand Accounts of the Night Eazy-E & Ice Cube Ended Their Feud," NahRight.com, September 11, 2015.

222   *"I told Eazy I was down"*: Ice Cube, quoted in Ben Westhoff, "Straight Outta Compton: Fact-Checking the Film . . . with Ice Cube," *Guardian*, August 13, 2015.

222   *"We gonna get the whole family back together"*: Hutchinson interview.

ETERNAL E

223   *"Before we went out"*: Krayzie Bone, quoted in Meara, "Firsthand Accounts of the Night Eazy-E & Ice Cube Ended Their Feud."

223   *"It was never anything serious"*: Mack interview.

224   *"In the studio, I knew something was wrong with him"*: MC Ren, quoted in Neil Strauss, "The Pop Life," *New York Times*, February 1, 1996.

224   *"He sounded worse than I'd ever heard him"*: Mark "Big Man" Rucker, quoted in Carter Harris, "Eazy Living," *Vibe*, June/July 1995.

224   *"I got a call from him"*: Tomica Woods-Wright, *N.W.A: The World's Most Dangerous Group.*

226   *"I was too young to understand that my dad was sick"*: Ebie Wright interview.

226   *"It got chaotic. Everyone was lost"*: Jernagin interview.

226   *"He went through the whole list of who to trust"*: Tomica Woods-Wright, *N.W.A: The World's Most Dangerous Group.*

227   *"By the time I seen my dad"*: Erica Wright interview.

228   *"I can remember the way everybody looked"*: Dr. Dre, *N.W.A: The World's Most Dangerous Group.*

229   *"I've never seen anybody die that quick"*: Hutchinson interview.

229   *"Eazy's right in the middle"*: Mack interview.

229 *"I don't think he was any more promiscuous"*: Jernagin interview.

229 *"Do I think something fishy happened to Eazy?"*: Jerry Heller, interview, First Fam Radio, March 20, 2014.

230 *"None of us have anything"*: Erica Wright interview.

230 *"I believe he was murdered"*: Ebie Wright interview.

230 *"We'd be like, 'Man, get that shit away from us'"*: Mack interview.

231 *"That is a strong lady"*: Ibid.

232 *"We got the short end of the stick"*: Ebie Wright interview.

232 *"I never turned my back on him"*: DJ Yella, quoted in Strauss, "The Pop Life."

EPILOGUE

236 *"'Fuck tha Police' did change the world"*: Ice Cube interview.

238 *"When he died, to me, Ruthless died"*: DJ Yella, interview by Clean.

239 *"He's not just some rapper who died from AIDS"*: Hutchinson interview.

240 *"Nobody was talking about old beefs"*: MC Ren, quoted in Ro, *Dr. Dre.*

240 *"The chemistry is just incredible"*: Mel-Man, quoted in Christopher O'Connor, "Reunited N.W.A Get Serious about Recording Album," MTV.com, December 7, 1999.

241 *On a film set in Leimert Park*: outtakes from Lorraine Ali, "Dr. Dre and Ice Cube Relive Youth on 'Straight Outta Compton' Set," *Los Angeles Times,* July 30, 2015.

241 *"It's fucking weird"*: Dr. Dre, unpublished interview by Lorraine Ali, fall 2014.

242 *"Ultimately Suge was gonna destroy it"*: The D.O.C. interview.

243 *"It makes no sense"*: Bhadreshwar interview.

243 *"They were our family"*: Dania "Baby D" Birks, quoted in Randall Roberts, "Jerry Heller on the Other Women 'Straight Outta Compton' Forgot," *Los Angeles Times,* August 27, 2015.

243 *"It was like seventy-five percent accurate"*: Ebie Wright interview.

244 *"There's been several movies made about Elvis"*: Ice Cube interview.

244 *"This movie was just a blip on the radar"*: Ibid.

244 *"I want to concentrate on other important areas right now"*: Jerry Heller, author interview via email, February 19, 2016.

245 *"I don't think [my abuse] should have been in the movie"*: Toussaint interview.

247 *"When we all come back together"*: Ice Cube interview.

247 *"It was amazing, like magic"*: Ibid.